# Media and the Marketplace
## Ethical Perspectives

# MEDIA AND THE MARKETPLACE

## Ethical Perspectives

*Edited by*
Eoin G. Cassidy
Andrew G. McGrady

First published 2001
by the Institute of Public Administration
57-61 Lansdowne Road
Dublin 4

© 2001 Institute of Public Administration
and individual authors

ISBN 1 902448 52 9

British Library Cataloguing in Publication Data
A catalogue record of this book is available from the
British Library

Cover design by Principle Concepts, Dublin
Typeset by CM Print & Design, Dublin
Printed by Techman

# Contents

# Acknowledgements

This publication arose out of a European Union SOCRATES post-graduate Intensive Programme and accompanying public symposium held in Dublin in February 1999. The ongoing theme of the Intensive Programme is Economy and Ethics, and it is co-ordinated by Professor Egidius Berns of the University of Brabant, Tilberg, the Netherlands. Faculty and postgraduate students from a number of European Universities participated in the two week programme which was hosted by the Irish partner, Mater Dei Institute of Education, Dublin, and organised by the two editors of this publication.

Funding for the Intensive Programme was obtained from the European Commission and from the Board of Mater Dei Institute of Education. The editors wish to acknowledge their gratitude to the Rev Dr Dermot A. Lane, President of Mater Dei Institute, and Dr Marcellina O'Sullivan, Director of Studies of Mater Dei Institute for their support with the organisation of the Intensive Programme.

This publication, arising from papers presented in the Intensive Programme and Symposium, has been made possible by grants from the Irish Centre for Faith and Culture, Maynooth, and United Beverages Group Ltd. The editors wish to record their gratitude to Rev Professor James McEvoy of the Irish Centre for Faith and Culture, and Conal Cassidy of United Beverages Group Ltd for their welcome support.

Finally the editors wish to acknowledge the assistance of John Devitt, Patrick Devitt, Ursula Kearney, Brendan McDonnell, and Kevin Williams of Mater Dei Institute, and Tony McNamara of the Instutute of Public Administration for their help in editing and publishing this collection of papers.

This publication was supported by a grant from the
**Irish Centre for Faith and Culture**
St Patrick's College, Maynooth, Ireland

# Contributors

**Marcel Becker** studied history and philosophy at the Catholic University Nijmegen, Holland. After he wrote his dissertation about application Aristotelian/Thomistic virtue-ethics in current ethical debates about war and peace, he became assistant professor, Philosophical Ethics, Faculty of Philosophy, Catholic University Nijmegen. He is mainly interested in the relation ethics-politics and the possibilities of using virtue-ethics in fields of applied ethics.

**Egidius E. Berns** studied philosophy and economics in Leuven and is professor of Social Philosopy and Social Ethics at Tilburg University, Holland. He is also research director at the Collège International de Philosophie in Paris and co-ordinator of the SOCRATES ERASMUS Intensive Programme "Economy and Ethics". He has published on the history of eco-nomic thought and contemporary philosophy. His most recent book (in Dutch) is entitled *Circularity and Usury: a deconstructive philosophy of economy*.

**Michael J. Breen** is a priest of the archdiocese of Dublin. At present he is head of department and senior lecturer in Media and Communication Studies, Mary Immaculate College, University of Limerick. His primary research interest is in the area of media effects and public opinion.

**Paul Brian Campbell SJ** is a Jesuit of the New York province. Born in Ireland he was educated in Dublin, Paris, Tokyo and New York. He is professor of English at Le Moyne College, Syracuse, New York. His research interests are in the area of new technologies.

**Eoin G. Cassidy** is a senior lecturer in Philosophy at Mater Dei Institute, Dublin City University. He obtained his doctorate in Philosophy in 1990 from the Institut Superieur de Philosophie, Louvain, Belgium. He has contributed to a series of international conferences on Ethics and Economics and published widely in the area of Faith and Culture. He is currently executive secretary of the Irish Centre for Faith and Culture.

**Farrel Corcoran** has held academic appointments in the University of Oregon, where he received his PhD in 1978, the University of New Mexico, Northern Illinois University and Dublin City University, where he is currently professor of Communication. He has been involved in academic administration as head of school and dean of faculty in DCU. He has held the post of chairperson of the RTE Authority. Academic interests include: Political Economy of Broadcasting; European Media Policy; International Communication, and Media Influence.

**Geert Demuijnck** is a research fellow at the Centre for Contemporary Ethics at Lille Catholic University, France. His interests are varied and include the ethical aspects of business and economics. He is particularly concerned with questions of distributive justice, and the ethical foundations of the welfare state.

**John Horgan** is Professor of Journalism at Dublin City University. He was a member of the Republic of Ireland's Commission on the Newspaper Industry (1995-1996).

**Damien Kiberd** is editor of the *Sunday Business Post*. He has recently edited two books on media ethics, *Media in Ireland, The Search for Diversity* (Dublin, Open Air, 1997) and *Media in Ireland, the Search for Ethical Journalism* (Dublin, Open Air, 1999).

**Marthe Lievens** was born in Ostend, Belgium. She pursued her undergraduate studies at St Andrews College of Education, Bruges. She pursued her postgraduate studies at Mater Dei Institute of Education, Dublin. In 1999, she successfully completed a thesis, *The Privacy of the Individual: An Ethical Challenge for Contemporary Journalism*. She is currently teaching in Virginia vocational school, Co Cavan.

**Andrew G. McGrady** is lecturer in Education at Mater Dei Institute of Education, a college of Dublin City University. His teaching and research interests include media and religion, moral and religious change throughout the life cycle, values education, and experience-based learning.

**Hendrik Opdebeeck** studied Economics and Philosophy in Ghent and Louvain (Belgium). At the Antwerp University he lectures in a variety of courses in the areas of applied and business ethics. He is a staff member of the Centre for Ethics at the Antwerp University. One of his recent publications is *The foundation and application of Moral Philosophy: Ricoeur's Ethical Order* (Peeters, Louvain, 2000).

**Bart Pattyn** (born 1962, Gent) studied theology and philosophy in Leuven, Belgium, where he completed his doctoral dissertation on the concept of "identity" in relation to the classical way of talking about oneself. He is working at the European Centre for Ethics organising different congresses and promoting interdisciplinary discussions among academics from different faculties on relevant political and ethical questions. He is responsible for *Ethical Perspectives, the Journal of the European Ethics Network*, and is working in the field of media ethics.

**Bert van de Ven** gained his masters degree in Economics and Philosophy at Tilburg University. He obtained his PhD in philosophy with a thesis entitled *Rationality and Ethics in Business: Foundations of Business Ethics* (in Dutch). Currently he teaches Business Ethics at Tilburg University, The Netherlands. His research is concerned with ethical aspects of business and the economy. He has published several articles in this field and a book on Marketing Ethics.

**Herman van Erp** is associate professor of Social Philosophy and Ethics at Tilburg University, The Netherlands. His main research subject is Political Philosophy. He is particularly interested in connections and comparisons between Kant, Marx, Hegel and Rawls. An English translation of his book *Het Politiek Belang* is in press. At the moment he is preparing a book on General Ethics. His publications in English include: "Democracy: Pragmatic Conceptions and Ethical Justification", in *Archiv für Rechts und Sozialphilosophie,* Beiheft 42; "Law and the States in Modern Times", in W. Maihofer and G. Sprenger (eds.), Stuttgart, 1990; "The End of History and Hegel'sonception of Modernity", in *Ideas y valores*, Revista Colombiana de filosofia, No. 107 (1998).

**Paul J.M. van Tongeren** (born 1950 Deventer, The Netherlands) studied theology in Utrecht and philosophy in Louvain (Belgium). He was awarded his PhD also from the Superior Institute of Philosophy of the Catholic University in Louvain (1984). He was "special professor of philosophy" at the State University of Leiden from 1985 to 1990, and is since 1987 professor of moral philosophy at the University of Nymegen. Most of his publications are in the field of ethics or of the history of philosophy, some in the field of philosophy of religion. He is a member of the editorial board of several journals of philosophy and of theology; he is editor in chief of a series entitled *Morality and the Meaning of Life*, and of a series of publications of the Dutch Association of Christian Intellectuals.

**Kevin Williams** PhD lectures in Mater Dei Institute of Education and is a past-president of the Educational Studies Association of Ireland. He is author/editor of several books and has published many articles on philosophical and educational issues in Irish and international journals. His most recent publications include the co-edited collections: *The Future of Religion in Irish Education* (Dublin, Veritas, 1997); *Words Alone: The Teaching and Usage of English in Contemporary Ireland* (Dublin, University College Dublin Press, 2000) and a forthcoming monograph on language education commissioned by the Philosophy of Education Society of Great Britain. The paper in this volume derives from his current research interest on the notions of identity and allegiance in civic life. It is one of a series of philosophical essays on the role of national and cultural/ethnic identity in contemporary society.

———— Introduction ————

# Ethical Inquiry and Media Practice

## *Eoin G. Cassidy*

What constitutes the ethical realm and how does it relate to other realms such as the legal, the economic or the religious? What is the nature of moral responsibility and obligation? What is the source of morality and how does it relate to human dignity, human rights and individual freedom? Questions such as these form the basis of the philosophical discipline that is ethics and are of concern to anyone engaged in fostering a morally literate society. In this context, one of the advantages of a homogeneous culture is that it provides an understanding and a level of acceptance of both the sources of moral authority and the nature of moral responsibility within which society can construct an ethical framework for its citizens. While there may be disagreement on particular ethical issues, the parameters nevertheless exist within which such disagreements may be satisfactorily resolved. Our contemporary "western" liberal culture is premised upon the fact that such homogeneity no longer exists. It is argued that, for better or worse, we live in a pluralist culture with competing and, in many cases, conflicting views as to what constitutes the right or the good and how these can be known. Furthermore, if one accepts the pluralist character of contemporary culture, it could be argued that even if there are universal and absolute moral principles, there is nevertheless little realistic possibility of achieving consensus on either the nature of these principles or their role in determining acceptable limits of human behaviour.

Such is the environment within which any treatment of media ethics must be situated today. Is it possible to construct a set of guidelines within which the ethical responsibilities of journalists and media providers can be situated and evaluated? And yet, what is the alternative – a society in which only the fittest survive, or an ethic based ultimately on the premise that "might is right"? The challenge facing those concerned with promoting the ideal of media ethics is to provide a coherent alternative to exclusively relativist, pragmatic, or subjectivist ethical stances. In this context, it is not sufficient to merely acknowledge that there is an ethical dimension to the world in which we live. This challenge can only be met by affirming the rational character of human nature against all forms of emotivism. Relativism argues that, even if there is a realm which allows one to affirm a difference between an "ought" and an "is", there is no possibility of rationally determining how one would distinguish them. In this scenario, media ethics is little more than a product of culturally conditioned behaviour patterns. Of the two other alternatives, pragmatism argues that ethical inquiry is a luxury and that market forces should determine media output within the requirements set by the law, while subjectivism argues that media providers should simply cater for the taste of media consumers.

The study of media ethics as outlined in this book is premised upon either a rejection of, or an unease with, the above market-driven stances. It insists that there is such a thing as an ethical life with associated personal obligations and responsibilities, and that this ethical imperative is of a higher order than that reflected simply in a producer-consumer relationship. In this context, there is need both to foster those virtues which underpin the classical idea of "the good" and to affirm the possibility of rationally discerning that which constitutes "the good" other than by relying on the good that is profit and/or what might be described as "a feel good factor". In addition, while acknowledging the difficulty of discerning the extent to which particular ethical principles are culturally conditioned, this study of media ethics will argue that there are ethical principles which transcend cultural boundaries. It will be argued that the existence of these universal ethical norms provides the indispensable context within which legitimate rights such as the freedom of the press or the right to individual privacy can be effectively protected.

In approaching the topic of media ethics I am conscious of the specificity of the theme. As with the study of any topic in applied ethics, it should not be forgotten that the point of departure must be rooted in the practices of the particular discipline. In this context, three broad avenues of enquiry suggest themselves as worthy of study. These are: media, democracy and the public space; media, culture and the shaping of identity; and media ethics and the dynamics of the marketplace.

## Media, democracy and the public space

Democracy depends upon an educated and aware citizenry. Two primary functions of the mass media are to educate and inform. The media has a function as a gatekeeper to the public space, setting the agendas for public discussion, defining the issues of the day, and orchestrating the participants in the resulting debates. While in the western media, the electronic mass media (television and radio) operate on the twin platforms of public service broadcasting and commercial broadcasting, the press has usually operated on a commercial basis. Furthermore, emerging media forms, such as the Internet, rely solely on a commercial platform. Clearly democracy depends upon media which respect the public space. In this regard, the influences of market forces vis-a-vis media ownership and output raise legitimate concerns. Market driven developments may marginalise minority viewpoints and undermine the exercise of a genuine pluralism of opinions. In a culture increasingly dominated by the forces of market economics, the question of the role of the media in the protection of minority interests is one that exercises the minds of public policy makers. Furthermore, it is this issue that unquestionably provides the most telling argument in favour of public service broadcasting. This is an ethical argument that hinges upon the view that the media has a social responsibility to serve the general interest as distinct from the most powerful sectional interests. However, even if one accepts this view point, there remains the problem of finding an appropriate forum for deciding on criteria for discerning the general interest.

In the opening paper, *Cultural Rights and Media Performance*, Farrel

Corcoran offers an impressive defence of public service broadcasting. In this context, he cautions against minimising the role of the media in shaping a healthy civic culture in which the liberties of individual citizens are supported. He bases his argument on a detailed analysis of the links between individual and cultural rights. The threat posed by market liberalisation to the continued existence of public service broadcasting cannot be ignored if one is sensitive to this issue. He concludes by reflecting on whether the politico-ethical foundation of public broadcasting will be strong enough to withstand the increasing pressures towards concentration of ownership power in private broadcasting.

The argument in favour of public service broadcasting is developed in the paper *Public Funds and Minority Broadcasting* by Kevin Williams. He considers the recent establishment of a publicly funded Irish language broadcasting service (TG4) and argues that its funding can be justified as a response to a very reasonable demand. Citizens have a right to a publicly sponsored service in the language of their choice. His carefully argued thesis draws upon the philosophical culture of human rights and reflects a commitment to respecting diversity. Over and above these considerations, Williams perceptively recognises that: "Encounters with diversity open us to what Louis McNeice in the poem, *Snow*, refers to as the "drunkenness of things being various." This diversity, both societal and within individuals, contributes to the common good". Another paper with an Irish focus in this section is *Newspaper Ownership in Ireland and its Effects on Media Diversity: The Commission on the Newspaper Industry Re-visited*. Written by John Horgan it examines the changing profile of newspaper ownership in Ireland and discusses the effect of the highly concentrated pattern of ownership of the print media in Ireland upon the culture of newspapers and the freedom of the press. Horgan is acutely conscious of the fact that the issues of press freedom and diversity of ownership are by no means unrelated. Furthermore, few would deny that media pluralism and the diversity of editorial opinion are basic prerequisites for the existence of a healthy democracy. The article concludes by exploring a number of possible ways in which diversity can be promoted.

The notion of freedom is of critical importance in the promotion of democratic values. Thus the issue of freedom of the press is universally regarded as one of the pillars upon which democracy rests. In the fourth paper in this section, *The Notion of Freedom and Current Developments in the Media*, Marcel Becker explores the development of this philosophical theme in the writings of John Milton and John Stuart Mill. In particular he explores the tension between the classic ideas of freedom and current journalistic practice. In the fifth paper in the section, *Media, Democracy and the Safeguarding of Minority Interests*, Herman van Erp acknowledges that market mechanisms can be defended but also criticised as being instruments for the satisfaction of majority wants. He argues that the social responsibility of journalists within a democracy is to confront the market mechanisms in a manner that promotes the interests of minorities by giving a public voice to rational debate on important social and political issues. In the final paper in this section, *Media, Democracy and Economic Power*, Hendrick Opdebeeck raises the question as to whether the power of the media increasingly lies in its capacity to ignore democratic values in order to serve the economic purposes of the market place. While acknowledging that the media has the power to subvert the democratic ideal he suggests that this is not an inevitable outcome of current developments. He argues that the tension between merits, needs and progress can be resolved in a satisfactory manner by moving from what is understood in economics as a data circle to a circle of responsibility.

## Media, culture and the shaping of identity

A further perspective from which to view the ethical issues relating to the mass media is that of their relationship with culture. Such a perspective takes on increased urgency when it is further recognised that the culture in which we are immersed provides the environment in which personal identity is forged. Culture is never neutral and can be exploited and shaped in ways that can create societal goals and/or reinforce societal stereotypes and prejudices. The centrality of such a focus is evident in many ways. In large part, the media are shaping a transnational western popular culture which exerts a stronger influence on young people than their local national culture.

Within the context of such acculturation, the protection and promotion of national culture has become an important issue. The increasing diversification of media, which current technological innovation allows, underpins the concept of narrow-casting (as opposed to broadcasting), which is directed at particular sub-cultures. Paradoxically, both the emergence of a "super-culture" and increased cultural fragmentation are evident in contemporary western society, both made possible by the technology of mass media. The ethical dimensions of technological opportunities such as digital broadcasting, satellite broadcasting and the Internet, can only be discussed in the wider context of the nature of culture and its impact upon social cohesion and personal identity. Furthermore, there is increasing evidence that, to the extent that the influence of the media diminishes other forms of social interaction, people are more receptive to forms of undemocratic propaganda communicated through the sensational reporting of news events. Today we are only too aware of the destructive effects of such propaganda. We must also remember that it is in and through culture that each generation transmits the defining patterns of meaning to the next generation. There are clear ethical as well as sociological issues at stake here. Thus the responsibilities attendant upon journalists and media providers inevitably transcend the boundaries of the here and now.

The first paper within this section is one which directs its attention to media users. Readers, listeners and viewers make personal choices with respect to the media products they use. The range of media products from which such selections can be made is increasing exponentially. Why, for instance, do people spend so much time watching television or develop loyalty to particular television programmes or a particular newspaper? Is it because they are consumers of a market-driven production, or is it because of something deeper, the need to identify with a mass group? In the first paper, *The Need for Understanding Mass Psychology in Media Ethics*, Bart Pattyn draws on Emile Durkheim's idea of the collective consciousness and on Freud's analysis of the process of identification to suggest the appropriate conceptual focus for understanding the power of the media. He concludes by alerting us to the disturbing reality that, if Freud is correct in asserting that people owe their critical powers to membership of various groups, then the reduction of social participation as a result of television will have serious negative consequences for society. He argues that there will be a discernable decrease in the ability of citizens to critique the institutions and structures of the society in which they live.

Culture is ceaselessly intertwined with narrative; in and through stories we shape identity, articulate self-experience and try to understand each other. Contemporary movements in philosophy have made us increasingly conscious of this narrative structure within which reality is perceived – the search for the truth is the search for the true story. A narrative-based methodology provides a powerful tool with which to assess the significance of the mass media not only with respect to its ability to shape consumer tastes but, more importantly, with respect to its function as a storyteller or, more precisely, with respect to its ability to provide the main narrative framework of interpretation of all other personal and social stories. To what extent has the media the power to impose its own ideology or "meta-story" to the detriment of other stories? If, as many might suspect, the media's power to impose its own "meta-story" is considerable, what are the ethical questions that emerge? In his paper *Narrativity, Ethics and the Media*, Paul van Tongeren raises these and other related issues. In particular, he alerts us to the meta-stories that shape our identity and the role of the mass media in creating these meta-stories. He perceptively recognises that the challenge facing journalists is to foster stories that enhance rather than restrict the moral imagination of the public and to do so in a manner that enables us to critique and transform the dominant ideologies of society.

In the final paper in this section *Cultural Ecology and Media Ethics: A Perspective from a Christian Philosophy of Communication*, Andrew G. McGrady situates the discussion about media ethics within the wider context of the inter-relationship between human culture and personal identity. He alerts us to the reality that the mass media does not only reflect or shape culture but is increasingly recognised as constituting culture – a "virtual culture" – that directs not only our knowledge of the world, but also our knowledge of ways of knowing. This provocative and, to the eyes of many, prophetic assessment of the relationship between media, culture and personal well-being raises ethical questions of a fundamental nature. Based on the premise that it is the spiritual and imaginative aspects of culture that underpin human social and interpersonal communication, McGrady argues the need for media professionals to develop an ethic based upon cultural ecology, noting that the way in which we create and use our cultural environment is as much an ethical concern as our relationship with the physical environment. Such an ethical sense requires a personal ethic of care on the part of each individual media professional, a personal responsibility that transcends the requirements of legal frameworks and codes of practice.

## Media ethics and the dynamics of the marketplace

In the above section of this book, the influence of market capitalism upon media ownership and output is repeatedly acknowledged. Here we turn our attention to the manner in which day-to-day media decisions are influenced by the culture of the marketplace. The dominant viewpoint in western capitalism is that the media is simply a business and that the primary function of this and every other business is the generation of profits. Regardless of whether or not one welcomes this development, the reality is that the constraints of the contemporary business ethos exercise considerable influences on developments in the media. An obvious example of one such development is the way in which media coverage of the distinction between the public sphere and the private sphere is becoming increasingly blurred. Faced with the public's desire for information, or simply public curiosity, it would appear that commercial pressures are making it increasingly difficult for journalists and media providers to respect the boundaries protecting the right to individual privacy. Whilst not denying the responsibility of the media to assist the public in realising its legitimate right to information, few would deny that commercial pressures make it difficult for journalists always to be attentive to the ethical issues surrounding the right to privacy. Another obvious example of the effect of commercial pressures on the media is to be found in the area of advertising, which exerts a profound structural influence on the mass media. The contemporary business environment in which the media operates is one where, in virtue of large budgets, advertisers can wield substantial influence on every organ of the media. In this context, one must be sensitive to the fact that in the world of advertising, the line between fact and fiction, truth and propaganda is finely drawn. Furthermore, commercial pressures can make it difficult for journalists to avoid acting in a manner that gives advertisers an indirect influence on editorial policy.

In the first paper in this section, *Must a Good Journalist be Morally Good? Media Ethics in a Liberal Culture*, I argue that the ethics of the free market achieves a balance between opposing forces but that it is a balance whose pragmatism ultimately destroys the very possibility of an ethical commitment to virtues such as truthfulness, fairness or honesty. Furthermore, I argue that if the values of the market come to dominate the ethical thinking of the media, the very foundations upon which liberal democracy rests will be in danger of being undermined. In this context, the question that must be posed is to what extent one can treat of the media simply as a business. Focusing on an Irish context, the paper by Damien Kiberd, *The Impact of Law and Ethics on the Practice of Journalism in Ireland*, offers tangible evidence of the commercial realities within which any discussion of media ethics in Ireland must be situated. Kiberd raises issues that question the assumption that journalism can be viewed as a profession rather than as a trade. Furthermore, he describes how commercial pressures can determine the way in which ethical questions, such as those surrounding privacy, are treated. He reminds us of the danger of adopting a too theoretical approach to the discussion of any issue in applied ethics. It must not be forgotten that media ethics as a discipline must be based upon reflection on the actual day-to-day practice of the media. Any theoretical discussion of this discipline must never lose sight of the reality that ethics is the science of practical reason.

Geert Demuijnck's paper, *Market Forces and Mass Media: Competing for an Audience of Consumers*, draws on the work of the renowned French sociologist Pierre Bourdieu to illustrate some of the negative influence of the media's commercial agenda on political and cultural life. He does however recognise that Bourdieu's rather pessimistic attitude is not immune from criticism. The commercial realities within which the media operates is the focus of Bert van de Ven's paper, *What's Wrong with Advertising? An Ethical Perspective on Communication in Advertising*. He raises questions that challenge the uncritical assumption that advertising is in some way an ethically dubious enterprise. Is advertising to be criticised for furthering materialism, or rather for the way it often does this, or both? In the course of answering these questions van de Ven offers the reader a penetrating analysis of the nature of the ethical challenges that face advertisers. His paper offers evidence of the value of Jurgen Habermas' theory of communicative action.

Two papers in the section focus on the vexed question of the ethics of privacy and journalistic practice. In her paper, *The Privacy of the Individual: An Ethical Challenge for Contemporary Journalism*, Marthe Lievens draws attention to a key moment in this ethical tension, namely that between the freedom of the journalist to engage in investigative journalism and the freedom of the individual to have his or her privacy respected. No other media ethical issue has proved to be as contentious as that which touches upon the privacy of the individual. In a detailed treatment of the question Lievens argues for the need to provide an ethical as distinct from a purely legal foundation for a code of journalistic practice. She concludes by arguing persuasively for the need for ethics to be included in media and communication courses. In his paper, *Between Clinton and Mitterand: On the distinction between the Public and the Private in the Media*, Egidius Berns offers a further reflection on this contentious media ethical issue of privacy. Through his analysis of media coverage of two recent public scandals, Monica-gate and the Mazarine-case, he reflects on the distinction between "the public" and "the private", and treats of the historical and cultural contexts within which they have developed their present currency.

The final paper in the publication, *The Net, it's Gatekeepers, their Bait and its Victims: Ethical Issues relating to the Internet*, is jointly written by Paul B. Cambell and Michael J. Breen. It examines in some detail the significance of the Internet as a growing phenomenon that continues to exert significant influence on society. The paper offers a sobering analysis of the way in which the Internet can be used as an instrument to further the interests of big business. They conclude with a recognition of the need for critical evaluation of its place in terms of social change and social equality.

## The genesis of this publication

This publication has emerged from an inter-university initiative which brings together eight European universities under the auspices of an EU SOCRATES intensive graduate programme entitled "Ethics and Economics". The Irish partner in this programme, Mater Dei Institute of Education in Dublin, hosted the 1999 two-week conference. The initiative testifies to a belief among the participating universities as to the importance of media ethics for today's world. In an era when the media fills our homes with its presence and the influence of communications, media and technology is reflected in every aspect of contemporary culture, the importance of providing a philosophically literate ethical education for media providers and journalists cannot be under-estimated. Media providers and journalists bear a heavy responsibility not only for the integrity of their profession but also to society at large. Acquiring the tools with which to execute this responsibility is not an easy task. At the dawn of a new millennium the media is increasingly perceived to be shaping our lives in its image. Perhaps, this is a time to strive towards a sense of the importance of philosophy within media and communication studies; and, in particular, the branch of philosophy that is ethics.

# Section 1

# Media, Democracy and the Public Space

# CHAPTER 1

# Cultural Rights and Media Performance

## Farrel Corcoran

*The thrust of this paper is to emphasise the links between individual and cultural rights and to stress the role of media in shaping a healthy civic culture in which the liberties of individual citizens are supported. It is argued that the justification for public service broadcasting lies in its production of merit goods.*

## Introduction – cultural rights

Various attempts have been made over recent decades to articulate a theory of public service broadcasting strong enough not only to guide actual broadcasting practice but to inform decisions in the political arena that bear on its funding and regulation. Once the move towards deregulation of broadcasting was completed in various European countries in the 1980s, these attempts quickened as a result of the arrival of the second generation of broadcasters, mostly working to a market rather than a public service imperative and mostly utilising cable and satellite technologies to distribute their programmes. But in many ways the debate about broadcasting has produced patently self-serving attacks on the very concept of public service broadcasting from private broadcasters whose first commitment is to a rising share price rather than culture and democracy, and in response a heightened tendency towards defensive manoeuvres among public service broadcasters themselves. The aim here is to step back from the fray and explore the philosophical underpinnings of broadcasting policy, to identify some key principles and concepts which should form the building blocks of a human rights based approach to a normative theory of broadcasting in democratic societies.

In their different ways both the liberal and the socialist traditions have placed considerable emphasis not only on the position of the universal rights of individuals within a comprehensive theory of justice but also of certain group-differentiated rights for minority cultures, indigenous people, national minorities and ethnic groups. This emphasis on minority rights is foregrounded in the policies and declarations of various supranational organisations in recent times. Thus the UN General Assembly in 1992 passed a resolution to adopt a "declaration of the rights of persons belonging to national, religious and ethnic minorities". Earlier General Assembly resolutions had brought the role of mass media into clear focus, as in Article 17 of the Convention on The Rights of the Child (1989) which asserted that "State parties recognised the important function performed by the mass media and shall ensure that the child has access to information and material from a diversity of national and international sources, especially those aimed at the promotion of his or her social, spiritual and moral well-being and physical and mental health". The Conference on Security and Co-operation in Europe (now OSCE) established a High Commissioner on national minorities in 1993 and the Council of Europe adopted a declaration on minority language rights in 1992.

It can be argued, of course, that many of these assertions rarely go beyond pious aspirations because they fail to identify implementation strategies, monitoring mechanisms and duty holders who can be held to account. Many are vaguely worded, do not get ratified in national legislation and lack enforcement support. The present difficulties of *Med-TV*, the satellite broadcast service directed towards Kurdish communities located in Kurdistan and in the Kurdish diaspora spread over seventy countries, illustrate the problem. Its objective has been to preserve Kurdish language and culture, to open up a public sphere in which a full range of Kurdish public opinion can be explored and to provide educational services to children and teenagers. Despite these lofty aims (or perhaps because of them) *Med-TV* has been raided by police in London and Brussels, has had its satellite links jammed, has been subjected to intense diplomatic pressure from Turkey and has finally been forced to cease broadcasting. No protection has so far been provided by the various international and regional bodies that assert the cultural rights of persons belonging to national minorities, which include the rights to preserve and develop their ethnic, cultural, linguistic and religious identity, freely use their national language, create and maintain their own educational and cultural institutions, maintain contact with persons of common ethnic origin within and outside their country and take part in public affairs. Some of the contradictions regarding *Med-TV* have already surfaced in Ireland in debates about government support for *TG4* and the issue of "parity of esteem" for minorities within Northern Ireland.

With the end of the Cold War and the consolidation of a more globalised capitalist order, concern about the targeting of centralised state pressures against cultural freedoms, as in the case of Turkey's hostility towards the very concept of Kurdish TV, is now being over-shadowed by anxiety about other less centralised but perhaps more powerful forces working against cultural freedoms. Embedded in powerful institutions, these operate at a level above that of the nation state, such as international trade agreements (World Trade Organisation) or international competition law (the European Commission). In this new re-regulatory environment, there is a growing tendency to attack cultural policies which attempt to address the "public good" in ways that resist the pressures of market forces and to reframe them as "unfair barriers to trade". So it is important to focus attention now to the notion of cultural rights not only in the context of the needs of linguistic, ethnic and other minorities but also as these rights apply to majority groups, and to trace the roots of these rights in the freedoms that should pertain to individuals in a democratic order.

"Cultural rights", in this majoritarian sense beyond the concerns of threatened minorities, is an underdeveloped category of human rights that is in need of elaboration into its components. Only then can we see how a theory of cultural rights can have pragmatic usefulness in underpinning national laws and inter-national agreements and informing professional ethics and practices in various cultural industries, but particularly broadcasting. A clarification of cultural rights is all the more urgent now because of the vast new landscape of possibilities for cultural production, distribution and consumption that has opened up with the convergence of computing and telecommunications with broadcasting and the rolling out of digital interactive media.

If we look again at the declarations of such supranational bodies as the UN and UNESCO, we see some references to cultural rights in a universal context. The Universal Declaration of Human Rights, published in 1948, declares in Article 27 that "everyone has the right freely to participate in the cultural life of the community". Article 22 goes a little further. "Everyone is entitled to the realisation, through national effort and international co-operation, of the cultural rights indispensable for his/her dignity and the free development of his/her personality". Various UNESCO conventions and declarations also call for protection of the rights to "cultural identity" and the right to "participate in cultural life". The 1995 report of UNESCO's World Commission on Culture and Development calls for the protection of "cultural rights as human rights" so that local cultures can realise their potential and the importance of cultures can be recognised at individual social and national levels.

While it is clear that culture is being used in these texts in the anthropological sense, to include a society's material as well as its symbolic culture, there is still a suggestion that the underlying concern is mainly for minority cultures. And it must be noted once more that these declarations operate more as pious aspirations, having little impact on how societies actually organise themselves, rather than as arguments that establish convincing links between the quality of life at the level of the individual citizen and the quality of public culture.

## The theory and practice of liberal democracy

A useful starting point in thinking about the links between personal fulfillment and public culture is the theory and practice of liberal democracy. The liberal tradition of foregrounding the ideals of personal liberty can be traced through the work of John Locke, Immanuel Kant and John Stuart Mill, which reflect on the emergence of liberal democracy out of older feudal and pre-modern formations, including absolute monarchies, in which people's political status was determined by their religious, ethnic and class membership. In political theory at least, the primary commitment of the modern liberal democratic state is to the freedom and equality of individual citizens, positively nurturing individual fulfillment or alternatively responding to the challenge with "benign neglect". Marx and Engels, however, set down the markers of a strong socialist critique in cautioning that in practice most states are materially and ideologically structured to support the interests of a minority ruling class at the expense of the needs of the majority. They warned that individual citizens' perceptions of their true position within society is filtered through the heavily ideological miasma of the ideas dominant at any particular time in each society's cultural superstructure, ideas that favour the interests of powerful elites. These ideological structures within which people live their lives are ultimately determined by the material base of society which defines in an uneven way how different social classes have access to the resources needed for a fulfilled life.

Are there cultural preconditions which underpin the liberal value of freedom of individual choice and can issues of cultural membership be incorporated into liberal principles of human rights? Or must we continually yield to the seductions of market ideology, which today offers itself ever more persuasively as the guarantor of all individual freedoms? The notion of cultural, as opposed to individual, rights is crucial here.

## Cultural rights and individual liberties

The practices and institutions which comprise a society's culture cover the full range of human activities, material and symbolic, public and private. Cultures tend to be territorially concentrated and based on a shared language and history, though there are also subcultures (for instance "youth", "gay", "neo-Nazi" and so on) which cut across the borders of societal cultures and may have an international or diasporic dimension. Cultures provide their members with a meaningful way of life across a full range of human activities and involve shared values, memories and orientations to the future. They are societal in so far as they are embodied in common institutions, in government structures, media, schools, trade unions, churches, legal systems and so on. These institutions underpin a culture's survival by diffusing a common culture throughout society. They have enormous significance in our lives because they determine individual options. National cultures emerged in many parts of the world in the nineteenth century as disparate groups formed deep bonds with each other in "imagined communities" which extended back into time immemorial and forward into the indefinite future, thus transcending individual mortality. In many situations what began as an audience (of newspapers, plays, pamphlets, music, novels) grew culturally into a "nation" through the diffusion of common notions of space and time, before it developed a political or military aspect (Anderson, 1983).

A common national culture enables a modern economy to function by allowing a literate, educated, mobile workforce to develop. A common language, identity and set of collective memories facilitates a strong sense of common membership of society to emerge. High levels of solidarity and willingness to make sacrifices for fellow citizens provide the ground on which the structures of a welfare state can be built. A commitment to equality of opportunity for people from different parts of society (classes, regions, races) is one of the major civic outcomes of the diffusion of a culture (Kymlicka, 1995).

From the point of view of the individual citizen and the existential choices she makes in exercising her freedom to choose how to lead her life in its many different dimensions, the resources of the culture are crucially important. The real effects of a lack of access to such cultural capital dramatises the point. The low level of life chances available to the mentally and emotionally disadvantaged and other radically marginalised groups is directly related to the constraints that shape their personal identities within what is for them largely a cultural vacuum. A fully diffused, healthy culture in principle allows everyone to form a conception of the "good life" and to revise it radically if necessary by questioning and rejecting dominant conceptions, without being guilty of apostasy. Our culture provides resources – information, examples, models, arguments, perspectives – with which we become aware of alternative visions of the good life, examine them critically and accept or reject them without penalty. The shared vocabulary of one's culture provides options for decision and points of view through which to see value in particular directions and make them meaningful, provided one enjoys social conditions which allow access to such resources as a liberal education, a pluralistic media system and opportunities for freedom of expression and association.

The notion of a "healthy" culture, supporting individual liberties, suggests the possibility of its opposite, the structural decay of a culture in which cultural identity ceases to be an anchor for individual identity. This in turn presses home the need to protect cultures from decay and debasement by ensuring that they are institutionally complete and that their practices are in tune with the cultural rights of citizens. Dramatic examples of cultural decay can be seen in the plight of various indigenous people in Australia, North America, the Amazon Valley and elsewhere and in parts of Africa where prolonged civil conflict has disrupted the functioning of cultural institutions for very long periods. Closer to home the notion of cultural debasement surfaces in debates about "parity of esteem" in Northern Ireland and in arguments, derived from theories of decolonisation, that the esteem in which Irish language-speaking culture is held in Ireland today (and therefore, arguably, the self respect of its members) can be protected from debasement by boosting the effectiveness of its cultural institutions, especially television. Reversing the process of decay facilitates participation in public affairs as a distinct public sphere becomes clearer and relationships of mutual responsibility, solidarity and trust promote a renewed sense of belonging.

A common culture holds the disparate elements of society together in many ways, not least by fostering a willingness among citizens for the mutual accommodations and sacrifices necessary for a functioning democracy. Stable democracies require a shared civic identity in order to sustain adequate levels of mutual concern, for example to agree to pay taxes for services which one will never use oneself. There are many places in the world where civic culture doesn't adequately take hold, even when parliamentary democracy is initiated, or where social unity becomes extremely fragile and then breaks down, as in Yugoslavia in recent years. Less violent attacks on the mutual concern underpinning civic culture can be seen in politico-cultural movements like Reaganism and Thatcherism and their variants elsewhere, whose corrosive effects still exert pressure on the very notion of a civic need for adequate levels of respect, tolerance, accommodation and sacrifice among citizens. It is evident that if democracies are to remain stable, we should be concerned not just about the justice of basic institutions but also about the attitudes of citizens, their sense of justice and interest in promoting the public good, their motivation to participate in the political process and hold political authorities accountable, their commitment to a fair distribution of resources and a willingness to show restraint in their economic demands.

All of this is vulnerable, however, and cannot be taken for granted as an inevitable outcome of the setting up of parliamentary democracy. Voter apathy is on the increase, even in Ireland which used to pride itself on its voting behaviour. There is a backlash against the notion of the welfare state in western democracies. Europe, in general (and Ireland in particular in recent years), is feeling the stresses associated with the emergence of multicultural societies, as large numbers of people seek asylum from civil strife in Eastern Europe and Africa. According to a recent survey, only 12% of American teenagers think voting is important to being a good citizen. Comparison with other surveys across time suggest that "the current cohort knows less, cares less, votes less and is less critical of its leaders and institutions than young people have been at any time over the past five decades"[1] Evidence from Britain is similar.[2]

## Public service

The health of societal culture, or what Habermas (1989) has called "the public sphere", should therefore be of concern to anyone interested in advancing the rights of the individual. This concern lies at the root of the tradition of public service broadcasting that emerged between the two World Wars in Europe. After the Great War period of military monopolisation of radio, the US decision was to turn over control of broadcasting to large private companies, including General Electric, RCA, Westinghouse and AT&T. This was partly in response to the patriotic pressure to balance perceived British dominance of worldwide cable communication, linked to its interests as a world maritime power, and to fend off an emerging British global monopoly of wireless communication by blocking Marconi's US ambitions. It was also an outcome of the dominant American political culture in which private capital was preferred to public control in the development of new industries. In Europe, by contrast, broadcasting was retained under democratic control and the early social embedding of radio laid the institutional and philosophical foundations for television some decades later, as both evolved from a "state broadcasting" model to one of "public service".

Public ownership of media implies an interest in generating a plurality of understandings in society that will maximise people's ability to interpret their social experience, question the assumptions of dominant voices and relate to alternative conceptions of society. This translates editorially into policies to provide access to a diversity of perspectives, values, expressive forms and representations of social reality, not only through factual material but also through fiction, which has its own enormous imaginative power to promote empathy and a sense of what it is like to be "other". A core objective in public service broadcasting, as distinct from its private counterpart, is to offer audiences a wide range of programme genres (news, current affairs, documentaries, drama, childrens' programming) and to ensure that a substantial proportion of these will be home produced and will get their fair share of prime time scheduling. Good broadcasting has the potential to invigorate civil society by allowing alternative points of view to flourish, so that effective protest can be registered and public support mobilised. Good broadcasting should create the cultural conditions for resolving conflict democratically, facilitating compromise and defining collective aims. Elections as defining moments in collective decision-making require special care for impartiality, but they are not the only significant moments when informed and involved citizens, free of both political and commercial pressures, need access to information that is presented as a public good rather than as a commodity.

The tradition of public service broadcasting has emphasised

respecting all taste cultures in a framework of representative pluralism which includes minority tastes, whether these are seen as regional, linguistic or generational. The logic of this flows from the commitment to charge a universal tax (licence fee) as the financial underpinning of a public service system. In purely private systems, programmes are predominantly seen as the means to generate revenue. In public service systems on the other hand, funding is provided to make programmes and broadcasters have, therefore, to be accountable to the public (directly in town hall meetings, indirectly through government departments and parliamentary committees). Most public service broadcasters have also assumed the role of sustaining a sense of national culture, creating the conditions for a "national conversation" on the airwaves and marking key national events and rituals in the nation's life cycle. Indeed, some broadcasters articulate the fear that the notion of a common cultural reference point for all will suffer from the fragmentation of national audiences that may accompany the proliferation of channels made possible by compression technologies. There is thus an important link between media performance and a public culture in which citizens have affordable access through broadcasting to a wide range of ideas, points of view, arguments, role models and genres. This link is most commonly elucidated these days by reference to Habermas's (1989) notion of the public sphere, but it has precursors in earlier notions of political rights, for example in Thomas Jefferson's "condition of political freedom" and Immanuel Kant's "principle of liberty," which define the legitimacy of social power in a valid democracy in terms of its diversity of opinion and expressive forms. From this perspective it is possible to examine examples of media performance which serve the public sphere very badly. In totally commercial systems that have no public service obligations, information is seen not as a public good but purely as a commodity in a circuit of exchange in which broadcasters' sole goal is to maximise audiences, advertising income and return to investors. Home production is kept to a minimum because of its expense or else it consists largely of packages of material produced overseas but "topped and tailed" by local presenters. Despite an increase in the number of privately-owned channels coming onstream in many Western countries in recent years, genre diversity is shrinking and yielding to a steady diet of low cost films and sports (famously described by Rupert Murdoch as his "battering ram" for breaking into global television markets). When ratings and market share become the sole drivers of broadcasting which is sensitive to audience size but insensitive to demand intensity, minority tastes are neglected.

## Information liberalisation

If public service broadcasting, at least in its ideal form, is so vital to the health of the public sphere in which individuals have the best chance of maximising their potential, is its usefulness self-evident and is its future secure? The answer lies in the way individual societies negotiate a place for public service broadcasting in a world that has become much more hostile to it over the last decade. Firstly, the discourse of "globalisation" which is in the ascendant among academics, policy makers and opinion leaders throughout the post-Communist 1990s, leaves little room for continued concern for the communication rights of nation states and national minorities, such as those articulated in the UN and UNESCO in the 1970s and 1980s. Some uses of the term have become decidedly ideological, when they lay down a "common sense" of inevitability to justify a global regulatory order in which a balance between commercial and public interest is allowed to mutate into wholehearted adoption of an unaccountable self-regulating economic system in which market forces achieve greater freedom than they ever experienced within democracies in previous times. As Ferguson[3] points out, globalisation can sometimes sound like a value-neutral descriptor of a supranational universe of media interconnectivity and material and symbolic goods exchange while it is at the same time concealing "extensive normative judgements, normative intentions and value judgements".

This shift in policy-making discourse is paralleled by a surge in global conglomeration in the major cultural industries as media giants become vertically and horizontally integrated to control the totality of their supply chain and spread investment risk. This vast array of strategic alliances, joint ventures and cross ownerships (News Corporation, Time-Warner, Disney, Viacom, Bertelsman,

TCI, CLT, the Kirch Group) is still in a process of rapid change as it prepares to dominate digital television. With their access to vast borrowings and solid reserves of corporate patience as they wait for huge world regions to yield up their disposable incomes (especially China, India and other large Asian countries) these conglomerates establish substantial barriers to entry for smaller companies that might have a more public service orientation. There is no doubt that the dynamism of the private global television system is now exerting serious pressure on content pluralism on the world's television screens and spreading the message that market forces alone will cater for all communication needs if allowed to operate unhindered.

There is a new global ideological underpinning for all of these corporate manoeuvres, which can be traced to key initiatives, especially the Clinton-Gore vision of a Global Information Infrastructure (GII) for an idealised neo-McLuhanesque "global society". The rhetoric promoting all this is a refinement of the market liberalisation ideology of Thatcher-Reagan, which purported to support a public purpose via private enterprise. The main players are giant corporations. Nation states, now more law takers than law makers, have become brokers of agreements articulated in supra-national agencies which have become the real sites of policy-making: the WTO, ITU, OECD, G-7, World Intellectual Property Organisation. In such a liberal market system, the goal is economic investment not human development. The ideology of the GII has advanced itself on the notion of the decline of totalitarian social models in Europe and the USSR but it has done so at the expense of public service social models. It is increasingly difficult to assert "cultural exceptions" in transnational trade negotiations and insert a non-economic recognition into the meaning of communication. Where once it was assumed, now it has to be argued that the information sector has a higher claim on public policy in trade negotiations than shoes, soap or ball bearings.

Some commentators[4] trace the emergence of information liberalisation, which invokes a vision of unprecedented transfers of knowledge through modern communication networks to individuals worldwide, to the ideological revival of John Locke's late seventeenth century theory of limited government, justifying political authority based on proprietary (as against divine or democratic) power. The goodness of the liberal social order is rooted in the contractual socio-economic relations of a market society. In this scheme of things, contractual and private law is in the ascendant over other legal traditions, such as the application of public and constitutional law to issues of public interest. It is difficult to escape the conclusion that in terms of depth of influence, information liberalisation is one of the major social movements of the modern age. As a political project, utilising supply-side regulation alone, its goal is to achieve a dramatic redistribution of power from the public to the private sector. It involves what Habermas (1989) described as a concentration of expression under proprietary governance on a scale not encountered since the passing of feudal society.

The paradox here is that this seismic shift of power away from democratically controlled institutions is being brought about by the actions of nation states themselves as governments confer unprecedented power of governance on a range of supranational agencies with no democratic accountability. For true believers in market liberalisation, the driving vision is to restore competition "to its natural state" and push back the power of the state to its proper minimal terrain, guaranteeing law and order and property rights. Calls for the ending of "the inflation of political demands" in trade in the information sector mean no place for content diversity and other public interest criteria. The most dramatic example of public-private dichotomies can be seen in the contrast between trade press discourse about globally distributed children's television (the ambition to take over all aspects of children's play and imagination through product-based programming licensed to food chains, toy stores, etc) and European sensitivities about quotas, advertising minutage, protection from exploitation through programme length commercials, etc.

Where do cultural rights fit with market liberalisation? Must cultural policies to enforce obligations of pluralism be invalidated because they are "barriers to trade in information services"? Must anti-concentration policies, aimed at ensuring fairer competition, be rejected as interventionist distortions of trade? Must subsidies to protect the common welfare in the public sphere (for example a licence fee for public service broadcasting) be seen as interfering with free trade and limiting the proprietary rights of communications industries? A pessimistic view of the future would see a growing de-legitimation of national policies to the point of threatening the inherent relationship that exists between information conditions and democratic conditions and concentrating regulatory force only on the media supply side (that is to remove barriers to trade), regardless of cultural effects. If this is the future, it represents a dusting off and revival of the post-World War II doctrine of the "free flow of information" enunciated at every opportunity by a succession of US administrations, until confronted from the 1960s onwards by Third World and Communist Bloc calls for a "free and balanced" information flow and a New World Information and Communication Order. This confrontation was neutered in 1985 when the US and Britain withdrew from UNESCO, one of the most important sites for the articulation of a non-western point of view on control of global communication.

For Ireland and other European countries, these tensions between the forces of market liberalisation and public service principles are in the process of being worked through at the level of the European Union, involving the Council of Ministers, the European Courts, the Parliament and the Commission. It is beyond the scope of this paper to explore the labyrinthine pathways of European cultural politics but it is worth noting that the recent enactment of the Treaty of Amsterdam, including its Protocol on Public Service Broadcasting brings the role of national Governments back into focus and it requires them to define what public service broadcasting means in their territories.

This, in turn, has motivated the new generation of private broadcasters, particularly in television, to lobby against the very idea of publicly funded broadcasting on the basis of competition law. Their opposition sometimes takes the form of an argument in favour of sharing the licence fee among all broadcasters who commit to producing particular types of programming deemed to be "public service" in nature. This would be done via a type of arts council of the air (Corcoran, 1996). More usually it takes the form of lobbying at national and European Commission levels for public funding to be spent by public service broadcasters only on a very restricted set of programme genres and for the programme cost-sharing arrangements of the European Broadcasting Union, which benefit small broadcasters like RTÉ in particular, to be curtailed. The working out of these tensions is taking place in the discursive and legal space that is still open between competition rules, with their focus on proprietorial rights, and the Amsterdam Protocol which protects the right of citizens to have access to public service broadcasting.

## Media economics

The thrust of this paper is to emphasise the links between individual and cultural rights and to stress the role of media in shaping a healthy civic culture in which the liberties of individual citizens are supported. Media performance is highly relevant here. Public service broadcasting is frequently criticised for failing to live up to its ideal performance and to fulfill its real potential, but there is no doubt that that ideal is now under sustained attack from private broadcasters and that the potential allowed by that ideal in shaping actual practice must be staunchly defended in the face of market liberalisation. The cultural argument has already been outlined here but there is also an economic argument because when free markets fail to function optimally, fail to provide all that is needed by individual consumers or society generally, then public sector intervention may be the most efficient way to supply the deficit. This is the case in broadcasting.

Economists define as "merit goods" those that are intrinsically by a majority of citizens even if they do not intend to use them – the work of museums, libraries, universities, art galleries, the output of concert halls, research institutes, arts organisations, heritage protection agencies and so on. Quality broadcasting is also a merit good whose value exceeds the valuation any individual would place upon it. Television and radio have the potential either to restrict or to expand the knowledge, experience and imagination of individuals and the stock of cultural capital available in society for general use. As the recent Davies Report (1999) notes, markets in general do not always work well where what is being sold is information or experience. This is because consumers do not know what they are buying until they have experienced it. "If all television is provided via the free market, there is a danger that consumers will under-invest in the development of their own tastes, experience and capacity to comprehend because it is only in retrospect that the benefits of such investment become apparent."[5]

Externalities also lead to market failure because the full costs and benefits of an activity (broadcasting) are not borne by producers or consumers. External benefits exist in broadcasting if it is assumed that television and radio have some influence on audiences. It has been argued here that these benefits can include improved social interaction, awareness of community needs and values, a greater empathy with "others", an increased sense of national solidarity and so forth. Broadcasting can, of course, also produce negative externalities where the wider social cost of, for example, violence, pornography or sensationalised news, are not borne by the broadcaster. While actual performance does not always match the ideal of course, the function of public service broadcasting is to produce positive externalities. Experience has shown that unregulated broadcasting markets, with no public intervention, will tend to provide more programmes with negative externalities than is socially desirable because the wider social costs of programming are not borne by the broadcaster.

If the market under-supplies merit goods that produce external benefits, then public funds are needed to redress this failure. The social importance of public service broadcasting in promoting citizenship (Kant's "Principle of Publicity") is the key justification for public funding to offset market failure. Many of the benefits of public service broadcasting as outlined here would be completely unprofitable in pure market terms and if there is no revenue from the markets to provide these benefits, the private broadcasting sector will produce far less than an optimum quantity of "merit goods" and there is widespread market failure. Governments must, therefore, rectify the under-supply of programmes providing external benefits. Pressures to conform to a neo-classical market economic model, though attacking the broadcast licence fee as a form of "state aid" that distorts the level playing pitch of pure competition, will result in the loss of welfare-enhancing programming and the decay of the public sphere. It also means that programmes which are highly valued by small audiences will not be produced. This can be empirically verified in the US, where broadcasting has been dominated by private capital since its inception and public broadcasting has been severely marginalised. If the justification for public service broadcasting lies in its production of merit goods, then it follows that public service broadcasting should be mainstreamed rather than marginalised. It has the duty to be popular, to strive to attract large audiences in order to maximise the social value of goods it produces. The public funding of merit goods makes little sense if they are viewed only by tiny audiences. The freedom to offer schedules which attract large audiences is particularly important for small European broadcasters that are dual-funded, like RTÉ, from the public purse as well as advertising budgets. It remains to be seen whether the economies of scale and the globalisation of distribution peculiar to digital television will increase pressures towards concentration of ownership power in private broadcasting or whether the politico-ethical foundation of public broadcasting will be strong enough to enhance the role of broadcasting in servicing an enriched public culture in which individual liberties can thrive.

## Notes

1 Glendon 1991:129.
2 Heater 1990.
3 Ferguson 1992:73.
4 e.g. Venturelli 1998.
5 Davies 1999:203.

## Bibliography

Anderson, B., *Imagined Communities: Reflections on the Origins and Spread of Nationalism*, London, Verso, 1983.

Corcoran, F., "Arts Council of the Air: Switching Attention from the Service to the Programme".*Javnost/The Public*, 3/2 (1996):7-22.

Davies, G., *The Future Funding of the BBC*, London, Department of Culture, Media and Sport, 1999.

Ferguson, M., "Mythology about Globalisation", *European Journal of Communication*, 7/2 (1992): 69-93.

Glendon, M. A., *Rights Talk: The Impoverishment of Political Discourse*, New York, Free Press, 1991.

Habermas, J., *The Structural Transformation of the Public Sphere*, Cambridge, Mass, MIT Press, 1989.

Heater, D., *Citizenship: The Civic Ideal in World History*, London, Longman, 1990.

Kymlicka, W., *Multicultural Citizenship: a Liberal Theory of Minority Rights*, Oxford, Clarendon Press, 1995.

Venturelli, S., "Cultural Rights and World Trade Agreements in the Information Society", *Gazette*, 60/1 (1998): 47-76.

─────── CHAPTER 2 ───────

# Public Funds and Minority Broadcasting

*Kevin Williams*

*In this chapter, I argue that the establishment of the Irish language television service, Teilefís na Gaeilge (TG4), was a response to a very reasonable demand and that citizens have a right to a publicly sponsored service in the language of their choice. Other arguments continue the defence, in principle, of the use of public funds to support TG4. The chapter concludes by drawing attention to some of the practical and ethical limits of this defence.*

## Introduction

Recent years in Ireland have witnessed an animated and sometimes bitter debate about the establishment of an Irish-language television station.[1] Like other stations serving minority language communities, and unlike sport or music channels, Teilefís na Gaeilge (TG4) could not expect to achieve financial viability based on advertising income or viewer subscriptions alone. In this chapter, I argue that the establishment TG4 was a response to a very reasonable demand and that citizens have a right to a publicly sponsored service in the language of their choice. Other arguments continue the defence, in principle, of the use of public funds to support TG4. The paper concludes by drawing attention to some of the practical and ethical limits of this defence.

## Is public funding a right?

Although I want to assert the right to public funds to support TG4, we must be very careful of the language of rights. The rhetoric of rights should not be promiscuously invoked in political discourse because when we make a claim based on rights, we invoke particularly weighty and compelling moral considerations. Rights have been described as the "heavy artillery in our moral arsenal"[2] and we must be sensitive to the limits of what can be demanded as a right, either as a liberty or as a claim right. A right in the sense of a liberty refers to an entitlement to pursue a particular course of action unless bound by some duty. I have a right to play soccer today unless bound by a duty of care to a sick member of my family. A right in the claim sense arises when another party has a corresponding duty towards us.[3] I have a claim right on the referee to protect me from the violent and dangerous play of an opponent.

But rights have their limits. The exercise of a right as a liberty, as we have just seen, may be limited by the presence of relevant duties, but it may also be limited by our human capacities. I have the right, in normal circumstances, to play a musical instrument but if I am tone deaf I cannot exercise this right – apart of course from making noise with the instrument. There are also logical limits to what we can assert as a claim right. For example, we can assert a right to receive an education, but it does not make sense to assert a right to a defined state of educatedness. In other words we can identify elements of adult commitment to the welfare of children and we can impose obligations on the community with regard to educational provision and educational opportunity, but it does not make sense to demand that the efforts of teachers meet with success.

Likewise it makes logical sense to assert a right to a minimum wage or a right to minimum standards of health care but it is not appropriate to assert a right to a minimum quality of life or to a minimum state of health. Some rights too may have to be qualified and curtailed due to considerations of the common good arising. For example, even the right, in the sense of the liberty, of individuals to set up a minority broadcasting service without public funding is qualified by the need to provide prior access to airwaves to other legally licensed services and by the law that prevents the dissemination of pornography. The assertion of a claim right on public funds, that is the direct imputation of a duty to the tax-paying community, is also qualified and limited by other demands on the public purse which I shall raise again in the conclusion to this chapter.

What sort of a rights-based argument can be made in favour of TG4? A case can be made, on the basis of what is entailed by the right to freedom of speech and expression, for a broadcasting service in the preferred language of a significant minority of tax-paying citizens. If a human interest, in this case in freedom of speech, is important enough to be enshrined in law as a right, then it will generate a complex series of corresponding duties or what Waldron (1989) refers to as "waves of duty". Waldron argues that

> if an individual's interest in speaking freely is important enough to hold the government to be under an obligation not to impose a regime of political censorship, it is likely also to be sufficiently important to generate other duties; a duty to protect those who make speeches in public from the wrath of those who are disturbed by what they say; a duty to establish rules of order so that possibilities for public speech do not evaporate in the noise of several loudspeakers vying for the attention of the same audience; and so on.[4]

Eamonn Callan (1997), who quotes this passage from Waldron, then invites us to dwell further on what other duties might be involved in the "and so on".

> If the interest in free speech is as much a matter of the speech we hear and understand as the speech we utter, as many liberal philosophers have claimed, then it will support duties to forestall the development of media monopolies.[5]

The right to public sponsorship of minority broadcasting is related to the right of citizens to have access to the language of their choice and not to be subject to linguistic monopoly on the part of the media. Without this access, an important aspect of the right to self-expression is infringed. This applies even more to the situation with regard to TG4 where the language in question, Irish, is the first official language of the state. This is not the case in the USA, where English is the only official language, although Spanish is widely spoken in parts of the country.

Yet the "waves of duty" incurred by respecting and vindicating any right are not all equally binding or compelling. The obligation to vindicate the right to freedom of expression means that the law will provide protection to citizens who hold extreme or eccentric political or religious views, but it does not entail an obligation to offer financial support to such individuals in order to give them access to the media. The former is more binding in the way the referee's duty to protect players from violent and dangerous play is more binding than the obligation to protect players from hearing abusive language from spectators. The duty to provide minority broadcasting in the language of choice is a strong one but this duty, as I argue in the conclusion, is not absolutely binding.

But the case for public funding for TG4/minority broadcasting is not only a right claim: it can also be defended on other grounds. Let us consider some of these.

**Respecting diversity**

State sponsorship of broadcasting for cultural minorities reflects a very practical commitment to respect for diversity. Diversity is a more pervasive and long-standing feature of Irish culture than is sometimes appreciated. Cultural diversity has been present among the inhabitants of the island long before the notion of diversity acquired its contemporary currency. To use some phrases from Louis McNeice's poem, *Snow*, our ethnic/cultural/moral landscape is "(i)ncorrigibly plural" and consequently "crazier and more of it than we think". The names to be found in Ireland today reflect wide and varied ethnic/cultural origins: Gaelic (the majority of Irish names); Norse (Harold, Sigerson, Sorensen); Norman (Norman itself, names with the prefix "Fitz"); English (English itself, Green, Brown, Black); Scots (Scott); British (Britain); Jewish (Bloom, Wolfson, Goldberg); Huguenot (Blanche, Champ, D'Olier, Boucicault, Le Fanu, La Touche). Then there are names such as Fleming, Holland, French and Spain that also derive from continental Europe. This diversity makes for a pluralism among the citizens of the country which is contrary to the homogeneous character that is sometimes mistakenly attributed to them. The moral diversity of contemporary Ireland was captured in the 1995 referendum on divorce where, as Taoiseach of the time, John Bruton, pointed out in response to the result, division on the issue was to be found not just between voters but even within the minds of many individuals who felt uncertainty about which way to vote.

## Linguistic diversity

The diversity offered by TG4 is linguistic and this represents a very special kind of diversity that is particularly important to cherish. By expressing something of the spirit of the culture of which it is part, language reflects the character of a nation in a unique way. Let us consider some examples of how language can embody the distinctive mindset of a people. In German, for instance, understanding of the word *gemütlich* entails appreciation of the cultural loading of the expression in terms of the notions of cosiness, intimacy and congeniality that are so valued in German culture. Think also, for example, of how difficult it would be to find single word equivalents in other languages for the terms chic, home, machismo, or chutzpah. In these words we find articulated something of the unique cultural psychology of the French, English, Spanish and Jewish peoples. And sometimes the vocabulary or idiom of one language can make us aware of bias in another. The socially invidious distinction marked in the English language by the terms trade and profession does not appear in the German term *Beruf* which is normally used to designate a person's occupation.

Let me here comment on two aspects of the Irish language that are very striking in this respect. These are its democratic forms and theological idiom. The distinction expressed in such pronominal forms as *tu/vous, du/Sie* and their equivalents in other languages is not marked in the Irish language. Irish young people are often nonplussed by the type of formality that these distinctions mark and the social distance which the terms express can appear odd to them. Later, however, they may come to appreciate the kind of intimacy that is communicated in the familiar form and come to see its value over the promiscuous "you". Or we could say that the use of *tú* in the second person to address individuals regardless of rank or degree of acquaintance with them expresses something of the convivial, companionable and democratic temper of Irish attitudes. The use of Christian names and the lack of authentic equivalent to *monsieur, signor, señor* or *Herr* (*uasal* is a bureaucratic coinage) further communicate the profoundly informal, democratic spirit of social intercourse in Ireland.

Secondly there is the theological idiom. For example, religious sensibility is to be found embedded in the Irish language itself. Such expressions as *Dia dhuit, Dia's Muire dhuit, Dia's Muire dhuit's Pádraig*, and *Beannacht Dé ort* communicate something of the orientation to the divine which is intrinsic to the Irish way of life. The invocations of God have a reality in these idioms which is certainly lost in the English "good-bye" and the Spanish *adíos*. Admittedly there are many common expressions such as *bail ó dhia ar an obair* or *go cumhdaí Dia sibh* that can be replaced by secular idioms, just as it is possible not to use *Grüss Gott* in the southern parts of the German-speaking world. Even in Irish, there are words such as *An Chéadaoin, Déardaoin* and *An Aoine*, meaning first fast, middle fast and fast, that have lost their liturgical significance. Nevertheless, it would be simply impossible to give or return a salutation without using, theological idiom.

Through TG4, the unique worldview of the Irish people, as embedded in the idiom of its language, is given expression in the public arena.

## Resisting the hegemony of English

The case for public funding of Irish-language television is especially important in a country where English is the dominant language. This is not just nationalistic negativity to the language of the former colonial power. In any case English is not just the dominant language in Ireland; its hegemony is worldwide as the lingua franca of commerce, of scholarship and of the media. This status is reinforced by the position of English as the key that provides access to the apparent glamour of Anglo-American media culture. Young people outside the English-speaking world are constantly surrounded by songs, films and television programmes in English, and this exposure serves as an incentive to learn English that is matched by no other language. In the English-speaking world, people are not exposed to the culture of any other speech community in the way that non-English speakers are exposed to the culture of the Anglophone world. Indeed, given the emphasis on learning English throughout the world, we should be less surprised at the competence of some foreigners in the language but instead be surprised that (thankfully) there still are people who do not speak English. The hegemony that the English language enjoys as a result of the ever-increasing eagerness of foreigners to learn English continues to reduce the need for English-speakers to learn other languages.[6] My exasperation in France and Germany in trying to find French or German speakers who did not attempt to foist their English on me has no doubt been shared by many Irish people wishing to learn these languages. Sometimes I wish that non-Anglophones would show evidence of more national pride and personal humility by using their own languages rather than attempting to speak English. In common with many others I normally consider it a courtesy not to be addressed in ubiquitous English. In the past the French were reputed to expect others to know French. And while this may have been true of the generation of Francois Mitterand, nowadays French politicians, sportsmen and writers seem as anxious as everyone else to parade their attempts at English. This development has dismayed some of their countrymen and women. For example, Jean Perrot quarrels with colleagues who use English at academic conferences in order to find an audience for their ideas.[7] But his is a voice against an inexorable trend. After all, a French Minister for Education has decreed that English is no longer a foreign language, stating that it has become a commodity like a computer on the Internet. TG4 is an initiative that serves to temper the Anglophone monopoly of the world and on these grounds alone should be welcomed.

## Affirming diversity

However, public sponsorship does more than simply concede a right or offer grudging respect to an unwelcome diversity. Encounters with diversity open us to what Louis McNeice, in the same poem, *Snow*, refers to as the "drunkenness of things being various". This diversity, both societal and within individuals, contributes to the common good. For example, the access to the cuisine of diverse nations and regions has added to the amenity of life for many Irish people, just as access to Irish music, song and pub culture has enriched the lives of citizens of other countries. TG4 provides access to a culture that is not a direct part of the everyday lives of many citizens. By encouraging linguistic diversity, both society and the individual are enriched. The personal enrichment offered by language is well captured in the insight of the Roman author, Quintus Ennius, who believed that knowledge of three languages gave him three hearts.[9] The enhancement which knowledge of language offers is also communicated in the view of Peadar O'Laoighre[10] that mastery of both English and Irish gave him two intellectual tools or weapons (*dhá arm aigne*). In contemporary idiom this might be called a "pluralism within". The linguistic diversity fostered by TG4 contributes to a very positive enhancement of this "pluralism within".

The production of programmes in Irish has also promoted the creativity of many people and has led to a flourishing of creative talent and energy on the part of programme makers and presenters. Providing an environment in which creativity can flourish in this way contributes to the common good and the creativity which is given an opportunity to express itself adds to the well being of the whole community.

## Irish beyond the classroom

A final reason in favour of the allocation of state funds to TG4 is that it marks a movement away from the classroom as the main, indeed almost sole, locus for the revival of Irish. Although very committed to the use of Irish, I have argued at some length[11] against the policy of compulsory Irish in schools. The policy has not been a success, and anecdotal evidence abounds of the alienating effect it has had on the attitudes of many young people towards the language. There is also strong research evidence that at least some pupils would not choose to study Irish at all at senior cycle if they were given a choice. The findings of a survey from

1993 suggest an unease among the general population about the compulsory status of Irish.[12] Sixty-eight percent of those from the general population surveyed felt that Irish should not be compulsory for the Leaving Certificate and a disturbingly high sixty-five percent felt that it should not even be compulsory for the Junior Certificate. Only thirty-one percent of school pupils questioned thought that Irish should be compulsory at Junior Certificate level and only twenty-four percent thought that it should be compulsory for Leaving Certificate students. There is at least a strong likelihood that many, if not most, of those pupils who thought that it should not be compulsory would not choose to study the language if given a choice. By offering a role for the language outside of the compulsory context of the classroom, TG4 offers a potentially far more fruitful way of ensuring the health of the language.

In spite of these arguments in defence of state sponsorship of TG4, I wish in conclusion to argue that this support should be conditional and subject to limits.

## Conditions and Limitations

To qualify for public funding, those who wish to benefit from such funds must meet certain conditions and preconditions. The most obvious is the need to offer full accountability for any funds disbursed by the state. Another is the obligation to respect the laws of the state and not promote illegal activity – such as support for violence to attain political ends or the encouragement of unlicensed distilling. This is different from offering room for individuals to argue in defence of their opinions; there is a difference between allowing the expressions of differing points of view, however unacceptable to most people, and uncritically promoting them. These are preconditions rather than conditions because it would be inconceivable for the state to sponsor any activity or institution that did not meet these conditions. Another condition is more subtle; it is the responsibility of citizens engaged in minority broadcasting to promote and sustain civic culture by actively fostering social cohesion between the minority and the wider community. No state could be expected to provide public funds for groups which seek to foment secession or in other ways to destroy its physical integrity. Minority broadcasting must contribute to the maintenance of the common civic culture and promote the virtues that sustain the democratic way of life. This is different from expecting uncritical adherence to government policy. Criticism is an intrinsic feature of the democratic way of life and the democratic state must accommodate it.

The most obvious and principal limit to the funding of TG4 or of broadcasting services for minorities is set by humankind's servitude to the scarce resources of the world. There is a strong case for the inclusion of financial provision for minority services in any state's budget, but its appropriateness in any particular circumstances will be a matter for political debate. The choices to be made can be invidious and it is disingenuous to pretend otherwise. We must consider the arguments for and against any particular disbursement of public funds. Choices have to be made regarding the priority that a society gives to health care, social welfare, education, sport and culture. Within any allocation on culture, choices have to be made about the appropriate level of funding for minority broadcasting. The burden of the argument of this paper has been that there is a good case to be made for supporting the use of public funds for this purpose. How this funding will weigh with other priorities is not a matter for me as a philosopher to determine. The tools of the philosopher are not those of direct political deliberation and decision.

## Notes

1 The number of native Irish speakers is low, probably fewer than 50,000. However, the significant minority seeking all-Irish schooling for their children suggests that increasing numbers have a very high commitment to extend their use of the language.

2 Lomasky, 1987:8.

3 See Riordan, 1996.

4 Waldron, 1989:510, quoted in Callan, 1997:184.

5 Callan, 1997:184.

6 The following comments by an Irish civil servant, James Murray (1993), who served on international committees for a number of years capture

what has certainly been my experience overseas. These committees included delegates from various European countries but, writes Murray, the "language used at all our meetings was English. Nobody ever questioned it or challenged it. It was taken for granted". Letter by James Murray to the Irish Independent, 7 January 1993, p.14.

7 Dupuis, 1998: 43-44.

8 See Cassen, 1998: 47.

9 *Quintus Ennius tria corda habere sese dicebat, quod loqui Graece et Osce et Latine sciret*, Gellius, 1928.

10 1973: 14-16; O'Laoighre, 1915: 30-36.

11 Williams, 1989: 1990.

12 These findings are taken from a survey conducted by Wilton Research and Marketing Ltd. (1993) on behalf of The Irish Independent, and published in that newspaper on December 13, 1993.

## Bibliography

Callan, E., Creating Citizens: Political education and liberal democracy. Oxford, Clarendon Press, 1997.

Cassen, B., "Le français n'est pas l'anglais", *Le Monde de 'Éducation, de la Culture et de la Formation*, No. 256, février, 1998, p. 48.

Dupuis, M., "Francophobies", *Le Monde de 'Éducation, de la Culture et de la Formation*, No. 256, février, 1998, pp. 42-44.

Gellius, A., Noctes Atticae/The Attic Nights of Aulus Gellius, translated by John Rolfe, The Loeb Classical Library, London, Heinemann, 1928.

Lomasky, L., Persons, Rights and the Moral Community, New York, Oxford University Press, 1987.

O'Laoighre, Peadar, My Own Story, translated by Sheila O'Sullivan, Dublin/London, Gill and Macmillan, 1973.

Waldron, J. "Rights in conflict", *Ethics*, 99, 1989, pp. 503-519.

Riordan, Patrick, *A Politics of the Common Good*, Dublin, Institute of Public Administration, 1996.

Ua Laoighre, Peadar, Mo Sgéal Féin, Dublin, Brún agus O'Noláin, 1915.

Williams, Kevin, "The limits of paternalism in educational relations", *Irish Educational Studies*, No. 10, 1991, pp. 110-121.

Williams, Kevin, "Reason and rhetoric in curriculum policy: an appraisal of the case for the inclusion of Irish in the school curriculum", *Studies*, No. 78, Vol. 2, 1989, pp. 191- 203.

# CHAPTER 3

# Newspaper Ownership in Ireland and its Effects on Media Diversity: the Commission on the Newspaper Industry Re-visited

## *John Horgan*

*The changing profile of newspaper ownership in Ireland during the mid-1990s led to the establishment of the Commission on the Newspaper Industry which reported in 1996. This paper discusses (in the context of the Commission on the Newspaper Industry) the effect of the highly concentrated pattern of ownership of the print media in Ireland upon the culture of newspapers, and explores a number of possibilities for promoting diversity.*

## The profile of newspaper ownership in Ireland

Recent controversy about the media in Ireland has tended to concentrate on questions of ethics. This is in no way a bad thing: professional standards in this area, and the public perception of the journalist's role and power, can both benefit from ongoing scrutiny and intelligent debate. There is, however, another area of media study which risks being overshadowed and which, in the long term, is at least as significant for the development of that heightened level of public consciousness which is essential for the proper functioning of a democratic society. This is the area of media ownership and control, which has important – if indistinct – implications for freedom and diversity of expression.

Less than five years ago,[1] the media scene in the Republic was both vigorous and variegated, even though underlying trends were giving cause for concern. The country had five morning, four evening (including the *Cork Evening Echo* and the short-lived *Evening News*), and five indigenous Sunday newspapers, quite apart from the plethora of British titles which covered our news stands with their (mostly) tabloid appeals. Today the number of morning papers has shrunk to four, the number of evening papers to two (one of which is effectively a local rather than a national paper), and although there are still five Sunday papers, their number has been kept up only by the emergence of *Ireland on Sunday*.

Is this merely a problem, or is it a crisis? At one level it could be argued that what has been happening over the past five years is no more than natural settlement. Newspaper readership in Ireland is still healthy. It is inevitable that, over time, changes will take place both in the number of titles and in the type of ownership. The most recent figures, indeed, show most Irish newspapers experiencing boom times, with increases both in circulation and in readership. So what is there to be worried about?

Looked at in more detail, the events of 1995 can, in retrospect, be seen to mark a watershed in Irish media history, although one which had been flagged for some time in advance. The key event of the year was the collapse of the Irish Press group of titles, which not only removed three national newspapers from our news-stands at a stroke, but which refashioned the print media landscape in a dramatic way.

That reshaping had already been under way for some time. In November 1990 Independent Newspapers had already acquired a large minority shareholding in the Tribune newspaper group (which at that time also included a number of Dublin free-sheets). In 1994 it moved again, this time to take a stake in the then ailing Irish Press Group. The collapse of the latter enterprise in 1995, although it put a certain amount of the Independent Group's shareholder funds at risk, created a new situation in which that group now controlled, directly or indirectly, a very large share of the indigenous Irish newspaper market. It owned directly the country's largest-selling indigenous newspapers in the daily, evening and Sunday categories. It had a fifty per cent shareholding in the joint venture *Irish Star*, which is also classed as an indigenous Irish newspaper (although of late it has taken on some of the more unwelcome characteristics of its UK partner). And although its stake in the *Sunday Tribune* was (and remains) a minority one, it has the degree of control inevitably associated with the fact that it has underwritten the *Tribune's* historic and continuing losses for almost a decade. In the indigenous Sunday newspaper field, there were only two titles outside its sphere of influence – the *Sunday Business Post* and *The Title* (later to undergo its metamorphosis into *Ireland on Sunday*).

## Concentration of ownership

This was the state of affairs which prompted the government to set up, after the collapse of the Press group in 1995, a Commission on the Newspaper Industry, headed by the former Chief Justice, Mr Tom Finlay, with a membership of twenty, reflecting just about every possible interest in the newspaper industry with the exception of printers. It was given eleven separate terms of reference (including the catch-all "any other matters which affect the industry"), held thirty nine full or sub-committee meetings between September 1995 and June 1996, and reported to the government after what must have been one of the most expeditious and intensely-focused commissions ever to have been established.[2]

This paper deals primarily with the Commission's response to the first of its terms of reference: "The need to guarantee plurality of ownership, to maintain diversity of editorial viewpoints necessary for a vigorous democracy and to promote cultural diversity in the industry".[3] Although the Report does not, and could not, state so directly, the drafting of this particular section represented a compromise between a number of powerful influences on the Commission, and needs to be read with a magnifying glass in order to elucidate the main lines of the arguments that took place. It also reflects the skill of the Chairman in ensuring that consensus of a kind was reached between opposing views, although this of necessity watered down the final recommendations.

The term of reference itself is notable for its assumption that plurality of ownership is something which is a societal good and therefore needs to be guaranteed. All members of the

Commission, as can be seen in particular in Report 1.4-1.5, did not share this view:

> There is a clear link between plurality of ownership and diversity of editorial viewpoint and of cultural content, but it is not an automatic connection nor is plurality of ownership the only feature contributing to such diversity. Plurality of titles is also a significant contributor to such diversity in any given newspaper market particularly in circumstances where a good standard of editorial independence is maintained.

It is difficult to see this finding other than as a partial derogation from the assumption contained in the original terms of reference. Decoded, it means in effect that the considerable – some would say overpowering, though this is arguable – presence of the Independent group titles in the indigenous newspaper industry is not necessarily *a bad thing*. The debate in effect was between two poles: plurality of ownership versus plurality of titles. It was not an abstract debate: the Independent, at the time the Report was written, owned or had substantial interests in seven out of the eleven indigenous morning, evening and Sunday newspapers.

A further clue to the origin of this compromise is to be found in Report 1.9:

> The role of Independent Newspapers in the domestic market and its effect both on editorial diversity and on the indigenous industry's ability to compete against imports led to a number of discussions within the Commission. In the course of these discussions the view was expressed that there are good grounds for believing that the ownership by Independent Newspapers of the *Sunday World* and its half share interest in the *Star* has had a marked effect on curtailing the imported dominance of the tabloid market in Sunday and daily papers in Ireland.

The first sentence in that paragraph must rank as one of the great understatements of the 1990s. What is important about the second sentence is that it records the view of Independent Newspapers but deliberately refrains from endorsing it. It depicts, in effect, a classic standoff. It was extremely important, from the Independent's point of view, that its wide and increasing ownership of Irish media titles, national and local, should not be portrayed by the Commission in an unfavourable light. The Commission opted for neutrality on this one, but at least put down a marker when it indicated its concern that "any further reduction of titles or increase in concentration of ownership in the indigenous industry could severely curtail the diversity required to maintain a vigorous democracy".[4]

The position of the Independent group has a certain crude logic to it. Although never expressed in precisely these terms, it might be summarised something like this: the greatest threat to the well-being of the indigenous newspaper industry is the financial and editorial muscle of the imports, and the war chest they can bring into play to make circulation gains in Ireland; the best way to keep them at bay is to support (or at least not to condemn) the policies of the major Irish player which, because of its size, is the player best equipped to see off the opposition; this means supporting plurality of titles rather than plurality of ownership; and, ergo, if the price of all of this is a slight diminution in the diversity of editorial opinion available to the Irish readership (which point is anyway not conceded) it is a small price to pay for keeping Irish newspapers in Irish hands.

Today, almost four years later, is an appropriate point to review the Commission's response to this problem and to look at what has happened in the meantime. As already noted, the indigenous newspaper industry seems to be on something of a roll. One new title, *Ireland on Sunday*, is looking moderately healthy, even if experiments like *The Evening News* have bitten the dust. Some newspapers are down a bit, but there are no signs of the wild swings in sales or advertising that betoken an industry crisis. In the electronic field, there is a new national TV channel, a new national radio channel, and there has been consolidation and success in the area of local broadcasting beyond the wildest dreams of the gloomy consultants who advised the Interim Radio Commission in 1985.

Beneath the surface, things are not quite so simple. It is now clear to anyone but the most wild-eyed optimist, for example, that the Irish Press titles are as dead as doornails. This is not because there is not a potential market for them, or for something like them: the track record of *Ireland on Sunday* suggests that there may well be. More significantly it is because the shareholding held by the Independent in the Press group, even more than the money it is owed by the latter, is an effective prophylactic against the possibility of reinvestment by any third party to help get the Press papers back on their feet. Who in their right minds would invest in the Press Group now if the first requirement of such an investment would be to enrich (or at least cut the losses of) the shareholders in Independent Newspapers?

The same is true, more or less, of the *Sunday Tribune* scenario. The publishing company which owns the Tribune, and which has two nominees of Independent Newspapers on its board of directors, now owes Independent newspapers in excess of £10 million. Although the paper has been improving and can make a publishing profit reasonably frequently, it is carrying a crippling burden of debt which it has no realistic prospect of repaying. This debt burden is an obvious reason why no other paper would want to take it over, and why anyone who wants to start a new Sunday newspaper would be better off starting from scratch. In the meantime the Tribune struggles on, doing an honourable job on life-support.

Conspiracy theorists please note: it is not necessary to believe that this was all planned by the Evil Empire in Middle Abbey Street in order to secure a stranglehold on the Irish publishing industry. There was a sound commercial logic behind both decisions. In the case of the Irish Press group, it was to keep Conrad Black and his cohorts (who at that stage included the *Sunday Business Post*) at bay. In the case of the *Sunday Tribune*, it was to prevent the Irish Times (or perhaps Murdoch) from snapping up a ready-made Sunday newspaper and financing its attacks on the soft underbelly of the *Sunday Independent*. It wasn't pretty – but then business rarely is.

Is there, therefore, nothing to worry about? If only life was that simple. Viewed in a wider context, the substantial concentration of media power in the hands of one corporate interest, although it may be commercially rather than ideologically or politically driven (as indeed seems to be the case) can be argued to have potentially serious disadvantages for the maintenance of media pluralism and of diversity of editorial opinion as an integral part of Irish culture. And this is all in spite of the fact that the Independent Group employs many fine journalists and has developed a lively, aggressive sense of journalism which can sometimes make up in immediacy for what it occasionally lacks in depth.

The most obvious disadvantage would arise in a situation in which the very size of the Independent empire, instead of providing a bulwark against predators, in fact whets their appetite. We should not be so bemused by the evident wealth of some Independent shareholders that we forget (a) that they are not the only shareholders in the company, and in fact own considerably less than 40% of the stock, (b) that they are not immortal, and (c) that, wealthy as the Independent group is, it is still a relatively small fish in the ocean in which the Murdochs, the Bertelsmanns and the other media giants swim. We have seen, in very recent times, the relative ease with which even comparatively small players move into the Irish media market: the *Mirror* gobbles up a few local papers; the *Sunday Business Post* – one of the publishing successes of recent times – is added to the portfolio of a UK conglomerate without so much as a hiccup; and the *Belfast Telegraph*, probably the most profitable single newspaper on the island, is put up for auction yet again. The bottom line is that media properties are properties like any other: they will be bought and sold on the basis of their profitability by a succession of owners who are swayed not by feelings of national pride and patriotism but by figures on a balance sheet. The story of Irish Distillers is a cautionary tale that could be borne in mind: it consumed and digested almost all its Irish rivals, only to find itself, at the end of the day, a mere pawn in a battle between two giants of the drinks business, one British and the other French. Irish whiskey is still Irish whiskey, of course – but the glass pauses momentarily on its way to the lips when the drinker reflects on the fact that he is swelling the coffers of Messrs Pernod Ricard.

I happen to believe that Dr A.J.F. O'Reilly is a media owner who has other agendas beside profitability (nobody dedicated to profit alone could pour all that money into the London Independent without a qualm), although I might not subscribe to many of them. But when all is said and done the future of the publishing empire in which he currently has such a large say will not, in a couple of decades, be decided by him; and the measure of good-will he has for his native country and its enterprises may not be easily transplanted into a new culture and new owners. Size does matter, but in a perverse kind of way it is also a threat.

## Effect on the culture of print media in Ireland

There are other aspects of the current situation which also pose problems. Newspaper culture in any given society is interdependent with the generality of culture, and there are perverse aspects of newspaper culture which are enhanced by the dominance of any particular title or set of titles. One is the tendency to limit, or even to skew, the media agenda. The nature of the market as it exists at the moment (and I will return to this later) with its heavy dependence on advertising, which now accounts for generally more than half of the gross revenues of any newspaper, means that newspapers, in common with other media, target particular groups of readers (for readers, read consumers) with considerable avidity. This has an inevitable effect, not only on the choice of topics deemed suitable for treatment, but often on the treatment of these topics as well. The most dramatic example of this in recent times (although it may well have been counter-productive) was the famous *Independent* front page editorial on the morning of the 1997 general election, written explicitly on behalf of that part of the population which pays income tax, and implicitly ignoring or belittling the equally legitimate claims of those among us who pay no income tax because their earnings are too low or because they are social welfare recipients. In other areas, the perception seems to be growing that it is easier, and more profitable, to entertain people or to frighten them than to educate or inform them. Entertainment comes in many forms, from the soft-centred stories dealing with the lives and loves of the famous or notorious, to the quirky and the bizarre. Fear is almost as easy to purvey: in its most traditional form, it occurs as the extravagant reporting of natural or man-made disasters. In its more refined form, it occurs as sensational, and often misleading, reporting about crime and the victims of crime. In a 1999 MORI poll in Britain, half of those questioned expressed the belief that tabloid newspapers had a vested interest in making people more afraid of crime, in spite of the fact that the overall murder rate in Britain, at roughly 13 per million of the population each year, is exactly the same as it was in 1857.[5]

In media which are striving to attain dominance, or to protect a dominance already acquired, these characteristics are inevitably magnified. And their malign effect on the diet served up to readers generally is intensified by another phenomenon which is well documented in the academic literature: the tendency of journalists to write the stories that they know will get printed, rather than the stories to which, given a completely free hand, they would primarily devote their time and energy. This is because the internal culture of media organisations is not unrelated to questions of career and advancement.

This is not more conspiracy theory stuff, but a view well grounded in academic research. Writers like Breed[6] and Sigelman[7] pointed out many years ago that there are several organic features of media organisations which have an important determinant effect on ideology. Breed, for example, effectively dismantles the classic reporter's belief in his own intrinsic independence and shows it as being more akin to the state which would, in more modern parlance, be described as being, as it were, in denial.

> No paper in the survey had a "training" program for its new men; some had a "style" book, but this deals with literary style, not policy ... Yet all but the newest staffers know what policy is. On being asked, they say they learn it "by osmosis". Sociologically, this means that they become socialised and "learn the ropes", like a neophyte in any sub-culture. Basically, the learning of policy is a process by which the recruit discovers and internalises the rights and obligations of his status and its norms and values. He learns to anticipate what is expected of him so as to win rewards and avoid punishments.[8]

Put more crudely, reporters learn that some kinds of stories are more likely to be published than others and, the more stories they succeed in getting published, the better their prospects of reward – both the tangible reward which appears in financial form, and the often no less significant reward of peer praise or envy. Policy arrives, not by diktat, but, in Breed's words, by osmosis. There is no need for media magnates to specify every comma and epithet in their publications: effortlessly, it just happens.

The fewer media organisations there are, the fewer media cultures there are. It is also the case, indeed, that the culture of any media organisation is influenced not only by its internal reward system but by the cultures of competing organisations. In this context, it is difficult to ignore the effect on Irish media culture of the UK journalistic culture, and more specifically of its tabloid component – but that is scope for a different article.

## Promoting diversity in the print media

To sum up at this stage: the print media in Ireland, in which one organisation at present has an overweening role, is (partly because of this fact) subject to forces which limit its agenda, impoverish it culturally, and render it more vulnerable to external forces, both commercial and ideological. What, if anything, can be done about it?

The Commission backed away from this problem, observing merely that the present level of cultural diversity in the Irish media was adequate, while warning that any further concentration of ownership would be viewed with concern. This is not to say that policy options were not canvassed, some more vigorously than others.

At the risk of being accused of breaching the secret of the confessional, I can disclose that at least one option which might be calculated to improve media diversity and widen the spread of ownership was discussed briefly by the Commission, but dismissed out of hand; and that a related matter – that of distribution – was touched on only briefly and unsatisfactorily.

To take the second point first, it can easily be seen that issues of distribution can have a huge effect on the availability of a wide range of media to consumers. In Ireland, we have only two print media distribution networks, one of which is owned by the Independent group. It is a situation which offers substantial possibilities for cartelisation, to say the least. The relevance of this to media diversity is, firstly, that media which have a vested interest in protecting their own publications can, if they choose, operate policies in relation to media distribution companies which they also own which can significantly increase the entry costs for new titles. The most classic case of this, historically speaking, was in 1932-33 when the then privately-owned Great Southern Railway Company refused to allow the newly-published *Irish Press* to be carried on the special newspaper trains hired by the existing newspaper proprietors. The fact that the managing director of Independent Newspapers at the time was also a board member of the GSR Company was, of course, no more than one of those happy coincidences with which the world of business and high finance is littered. Other countries are not content to leave media distribution to the laws of the market: in France, for example, many of the small news kiosks in cities throughout the country are State-owned, but leased to private individuals who, as a condition of their lease, have to display any publication that a hopeful editor sends them. This makes it far easier for the publishers of new (and indeed existing) titles to accurately assess the demand, and the geographical spread of the demand, for their publications.

I am not suggesting that such a scheme would be politically workable, or culturally consonant with existing Irish practices: I mention it simply to underline my argument that distribution is an important factor to be borne in mind when assessing the problems facing new media, and that any government which is in favour of promoting media diversity should be thinking creatively in the area of distribution as well as in the areas of taxation and other incentives.

Faced with the problem of actually promoting diversity in media (as opposed to the problem of protecting the media already in existence), the Commission sounded a very faint trumpet indeed. Most of the taxation and other measures it recommended would have primarily benefited existing media (strongly represented on the Commission) rather than doing much for new entrants.

One proposal, which was supported only by myself and a handful of other Commission members, was to explore the possibility of creating a Newspaper Fund which could provide working capital for new entrants to publishing and indeed help tide existing titles over a rough financial patch. The model chosen as an example was that of the Netherlands where, on the introduction of television in the early 1960s, such a fund was established and supported by top-slicing the revenue flowing away from newspapers and towards the new medium. The fund was created explicitly to recognise that the introduction of television advertising amounted to a major distortion of the traditional market for advertising in the media, and that newspapers should be compensated for this. It has, over the years, amassed a fund of such a size that it no longer needs additional capital and simply administers the interest from its fund. The use of the money is controlled by a group of government-appointed worthies who are independent in the exercise of their functions but answerable to parliament through a minister in the same way as many state-sponsored bodies are here.

This suggestion was greeted with cries of alarm and horror, especially from representatives of the newspaper managements on the Commission, who killed it stone dead with the verdict that it would amount to government interference in the freedom of the press. This is in spite of the fact that the proposal, as suggested, would have involved no additional taxation, and a net transfer of resources from the electronic to the print media. It would, in fact, have been cost-free, inasmuch as any of these measures is ever entirely cost free. This is because it could have been financed, as in the Dutch option, by a levy on TV advertising, but in a context in which RTE and any other TV stations involved would be allowed to increase the total amount of allowable advertising in each broadcast hour to produce revenue slightly in excess of that envisaged by the levy

What does "the freedom of the press" mean, if it is to be more than just a slogan? If the press in Ireland is free only to die, to engorge itself on its competitors, or to provide rich pickings for foreign raiders, do we not need to examine a little more coolly our traditionally suspicious attitude to government financing in the media (except, of course, when it is handed out to us by way of

VAT or other taxation reliefs)? Do we not need to accept that standards of probity and objectivity are not entirely absent from Irish public life? And we should think again about creative ways in which the freedom – and, just as important, the diversity – of the press in Ireland in the next century will become less of a knee-jerk response to real or imagined slights to journalists' sense of self-importance, and more of a concrete reality.

## Notes

1 This chapter was written in October 1999.
2 *Report of the Commission on the Newspaper Industry*, p. 2841. Referred to in later endnotes as Report.
3 Report p. 5. The relevant chapter of the Report dealing with this term of reference is at pp. 29-32.
4 Report, 1.10, p. 30.
5 "The Editor", in *The Guardian*, London, 8 October 1999.
6 Breed, 1955: 326-335.
7 Sigelman, 1973: 132-151.
8 Breed, p. 328.

## Bibliography

Breed, "Social Control in the Newsroom: A Functional Analysis", *Social Forces*, Vol. 33, 1955.

*Report of the Commission on the Newspaper Industry*, Dublin, the Stationery Office, June 1996.

Sigelman, "Reporting the News: An Organisational Analysis", *American Journal of Sociology*, Vol. 79, No. 1, 1973.

──────── CHAPTER 4 ────────

# Classical Ideas of Freedom and Current Journalistic Practice

*Marcel Becker*

*The practice of journalism as a profession involves many issues that have an ethical dimension. Most of these are related to the growing influence of commercial media and commercial thought on the media-landscape. This paper presents a reflection on the notion of freedom, an important notion in Enlightenment philosophy. The strongest defender of this idea is the nineteenth-century liberal philosopher John Stuart Mill who argues for "the most unlimited use of freedom". However, currently, "freedom of opinion" is often used as a justification for actions that are morally questionable. Some journalistic practices can impede our freedom and our capacity to engage in independent thought. This is especially so when entertainment is deemed more important than in-depth information or where the media, in order to survive economically, confirm rather than challenge society's existing values and beliefs. There is a tension between classic ideas of freedom and current journalistic practice. Today personal freedom is the final appeal that people make when they are asked to justify their actions; but such a use of freedom can be equated with arbitrariness. Mill and Milton's plea for freedom is to be understood against the background of a larger moral framework: they are convinced that there exists a deeper truth, which has to be recovered.*

## Introduction

The practice of journalism as a profession involves many issues that have an ethical dimension. Such issues can be classified into two broad categories. Firstly, there are questions about the particular behaviour of journalists. The dilemmas they face are many: should journalists use information from a source that does not want to be identified? must journalists always tell the truth, even when people would be severely damaged by its publication? how should they react to pressure from economically powerful institutions? A good journalist needs a range of information from many people, some of whom may be inclined to manipulate or improperly influence the flow of information. Such matters are frequently the focus of public debate, a debate which sometimes results in condemnation of the behaviour of those involved, and in the proposal of journalistic codes of conduct which contain clear rules to guide journalistic behaviour. The second category of ethical issues relates to the fundamental character of news-presentation. The enormous changes that are going on in the media-landscape are often accompanied by complaints about the growing superficiality of news coverage: the emergence of broadcast-stations such as CNN and Sky Television are often taken as examples and proof of such superficiality.

Both of these broad problems are closely related to the growing influence of commercial interests and perspectives on the mass media. The relationship between the "media" and the "market-place" is thus the critical issue in recent developments. While it is not the job of the philosophical ethicist to analyse the empirical situation (it is the responsibility of social scientists to gather and analyse data) or to present solutions (it is up to politicians and managers to solve problems), what the ethicist can do is to reflect on key issues: what are the central notions? how do they function? what is their meaning in the present time? This paper will concentrate on a discussion of the notion of "freedom", a notion that is, or should be, of central importance in debates concerning the commercialisation of the media.

## The task and responsibility of the media

There is an immediate difficulty in seeking an answer to the question of how the task of the news media is to be described. Journalistic codes of conduct usually describe what journalists should not do; there are currently few elaborated statements of the proper task of journalists, few positive indications of what they should do.[1] In the past twenty years many universities have commenced studies in mass media and there is now an abundant literature available. However, in spite of this, fundamental reflections about the task and responsibility of the mass media remain scarce and there is a gap to be filled by contemporary ethical literature.

A literature is, however, available from the nineteen twenties and thirties, and before, reflecting earlier dramatic changes to the social landscape as a result of the emergence of the new media. This earlier literature contains several positive statements that are elaborations of Enlightenment philosophy. The philosophers of the Enlightenment were convinced that spreading information was of considerable value in stimulating the cognitive abilities and culture of citizens. In the beginning of the twentieth century the view was held that the media could serve the emancipation of the people. For instance W. Lippmann, who in 1922 wrote his classic *Public Opinion*, saw in the media many possibilities for what he called "civic enlightenment": the media "maximize the public's understanding of its environment" and this in turn enriches human life.[2] Such "education" was not only valuable in itself, it had also a political aim: information could resist oppression by authoritarian rulers and help to uncover the truth. As a result the people would be equipped to participate in the political process.

In the few positive contemporary statements concerning the task of the media, the combination of these elements can still be seen: the media provide the information that makes it possible for people to participate in the political process. The flow of information concerning the major problems that the world and its people face underpins both democratic understanding and democratic action. A truly "democratic society" is not simply a society in which once in every four years votes are cast and counted; democracy is an institution which depends upon an ongoing public conversation in which informed citizens rationally debate the issues that face them.[3] In contemporary society the media are one of the important mechanisms which stimulate the process in which political choices are made[4] as journalists serve the public interest by publishing facts and opinions without which an informed electorate cannot make good decisions. In large measure journalists are responsible for the quality of the democratic process. The important question is: does this imply a *moral* responsibility on the part of the news media and the journalist?

Those who argue that the journalistic media should stimulate discussion in a pluralist society, focus, implicitly or explicitly, on an ethical task.[5] One of most important journalistic codes of ethics is the *Statement of Principles of the American Society of Newspaper Editors* (ASNE) which states that "The primary purpose of gathering and distributing news and opinion (is) to serve the general welfare by informing people and enabling them to make judgements on the issues of the time". The media fulfill this task in several ways. They report the news; they tell us what important things are happening. But they do more than present facts, they offer a broader interpretive framework and highlight the issues for discussion; they set agendas. While journalists may not tell us "what to think" they have an important voice in determining "what to think about".[6] Moreover the media provide a forum for critique and comment.[7] By providing a forum for different voices and by presenting their own comments, the news media contribute to the forming of public opinion. Thus the central notions (such as "fairness", "privacy" or "justice") in debates concerning media ethics in general and journalistic ethics in particular must be interpreted in the light of the media's task to inform public opinion. In this paper I will concentrate only on the complex notion of freedom.

The notion of "freedom" is often used to justify developments in the commercial media, the basic argument being that such commercial developments should be accepted because they give people "freedom of choice", "freedom of expression", and "freedom of opinion". Thus, it is argued, journalists should be free to write what they want and people should be free to read (or not read) what they want. However, the key question remains: how does the notion of freedom relate to the mission and task of the media? At first glance it seems that there should be a close relationship: a free market brings a free press, which promotes a diversity of opinion. And a free press supplies the access to information that citizens require in order to act in a democratic and responsible manner. Further, journalistic freedom is a necessary condition in the daily practice of journalism. To gather important facts and highlight abuses, freedom of movement is necessary. And closely related to this, the journalist should also be free in the sense of "being independent"; he should not accept gifts or bribes, or act in a way which would make him dependent upon others. Journalists should be free to express and articulate what they wish since freedom of speech is the absolute and necessary condition underpinning journalism. But how are we to understand freedom?

## Freedom: Milton and Mill

Freedom was one of the significant preoccupations of Enlightenment philosophy. In his work *Areopagitica* (1644) John Milton was one of the first to plead for a free press, and surely the first to compare the flow of opinions with economic trade. John Stuart Mill's *On Liberty* (1859) also counts as a later classic representation of the Enlightenment ideal of a free press in a democratic society.

In using the metaphor of the market place of ideas[8] John Milton presented strong arguments against censorship. Censorship involves a lack of esteem for the people and hampers the development of human capacities as people will "sicken into a muddy pool of conformity". Moreover truth has many parts and can be compared with a "firm root, out of which we all grow into branches".[9] A diversity of opinions does justice to this versatility. Milton was convinced of the contribution of the market place of ideas to human progress since if all possible ideas are widely known, the best idea will gain most support. People who argue for censorship doubt the strength of truth, but truth is strong enough to survive challenge and discussion. Milton's confidence reflects his religious convictions that Christian ideas form the root of all true knowledge,[10] and that ultimately it is in this direction that truth must be sought.

Milton's passionate defence against censorship is no longer frequently cited in justification of freedom of speech. The philosopher presented as the strongest defender of the idea is the nineteenth-century liberal philosopher John Stuart Mill. Several journalistic handbooks refer explicitly to Mill's *On Liberty*, quoting especially from chapter two, "On the Liberty of Thought and Discussion". Here Mill makes it clear that he is deeply worried about the suppression of opinions. It is not only governments who are responsible, for in public opinion itself there are tendencies to suppress deviant lines of thought. Mill vigorously rejects such obstruction and pleads for "the most unlimited use of freedom",[11] for which he presents two reasons. Firstly, people never can be finally sure if an opinion is wrong, since faced with the abundance of different and divergent opinions throughout history, we must conclude that the human being is fallible. Fortunately, it is also a human quality that mistakes can be corrected. So it is never justifiable to eradicate deviant opinions; ongoing debate is necessary and will bring us closer to truth. Mill shows himself an heir of the Enlightenment when he contends that humanity is involved in a process of developing its rational capacities. Over time, more and more people hold stronger and better opinions. This position is reached (and has to be sustained) by rational discussion and research. Open discussion brings the truth nearer: "When an opinion is true, it may be extinguished once, twice or many times, but in the course of ages there will generally be found persons to rediscover it".[12]

The second reason Mill gives in his plea for liberty flows from his ideas about what it means to "hold an opinion". It is more than loosely expressing a belief: having an opinion means having knowledge of the grounds and meaning of that opinion, a knowledge which can only be reached in discussion with deviant opinions. Only an opinion that has come into being in the struggle with other opinions can really count as an opinion: "... no man's opinions deserve the name of knowledge, unless he has either had forced upon him by others, or gone through of himself, the same mental process which would have been required of him in carrying on an active controversy with opponents". Without an intensive public debate, words are empty phrases. So a deviant opinion always has something to say, challenging us and forcing us to articulate a response. Pointing to the classical dialectic philosophical methods developed in the Platonic dialogues and in medieval scholasticism, Mill argues that we should be grateful to our opponents.

So Mill's explanation of liberty is inextricably bound up with his views on the role of discussion in society. In debate and discussion people influence each other's opinions and are brought closer to truth. However, "to influence an opinion" must be distinguished from seeking to "suppress" an opinion, and no one should seek to "*decide* a question for others" (italics mine). Mill strongly advocates an intensive debate, in which people try to persuade each other and are open to criticism of their opinions and conduct. This requires a certain attitude. Mill severely condemns the slavish attitude, speaking in a belittling manner about the "low abject servile type of character". An opinion that is not attacked leads to self-satisfaction, which is a moral weakness (which is in itself bad and is an obstruction on the path to truth). This recalls Mill's famous statement: "better a dissatisfied Socrates than a satisfied pig".

## Current developments

Currently we are witnessing journalistic developments that are contrary to the convictions of Mill and Milton. Amongst these developments, four trends are particularly important here.

Firstly, "freedom of opinion" is often used as a justification for actions that are morally questionable. For instance journalists who are accused of operating insensitively or too aggressively may justify their conduct by reference to "freedom". They maintain that freedom of opinion is an absolute right, which they can use arbitrarily. It may be arguable whether a clear distinction can be made between inquisitiveness and genuine truth seeking, but it is obvious that arbitrary or intrusive journalistic practices are far removed from Mill's serious search for truth.

Secondly, in the light of the urgent problems facing the world, the typical daily content of an American television news channel or a British tabloid newspaper is not just a shame but a crime. The French sociologist Pierre Bourdieu argues vigorously that such media only address primary feelings and do so in an exploitative manner. As a result, the possibility of making a strong argument on television is increasingly limited. Instead of thinking freely and independently we are dominated by the symbols that television fires at us. Accordingly, Bourdieu speaks of "symbolic violence". Since it is the ability to think in arguments that makes people free and independent, Bourdieu considers that what is at stake here is our *freedom and independence*, attributes that Mill considers vital.

Thirdly, there are several "free market" mechanisms that cause the press to work *against* the ideal of an informed and critical citizenry. When news is seen as a commodity, the press has to satisfy the preferences of its consumers. This has two important consequences. The aim of the media should be to tell the truth, but instead their efforts are directed at amusing their audience. To criticise a journalist for failing to report significant events truthfully is to accuse him of failing to perform a function that is fundamental to his profession. This is not to say that entertainment is not a dimension of the journalist's work, but it should be subordinate to reporting accurately and truthfully. Furthermore, even when journalists sincerely want to tell the truth, in their presentation of the news they often confirm the pre-existing values and beliefs in society, reproducing the preferences to which the audience responds. The problem is particularly acute when there is news that the consumer does not want to hear.

Fourthly, in order to survive economically most contemporary media conform to mass preferences and this leads to uniformity rather than the diversity of opinion that was proposed by Mill. There may be an ever-increasing range of media available, but there is a "sameness" in the message they present. Moreover, the media are more and more superficial in their treatment, with little intensive or substantive debates between them. This leads to a paradox: the more a news-medium is commercially successful in attracting an audience, the less its existence can be justified. The argument that quality journalism does not attract a large audience is incompatible with Mills "conviction that people are able to decide what is best for them".

These developments in modern journalism impede rather than facilitate informed discussion and debate in society. They tend to ensure that people's knowledge of important matters remains superficial and passive. This is unfortunate in the context of Mill's assertion that a person who uncritically assents to a proposition does not really have knowledge.

## Mill's notion of freedom

The tension between classic ideas of freedom and current journalistic practice suggests that something has changed with respect to our understanding of the notion of "freedom" itself. To understand what has happened it is necessary to look closely at the way the concept of "freedom" is used.

In contemporary society when no substantial arguments are left to justify an action, people in their last resort say "I am free to do as I wish", thus implying that the highest authority is their own preference. As ultimate justification, "freedom" means that "I am permitted to do as I want". In this sense freedom can be equated with arbitrariness. An arbitrary judgement is one that does not have a substantial relationship to the matter under consideration. Freedom understood in this sense suggests indifference in respect of the matter under consideration as well as a belief in one's own self-importance that could be interpreted as arrogance.

For Mill and Milton freedom does not have the function of presenting an ultimate, arbitrary justification for personal action. Their concept of freedom is to be understood against a different, wider framework. Milton refers to the common Christian values that free people will discover as the source of their freedom. Mill's main concern is with the mental well-being of humankind. In *On Liberty* he quotes Humboldt: "the end of man is the highest and most harmonious development of his powers to a complete and consistent whole".[16] In the concluding summary of his second chapter Mill writes: "We have now recognised the necessity to the mental well-being of mankind (on which all their other well-being depends) of freedom of opinion, and freedom of expression of opinion".[17] Absence of freedom impedes mental activity and impairs the development of human capacities. Thus Mill views freedom in connection with the need for a diversity of opinions and an intensive quest for the truth. When people are free they will dispute each other's opinions and in discussion and debate they will challenge each other to employ their capacities and faculties. This results in a diversity of opinions, enhances the quality of public debate and brings truth itself nearer. The difference between Mill and the modern notion of freedom is that in the modern identification of freedom with the arbitrary, substantial argumentation gives way to superficiality. To Mill, people can have an opinion only after intensive discussion, through which they gain a real sense of meaning and a firm foundation for their opinion.[18]

However, it could be argued that Mill's concept of freedom has turned out to be false. While his ideal of freedom remains valid, it has not resulted in the desired outcome. So what has gone wrong? By presenting freedom as a condition of human development Mill implicitly expresses an expectation about how human beings behave when they are free. He presupposes that people, when not impeded by constraints, will develop their talents. This presupposition is articulated in a paradoxical way when Mill states that "it is the duty of governments, and of individuals, to form the truest opinions they can ..."[19] Closely related to this, On Liberty contains another paradox. For Mill "rationality" means investigating a matter from all sides. But this cannot be done indefinitely or it will end in relativism and indifferentism. Mill does not reflect upon this problem: he is convinced that truth will survive critical discussion but he does not explain how it will do so. Both paradoxes point to the conviction that a truth exists which has only to be uncovered. In the former paradox Mill presupposes that some things are so valuable that they must be known, and that people will eventually discover them. In the latter he presupposes that ultimately a truth will appear that is resistant to all criticism.[20]

## Conclusion – application to journalistic practice

Mill's use of the notion of freedom must be understood against (and cannot exist without) a broader moral background. This enables us to reconsider the way the value of "freedom" is used in journalistic practice. An appeal to "personal freedom" cannot be used as a final justification; a broader moral framework is necessary.[21] This applies to current ethical debates concerning journalistic practice. Moral issues should not be treated as isolated: their relation with the broader framework should be reported and explored. Take for instance the notion of "journalistic responsibility" that accompanies "freedom of the press".[22] The interrelation of freedom and responsibility is clearly expressed in the ASNE code, which states: "the first Amendment, protecting freedom of expression from abridgement by law, guarantees to the people through their press a constitutional right, and thereby places on newspaper people a particular responsibility".[23] However, it is not always certain what is meant by such responsibility. Based upon Mill, it should be clear that journalistic responsibility goes beyond legal liability for harmful actions. The responsible journalist is conscious that his task is important for society as a whole and so he is willing to confront moral dilemmas even if this involves making associated painful personal decisions. However, such a journalist will always be able to give an account of his decisions and will not fall prey to the kind of journalism that evokes general indignation.

## Notes

1  Lambeth, E., *Committed Journalism: an Ethic for the Profession*, Bloomington 1992 (1986), p. 8 "What the media lacks is a positive statement on the ethics of journalism that is both conceptually rich *and* demonstrably useful".

2  Shanks, T., *Power, Truth and the Flow of Information*, in P. Rossi and P. Soukop (eds.), *Mass Media and the Moral Imagination*, Kansas, 1994, 43-51, p. 43.

3  Cf. Murray, who describes society as a "public conversation according to reasonable laws". Quoted in Sullivan, W., *The Democratisation of Moral Judgement*, in P. Rossi and P. Soukop, *Mass Media and the Moral Imagination*, p. 34-42.

4  Lambeth speaks of "public service"; McManus, p. 90 of "well-being in society". McManus, J., *Market-driven Journalism*, Thousand Oaks, 1994; Aggarwahl, p. 77 speaks of "public interest"; McManus, p. 24 of "general welfare". Belsey of "public interest", Belsey, A., "Privacy, Publicity and Politics", in A. Belsey, R. Chadwick (eds.) "Ethical Issues in Journalism and the Media", London, 1992, p. 77-92.

5 To Belsey/Chadwick it is the main reason to say that the journalistic profession has an honourable aim; it cares for the health of community. Belsey and Chadwick, "Ethics and Politics of the Media: the Quest for Quality", in Belsey and Chadwick, *Ethical Issues in Journalism and the Media*.

6 Shanks, p. 47.

7 Lambeth, p. 38.

8 Milton"s *Areopagitica. A Speech for the Liberty of Unlicensed Printing*. With introduction and notes by H. Cotterill, London, 1907, p. 29 and p. 37 – opinions are compared with merchandise.

9 Milton, p. 42.

10 Milton, p. 46: "Truth is strong next to the Almighty".

11 Mill, J.S., *On Liberty*. Edited with an Introduction by Gertrude Himmelfarb, London, 1974, p. 115.

12 *On Liberty*, p. 90.

13 *On Liberty*, p. 83.

14 *On Liberty*, Penguin, 1974, p.114.

15 Bourdieu, P., *Over televisie* (Dutch translation of *Sur la Television*, 1996), Amsterdam 1998.

16 Elsewhere freedom is called a condition: "Complete liberty of contradicting and disproving our opinion is the very condition which justifies us in assuming its truth for purposes of action", *On Liberty*, Penguin edition, 1974, p. 79. To reach this end there are two requisites: "freedom and variety of situations" (p.121).

17 *On Liberty*, p. 115.

18 As further evidence it can be noted that in the present time even the origin and meaning of the concept freedom seems to have been forgotten.

19 *On Liberty*, p. 78.

20 In this respect *On Liberty* is not far away from Milton's *Areopagitica* in which he makes clear that his plea for freedom is based on the conviction that the truth will prevail. It was Milton's Christian background that brought him to this conclusion. Mill also presumes the background of a Christian society, in which there was a consensus about what was good and valuable in human life. Mill was also strongly convinced that his upper-class ideology of the "good life" represented the best possible way of life, a conviction he held so firmly that he saw no need to make it explicit.

21 Belsey for instance says that the press must not only be free but also "vigorous". "A press could be free yet timid or torpid". Belsey and Chadwick, p. 6. In this context, see Eoin Cassidy's paper in the present volume.

22 Lambeth, chapter one, elaborates on this as a positive duty of the press.

23 Lambeth, p.28.

# Bibliography

Belsey, A. and Chadwick, R., "Ethics and Politics of the Media: the Quest for Quality", in Belsey, A. and Chadwick, R. (eds.) *Ethical Issues in Journalism and the Media*, London/New York, Routledge, 1992.

Berlin, I., "Two Concepts of Liberty", in *Four Essays on Liberty*, London, Oxford University Press, 1969.

Bourdieu, P., *On Television* (translated from the French *Sur la television*), Amsterdam, Boom, 1998.

Mill, J.S., *Autobiography* (1873), reprinted in Robson, J.M. (ed.), *Collected Works of J.S. Mill*, Routledge and Kegan Paul, Toronto, 1991.

Mill, J.S. *On Liberty* (1859), reprinted in Robson, J.M. (ed.), *Collected Works of J.S. Mill*, Routledge and Kegan Paul, Toronto, 1991.

Riley, J., Mill on Liberty, London/New York, Routledge, 1998.

--------- CHAPTER 5 ---------

# The Media and the Public Interest

## *Herman van Erp*

*A tension exists between two elements in the role of the mass media in promoting democratic values. Firstly, there is the ideal of a public forum (*agora*) as the centre of a democratic public domain where citizens meet and share opinions about matters of public interest. Secondly, there is the reality of those economic market mechanisms that influence the shape of modern mass media. Market mechanisms can be defended, but also criticised as being an instrument for the mere satisfaction of majority wants. In a democracy it is not sufficient for the media to be responsive to market forces alone. These forces will not guarantee citizens responsible and serious discussion of matters of public interest. In a democracy, the state has a duty to provide for a journalism which serves this interest.*

## The media and the public space

Greek democracy was a type of direct participation of all free individuals in legislation, jurisdiction and political decisions. The public forum, or *agora*, where the citizens held court in their capacity as equal and fully-fledged reasonable human beings, had to be a place of political virtues and had to be safeguarded against the spirit of merchandising, money-grabbing and the ambition of fulfilling one's own private desires. In major modern democracies, it is impossible for all citizens to participate directly. According to the American Commission on Freedom of the Press, the press has to be "a free market place of ideas, a forum for the exchange of comment and criticism, (and) ... a representative picture of constituent groups in a society".[1]   One role of the mass media is to take over the function of the Greek *agora*. Accordingly, the role of the press is to keep voters "well informed and capable of actively participating in public life, to subject politicians and governments to scrutiny and evaluation, and to express public feeling and to provide a platform for ideas".[2]

Merrit (1998) notes that journalism is an important democratic art. "In today's geographically dispersed and increasingly inward-looking society, only journalism can provide the shared information and the place for discussing it that are essential to the democratic process. At its best, it creates the *agora* where democracy is practised. But journalism must often be performed reflexively, under severe restrictions of time and space".[3]   In this respect, it is interesting to note that Plato already had a fundamental problem with the opinions and so-called truth of the *agora* because they were always formed under the pressure of time. People on the *agora* wanted to be informed quickly and they collected their information from the different and rather arbitrary sources that happened to be available.

In the modern mass media there is an increasing demand for information in the form of immediate news. Television, in particular, is characterised by a culture of presenting news as a kind of entertainment that must grip and fascinate the masses immediately. Under the influence of television, journalists are compelled to look incessantly for scoops and to confine most of their attention to what competing press agencies will present as news and, particularly, to what television companies are interested in for their talk shows. In this way, the interests of the media themselves largely determine the topics and processes that deserve the attention of the media. The French philosopher, Pierre Bourdieu, suggests that it is more likely that the media will manipulate the public for their own purposes rather than that they will give it the information and opportunities that are needed for a well-balanced exchange of ideas.[4]   In this context, the widespread complaints heard these days about the superficiality of the news media seem to be but a variation of the centuries-old judgement of the intellectual elite about the triviality, inconstancy and even danger of public opinion which has not been informed by responsible authorities.

Seen in this perspective, freedom of the press is a good thing, but it is another matter to make good use of it. That is the reason why classical liberals, who were strong defenders of an independent press without state censorship, did not always make a plea for universal access to this press. In their view the freedom of the press and the right to express one's opinion in a public forum was a privilege of those citizens who proved themselves to be truly independent thinkers. A famous example of this conception of the freedom of the press is to be found in the work of Immanuel Kant.

In his essay, *Zum ewigen Frieden*, Kant envisages the freedom of the press as the only palladium of civil rights. Today, a free press is still considered to be "a bastion of freedom, a safeguard against the various assaults that are made on democracy".[5] In another essay, Kant calls this freedom, which he describes as the public use of one's reason, the most harmless form of freedom.[6] Public use of reason, for Kant, is the way in which scholars can argue in front of the public that constitutes the world of readers. A scholar writes in his capacity as scholar for the whole community of world citizens, a public of which he is a part himself. What Kant says about public reason is interesting in at least two respects. On the one hand, he understands public reason to mean the public of the whole world. It is precisely the openness and universality of the spirit of scholars, who are presumed not to speak in the national interest or the interests of particular groups, that gives them the right to freedom in what they write, to free writing. On the other hand, Kant confines this open sphere of public thinking to those who engage in scholarly writing. Only in this kind of writing does he recognise expressions of public reason that can be trusted unconditionally. This type of public reason and freedom is harmless and cannot be a threat to the legal order because it is not accessible to what might be described as the unlettered masses. For Kant, therefore, this large category of unlettered people is not the public for which the freedom of press has to be guaranteed.

It would seem that Kant had a more limited conception of the extent of the learned public than many of his contemporaries. However, all would have accepted that the idea of the freedom of the press was restricted to journals published for those with the capacity to think independently and to discuss and write about arguments. Inhabitants of the age of Enlightenment saw themselves as members of a republic of letters where debate was the best defence against despotism. The contemporary critical theorist, Jurgen Habermas calls this the "bourgeois public sphere"[7] which, in its coffee houses and new periodicals criticised the Parliament and the Crown. "Because this criticism was carried, out in public, it had something of a transforming effect on Parliament and helped to usher in an era of parliamentary democracy".[8]

In present-day mass democracies and in a global market economy, both the idea of the global public and our conception of the meaning and value of publicity have radically changed. This change is itself largely the product of the development and growth of the public media into the mass media. Journalism is in danger of being reduced to a flat, neutral and detached reporting of fast news and entertainment, without regard for the quality of public discussion and argument. This has the effect of encouraging cynicism and undermining the credibility of journalism. However, a new conception of journalism described as public journalism is emerging to address these concerns. According to Davis Merrit, its objective is to find ways in which journalism would be able to serve a purpose beyond – but not in place of – telling the news: for the purpose of re-invigorating public life by re-engaging people in it. "This can only be done if journalists think of the people reached by their efforts not as an audience to be entertained or as spectators at an event, but as citizens capable of action."[9]

I would say that public journalism does not see the media as a public good in the merely economic sense, but as a good that has to be used by socially responsible journalists for the good of the public interest. For that purpose, journalism must involve not only private but also public virtues, the ability to translate the general ideals of a democratic public life into concrete examples of public reasoning.

## The social responsibility of the media

The public discussion of facts in the light of values and norms in the mass media facilitates participation by citizens in a democratic life. "Mass media can serve democracy only when those who manage them feel a passionate responsibility to create it and maintain it."[10] The acceptance of social responsibility is the moral duty of those who administer the mass media. They are, together with politicians, highly responsible for the way in which the public domain evolves and cannot hide themselves behind the demands of the majority that are driven by markets. There is a moral challenge for the mass media to look for new possibilities to promote the security of the public domain at national levels and particularly to find ways for the creation of a public forum for the European Community. European intellectuals are responsible for preventing the unification of Europe from remaining an undertaking with merely economic purposes. In the words of the Dutch sociologist, Bram de Swaan, "shortly, nothing will be heard in public other than the boom of entertainment, show and propaganda if the furnishing of the public room is left to the political economists".[11] For this reason, we need a journalism in the public interest based on certain virtues. The observance of prohibitions alone is not sufficient for this kind of journalism: it demands the development of special virtues.

So-called public or civic journalism is often associated with a communitarian conception of ethics.[12] In the ethical debate between liberals and communitarians, the former mostly opt for an ethic of general rules and duties, the latter for an ethic of virtue.[13] I would prefer to describe as civic or public the type of journalism that can be characterised as republican because it dedicates itself to the public interest. Public journalism should strive not for typical communitarian virtues that are important for the preservation of communities with shared beliefs, interests and identities, but rather for republican virtues, oriented at truth and universal ideals. We saw that Kant restricted the freedom of the press to what he called the public use of reason, but for present-day mass democracies this is too restricted a conception of freedom. Public reason, according to Rawls, is characteristic of a democratic people. It is "the reason of equal citizens who, as a collective body, exercise final political and coercive power over one another in enacting laws and in amending their constitution".[14] It is a political construction that has a strictly limited subject: the good of the public and the fostering of fundamental justice. It is limited because it is not concerned with all the aspects of what could be a good life. As politicians or candidates for political office, citizens are expected to care not only for their private interests or the non-public ideals of the groups to which they belong, but also to exercise virtues of public reason. Public journalism is not the same as public reason in this sense, because it is independent from the political structure and its subject matter is much wider. It is, however, connected with it in so far as it is interested in the actualisation of public reason. In this perspective, it can be regarded as a form of public reasoning.

Private undertakings and concerns always have social responsibilities that are primarily determined by the notion of negative freedom: in the use of one's own freedom one must not hinder the freedom of others disproportionately. In political liberalism, public law has a primary function to guarantee freedom and equality for all. That is the main reason why the rights of freedom of speech and press are constrained by the law. The media can operate unfettered at least until they collide with individual rights or institutional interests. However, the responsibility of public media cannot be restricted to the observance of the principles of negative freedom.

Negative freedom does not guarantee the more positive freedom that is a condition of the existence of public reason itself. Where the media are driven solely by public opinion, output will tend to be populist in order to secure audiences. In other words output will pander to majority taste rather than to the promotion of the public space, the *agora*, of reasoned political argument. Therefore, the democratic state has an obligation to create the conditions under which public journalism can flourish. This has a parallel in the obligation of the state, explored elsewhere in this volume by Kevin Williams, to provide a media service to linguistic minorities. The state has to support a media service that can resist the pressure of the market. This gives rise to a tension because, at the same time, journalists must be allowed the freedom to criticise the very politicians who ensure their freedom. Therefore, the state also has the obligation to safeguard public journalism by formal rules protecting its independence from the political institutions. The kind of tolerance required here is itself a moral ideal, a principle of enlightened thinking. It presumes that a free communication of ideas is a better basis for truth and a good social life than either political pressure or the demands of the market place.

## Notes

1 Van Cuilenburg, 1997: 80.
2 McQuail, 1998: 133.
3 Merrit, 1998: 119.
4 See Bourdieu, 1998: 90.
5 Murphy, 1998: 90.
6 Kant, Was is Aufklarung?: p. 37.
7 See Navasky, 1998: 113.
8 Ibid.
9 Merrit, 1998: 123.
10 Bogart, 1998: 11.
11 De Swann, 1999: p. 9.
12 See Dennis and Merril, 1998: 156-165.
13 See Alastair MacIntyre, 1985.
14 Rawls, 1993: 214.

## Bibliography

Bogart, L., "Media and Democracy", in Dennis E.E. and Snyder, R.W. (eds.), *Media and Democracy*, New Brunswick/London, Transaction Publishers, 1998.

Bourdieu, P., *On Television and Journalism*, Amsterdam, Boom, 1998 (originally: *Sur la Television*, Paris, 1996).

Dennis, E. E. and Merril, J. C., *Media Debates: Issues in Mass Communication*, New York, Longman, 1996.

Dennis, E. E. and Snyder, R.W. (eds.), *Media and Democracy*, New Brunswick/London, Transaction Publishers, 1998.

De Swaan, B., "Europa behoeft intellectueel debat", in *NRC Handelsblad*, 26th Jan., 1999.

Kant, I., *Was ist Aufklarung?* Berlin, Akademie-Ausgabe VIII.

Lijphardt, A., "Majority rule in theory and practice: the tenacity of a flawed paradigm", in *International Social Science Journal*, 129 (1991), pp. 483-493.

MacIntyre, A., *After Virtue: A Study in Moral Theory*, London,

Duckworth, 1985.

McQuail, D., "New Roles for New Times?", in Dennis E.E. and Snyder, R.W. (eds.), *Media and Democracy*, New Brunswick/London, Transaction Publishers, 1998.

Merrit, D., "Public Journalism – Defining a Democratic Art", in Dennis E.E. and Snyder, R.W. (eds.), *Media and Democracy*, New Brunswick/London, Transaction Publishers, 1998.

Murphy, D., *The Silent Watchdog: The Press in Local Politics*, London, Constable, 1976.

Navasky, V., "Scoping about Habermas", in Dennis E.E. and Snyder, R.W. (eds.), *Media and Democracy*, New Brunswick/London, Transaction Publishers, 1998.

Rawls, J., *Political Liberalism*, New York, Columbia University Press, 1993.

Van Cuilenburg, J. J., *Lezer, krant en politiek: een empirische studie naar Nederlandse dagbladen en hun lezers*, Amsterdam, VU Boekhandel, 1977.

———————— CHAPTER 6 ————————

# Media, Democracy and Economic Power

## Hendrick Opdebeeck

*The media, being a means of transferring and distributing knowledge and information represents an important part of the economic process and the wielding of economic power. Could it be argued that the power of the media increasingly lies in its capacity to ignore democratic values in order to serve the economic purposes of the market place? In this paper, I examine the concept of economic power and the tension that exists between economic power and the ideal of democracy. I suggest that the media has the power to subvert the democratic ideal but need not be so conceived. There is a way of combating this potentially subversive power by moving from what is understood in economics as a data circle to a circle of responsibility.*

### Introduction

The power of the media can be best understood in terms of its relationship with elements of political, economic and technological power. The fact is that the media both drives and is driven by technological innovation. Furthermore, media providers without a secure economic foundation are soon eliminated by competition; and finally, there is a two-way exchange of influence between the media and politics.[1] What is the goal to which media power is directed? Could it be argued that the power of the media increasingly lies in its capacity to ignore democratic values in order to serve the economic purposes of the market place? This is the question that provides the focus for this paper.

Power need not necessarily be classified as something to be condemned. The critical issue is the ethical foundations on which power is framed and exercised. In today's culture, utilitarianism is increasingly becoming the exclusive ethical benchmark of the concept of power. Unfortunately, utilitarianism reduces human activity to a tool or an instrument, with the consequence that human activity risks becoming detached from the democratic ideals of justice or fairness. In this context, the task before us is to examine to what extent justice is being used as a moral standard in the media's exercise of power and to what extent the media contributes to fostering a culture of justice or fairness in our democratic culture.

In examining this issue we will refer to democracy in the civic or *moral* sense. Charles Taylor states in his *Philosophical Arguments* (1995) that a democracy will only survive if the population embodies a moral project, if it turns towards the common good.[2] The democratic ideal in this civic or moral sense is to be found in the French *Declaration of Human Rights* (1789) where freedom as an ethical ideal was seen as the litmus test for the existence of democracy.[3] Today, due to the powerful influence of market economics on contemporary culture, the key civic or moral ideals of freedom, equality and justice risk being marginalised.

In the pre-modern society in which *homo-economicus* had no central position, life was, for the most part, ruled by moral principles that derived their orientation from a religious or metaphysical sphere. For the greater part, politics followed these principles and, in turn, helped to determine the shape of the economy. How times have changed. It is becoming clear that there has been what might be called an inversion of hierarchy. In today's culture, it is technology and the media that are determining social life rather than being determined by it. The economy is producing and distributing what technology, via the media, manages to persuade us to purchase and, slowly but surely, the market place has come to play a determinative role in the political sphere. Situated between utopias that criticise power and totalitarian systems that exalt power, democracy is now being threatened by the market place.

The media, being a means of transferring and distributing knowledge and information, represents an important dimension of economic power with implications in the context of the contemporary inversion of hierarchy. For instance many today would argue that politics is increasingly at the service of the media and the economy rather than the other way around, that it has chosen to adapt to rather than to confront the demands of economic power. This can be seen in the promotion or toleration of multi-national media stations that are saturating the public space and increasingly setting the agenda for public debate. The economic power of multi-national media corporations is creating a scenario that suggests that politics is the inverse of business, i.e. a public body with responsibility but without power.

Essential to this inversion of hierarchy is the one-dimensional influence of technology and the media upon both the economy and politics that has given rise to a culture increasingly influenced by a utilitarian ethic. The many-sided, rich, religious or metaphysical context has had to yield to the criteria of utility. To what extent will ideals such as fairness, equality and solidarity survive in a culture in which economic forces including the economic power of the media are omnipresent? To examine this issue we must focus our attention on the fundamental assumptions of power that underpin the structures of both the economy and the media.

## The fundamental assumptions of power

### *The assumption of the data circle*
The first fundamental assumption in economic theory on this topic is the data circle. By the assumption of the data circle is meant the variety of elements or data, such as human necessities, the conditions of nature or the environment, and the population with its working capacity, technology and money. These elements are supposed to be neutral; they are not supposed to be the creation of vested interests. Furthermore, as long as the economist does not alter one of these elements or data in framing a theory, these important sources of power are supposed not to change. While many media corporations like to represent themselves as neutral means to transmit information, their entanglement with the world of capital, their inter-dependence on technology and the power of the media to play on human wants and desires, make it impossible

for serious commentators to consider them as merely neutral data. Rather it is increasingly obvious that they play an important role in creating endless human needs rather than just reflecting those that already exist.

## The assumption of scarcity

The confrontation with scarce resources is the opposite of the endless human needs implied in the data circle. The presupposition of interminable human needs points to an unwillingness to consider the sensible possibility of confining one's needs instead of making them endlessly expand. Gandhi's famous comment is applicable here, teaching us that the earth is likely to produce enough to satisfy everyone's needs, but not everyone's greed. The constant whipping up of human needs is strongly encouraged by unrestrained non-selective advertising in the press and the audio-visual media. Every year, the American television industry earns thirty-four billion dollars in selling broadcasting time. Every day, the average North American spends one hour on reading advertisements, watching advertisements on television or listening to them on the radio. Clearly, advertising does not stimulate us to limit our wants; all too often the media misuse their enormous position of power, despite their capacity to play the opposite role of diminishing our unbridled needs.

## The assumption of utility

In economics the main preoccupation is with production/utility rather than the question of why certain targets are or are not aimed at. The economist can be blind to the qualitative distinction between sensible and senseless aims, or between aims that result in negative effects such as environmental pollution, unemployment or the ever-widening gap between the Western and the Third World. The preoccupation with maximum utility results in a concentration on short-term concerns: "In the long run, we're all dead" (Keynes). In the media this assumption of utility prevails. More and more the significance of what the media offer depends on the economic effect or its utility. In their own wording, this prerequisite of utility may best be called the assumption of enjoyment.

*The assumption of individuality*

The assumption of individuality is closely connected to that of utility. Only an individual can compare a utility desired with a utility acquired. The assumption of individuality does not mean that collective needs do not exist but the assumption refuses to see them on the collective level. Collective needs are to be considered as being derived only from individual needs. Consequently, the terms "economic acting" and "uneconomic acting" have acquired an overly restricted meaning. An act is regarded as uneconomic if it does not produce any utility for those who performed the act; the question whether something has or has not produced any utility for the community has been neglected. In the media the individual also is the master, because the customer is always right! Professional success is judged by circulation of printed material or ratings on television. Ratings, however, are the addition of individual options. Programmes are transmitted when individuals tune in to the channel of their choice. Issues surrounding the value of programmes for the community or the common good do not feature in a media culture that is dominated by ratings.

*The assumption of aim and means*

The systematic separation of objectives or aims: profit maximising, and means: labour, technology and land is a further point of departure in economics. Little scope is left for interchanging these aims and means, for believing that work of intrinsic quality may be considered as an objective in itself rather than just a means to increase profitability. For example, the present exertion of power to replace labour by "cheaper" capital goods signifies a one-sided view of work as simply a means of production rather than an end in itself. The distinction between aims and means in the manner outlined above creates a single norm, namely efficiency or efficacy. With the increasing acceptance of this assumption, economic criteria are placed on a higher footing than those that concern the fundamental quality of human life. With respect to the media, the separation of aims and means threatens to reduce the work of journalism or that of media providers to one whose sole concern is efficiency defined in terms of market share. In this context, questions associated with pride in the intrinsic quality of one's work fade into the background.

### The assumption of the price

Economics appears only to need a price and market mechanism to compare respective options and preferences and to find the adequate balance. Individual utility seekers have recourse to prices. Through them the supply and demand of aims and means becomes possible. However, from an ethical point of view the price and market mechanism could be labelled as institutionalised individualism and irresponsibility. For example, buyers and sellers are responsible for no one but themselves: a rich salesman would be perceived to act in an uneconomic manner if he sold his goods at a lower price to people who are less financially sound, and a wealthy buyer would not pay more because he happens to meet a poor supplier. Similarly, from the perspective of the world of economics – price and market mechanisms – the media, the viewer and the producer are responsible only for themselves. From this perspective, a broadcasting station need not concern itself about the commercial or moral effect of its transmissions on children or adolescents. Furthermore, a viewer need not account to anyone for his or her own programme choices. The radio or television guide has only to be consulted to find the time of a favourite programme, just as a consumer consults the prices in an advertising brochure: pressing the button may be compared to taking out one's wallet and paying the price. Larger ethical issues surrounding the quality of programming are not relevant in the culture of market economics.

## Economic power and the media versus democratic justice

To understand the precise nature of the confrontation between the use of economic power in the media and the ideals of democracy we will examine media power through the lenses of distributive justice. Traditionally, justice is seen as the moral quality that impels people to give others their proper entitlements. Distributive justice directs this concern to issues relating to the sharing of goods from the community to the individual. In this context, anyone concerned with promoting the ideal of distributive justice must be conscious of the need to balance two conflicting principles, namely "to everyone in accordance with their merits" and "to everyone in accordance with their needs".

The principle "to everyone in accordance with their merits" always refers to the past, to merits rising from a gift, diploma, knowledge, or working ability. This principle therefore has an inevitable tendency to promote inequality. In economics, the focus on merits frequently aims at an increase in economic production both quantitatively and qualitatively. In the process, inequalities are either tolerated or even created. In contrast to the first principle, the second principle of distributive justice, "to everyone in accordance with their needs" positively promotes equality. Its focus is on the basic necessities that are a prerequisite for humane existence.

The Belgian author Louis Duquesne de La Vinelle[4] offers an interesting perspective within which to analyse this issue. He firstly acknowledges the impossibility for one and the same body to make both principles of distributive justice come true, since the principle of merits implies inequality whereas the principle of needs implies equality. Duquesne's solution is to make both politics and the economy function as efficiently as possible. Therefore, he advocates both free competition and genuine democracy. This approach aims to realise the goal of the common good within the framework of an acceptance of both the liberal and the socialist traditions. The liberal approach supporting the free market mechanism solves the problem of merits, whereas socialism copes with the problem of needs by appealing to democratic decision-making.

Another approach would be to suggest that issues surrounding economic power and justice or media and democracy are most successfully co-ordinated in a mixed market economy, where the question of production (efficiency) may be most fittingly combined with the distributive matter in a manner that balances the principles of merit and needs. Government power is needed to keep the private exercise of power in the national community within the limits of the common interest. In the sphere of economic trading, this means that the media would not only be tested against the norm of economic efficacy, but also against the ideal of distributive justice, "to everyone in accordance with their needs".

## The tension between progress, power and justice

The mixed market economy may offer a seemingly logical way out of the tension between economic power and justice, but the question remains whether the division between economic or media efficiency and democratic justice – in other words, between the economy and ethics – can be resolved. For example, the principle of merit which is a central issue within economic power, and which often comes to the fore in the media, stimulates economic growth and progress but tends to favour inequality. This is in contrast to the principle of needs, which rather emphasises equality and curbs growth.

Economic progress has serious side effects. Since the "Club of Rome", people have become all too aware of the limits of growth and progress. One of the reports to the "Club of Rome" has the title: *Beyond the Limits of Growth* (1988). Here, it is stated that, in the growth of their economy, the western industrial nations should shift the accent from the current quantity growth to quality development. The report advocates the abandonment of the old idea of economic growth because it leads to a disproportionate seizure of scarce raw materials, to more environmental pollution and to a situation where gross inequality is tolerated. These opinions are at variance with policies adhered to in many western European countries. In these countries the growth of GNP and the Maastricht Norm are promoted alongside support for the free market sector. In such countries it could be argued that today's economic problems will be solved at the expense of a secure future.

Instead of addressing the justice issues of fairness and social justice, those who wield power in the world of economics end up following the iron law of so-called economic and technological progress that exclusively rewards merit and defines progress in terms of ever-increasing production and ever-rising standards of living. It is a world in which the media are trapped as well. This law can apparently afford to neglect its negative power effects on the Third World, on unemployment and on environmental pollution. Given the negative effects of unbridled economic growth, we are compelled to ask the question as to whether an exclusive reliance on the principle of merit is acceptable even on economic grounds. Bounds must be set to the so-called economic freedom based on merit that does so much to restrict the freedom of those without power

As a social science, economics contains normative elements which concern essential features of human existence. In meeting these real human needs and desires, the demand for justice cannot be evaded even by those who pursue a one-sided utilitarian ethics of merit. It is simply not possible to regard ethics based on the ideal of fairness as a secluded activity with no relevance to the world of economics or the business of the media. If one is to embrace shared responsibility and participation that alone is capable of respecting the dignity of human activities, an exclusive reliance on both an ethics of merit and a false opposition between the individual and the community must be critiqued.

## From a data circle to a responsibility circle in economics and the media

An ethical dimension to the economy and media resides in the six basic power assumptions mentioned above. In this context, data such as human needs, the environment, employment and technology can no longer be regarded as simply neutral quantitative data devoid of any qualitative or evaluative content. If we are to construct a truly ethical economic policy, this data circle must be turned into a responsibility circle. In the preface to one of the last reports of the "Club of Rome", it is rightly stated that the industrial nations carry a special responsibility commensurate with their power, wealth and technological ascendancy. Responsibility towards the needs of the environment as well as those towards technology cannot be evaded. One needs to restore the etymological meaning of the word economy, namely *oikonomia* (*nomos*: rule and *oikos*: house) or good housekeeping. Aristotle distinguished the term *oikonomia* (the art of the good use of wealth) from *chrematistics* (the art of acquiring wealth). In this scenario, a mass medium such as the media should focus on the good life or on the common good for society rather than simply on the profitability of growing circulation figures.

The acceptance of a responsible attitude towards human requirements raises questions regarding the assumption of the infinity of human needs. If only for the sake of the environment, it is sensible to recommend a restriction on human wants, the substitution of *the economy of the enough* for that based upon *the economy of scarcity*. Furthermore, if this substitution were to be accepted, the prosperity gap between the First and the Third World would be replaced by a fairer division of wealth on a basis other than a never-ending subjective scarcity which can never be satisfied. To promote such an ethical environment, the Canadian Lasne founded in 1988 the Media Foundation and began publishing a magazine entitled Adbusters. It currently has a circulation of 45,000 copies in the USA and Canada alone. In order to discourage an over-reliance on the consumer market that is generated by television, an international group of subscribers to the *Adbusters* magazine have recently organised themselves under the banner, "Greenpeace of the Mind". Their activities include promoting advertisements that encourage viewers both to watch less television and to be critical of consumer advertising.

The acceptance of the idea of a circle of responsibility inevitably questions the economic principle of rationality, according to which the economic subject is solely concerned to maximise utility. In the light of the circle of responsibility, one can legitimately place value on the higher human necessities and needs such as self-esteem and self-fulfillment rather than the purely physiological needs. In the context of the acceptance of the validity of these needs, economic growth could be redefined in a manner that includes services that are considered important in promoting cultural and ethical standards of living. Such an alternative, however, is difficult to achieve in a society that is encouraged to consume more and more material goods. However, it is only if one can break free of this limited view of utility that one will be able to recognise the intrinsic dignity of human activities that promote quality of life issues. It is only in the acceptance of the ideal of the circle of responsibility that one can grasp the truth that a human activity such as labour is a valid goal rather than just a means to the economic goal of profitability.

A lesser emphasis on utility maximisation has the further advantage that it would foster an environment that promotes interpersonal relations. In a utility culture, the focus is on the individual. It is only the individual who can compare the utility longed for with the utility acquired. Contrast this with the recognition that only by qualitatively rich interpersonal relationships can people meet the deeper human needs that transcend utility maximisation. In embracing this perspective the media has the potential to become a communication media in the full sense of the word. In a culture that embraces the economic ideal of utility maximisation media power will inevitably work to subvert the democratic ideal of justice or fairness because a narrow view of human needs coupled with an ethic of merit will undermine any ideal not promoted by concerns of economic utility. However, if one succeeds in the cultural task of shifting economic theory from a data circle to a circle of responsibility there is the potential to refocus the power of the media in such a manner that is capable of truly becoming a communications medium. In this context, it undoubtedly has the potential to strengthen the social fabric of society that is the bedrock of any true democracy.

## Notes

1 Sannel, P., "The Media and Democracy", in *Media, Culture and Society*, 14, 1992, pp. 325-328.
2 Compare to Ricoeur's definition of a moral project as "La visée de la "vie bonne" avec et poutr autrui dans des institutions justes". *Soi-même comme un autre*, Seuil, Paris, 1990.
3 Compare to J. Maritain in *Christianisme et démocratie*, Paris, 1943: "le mot démocratie, dans l'usage des peuples modernes, à un sens beaucoup plus large que dans les traités classiques de science du gouvernement. Il désigne d'abord et avant tout une philosophie générale de la vie humaine et de la vie politique, et un état d'esprit". (p. 23).
4 Duquesne de La Vinelle, L., *Le marché et la justice*, Duculot, Paris, 1987.

## Bibliography

Arendt, H., *The Human Condition*, University of Chicago Press, Chicago/London, 1958.

Barry, A., "Television, truth and democracy", in *Media, Culture and Society*, Vol. 15, 1993, pp. 487-496.

Duquesne de la Vinelle, L., *Le Marché et la Justice*, Duculot, Paris, 1987.

Ellul, J., *La technique ou l'enjeu du siècle*, Armand Collin, Paris, 1954.

Ferre, F., *Philosophy of Technology*, Prentice Hall, Paramus, 1987.

Garnham, N., *Capitalism and Communication*, Sage Publications, London, 1990.

Guillebaud, J-C., "Les médias contre la democratie?" in *Esprit*, 190, Mars-Avril 1993, pp. 80-101.

Heidegger, M., *Sein und Zeit*, Tübingen, 1928.

Jonas, H., *Das Prinzip Verantwortung. Versuch einer Ethik für die technologische Zivilisation*, Suhrkamp, Frankfurt/M, 1979.

Keane, J., *The Media and Democracy*, Polity Press, Cambridge, 1991.

Maritain, J., *Christianisme et démocratie*, Paris, 1943.

Miller, D., *The Lewis Mumford Reader*, Pantheon Books, New York, 1986.

Mitcham, D., *Thinking through Technology, The Path between Engineering and Philosophy*, The University of Chicago Press, Chicago/London, 1994.

Opdebeeck, H., "Technology, blessing or curse? A techno philosophical approach", *Ethicomp*, Erasmus University, Rotterdam, 1998.

Ricoeur, P., *Soi-même comme un autre*, Seuil, Paris, 1990.

Sannel, P., "The Media and Democracy", in *Media, Culture and Society*, 14 (2), 1992, pp. 325-328.

Pot, J., *Die Bewertung des technischen Fortschritts*, Van Gorcum, Assen/Maastricht, 1985.

Toffler, A., *The Third Wave*, Collins, London, 1980.

# Section 2

# Media, Culture and the Shaping of Identity

# CHAPTER 7

# Mass Psychology in Media-Ethics Revisited

*Bart Pattyn*

*Among the theoretical models employed to interpret social relations, the economic model is currently taken to be the most authoritative. This is also the case in discussions about the mass media, where owners, producers and users often think in terms of supply and demand, market share and preferences. Such economic discourse is attractive because it makes it possible to circumscribe any considerations about the moral acceptability of human motives. A more careful analysis of what makes contemporary mass media so enticing is required. This paper describes the relationship between self-respect and courage on the one hand, and the energy emanating from group solidarity on the other. The mass media suggest that they can bring individuals into contact with this vital energy. The fact that the mass media are so successful in exploiting this need for group solidarity means that the power acquired by the media has no counter-balance today. In the future this will compromise the critical sensibilities of the citizens.*

## Introduction

In Belgium the amount of time devoted to work in a normal working day in 1998, divided by the number of Belgians above the age of fifteen was 3.1 hours and the number of hours of television viewed per day was 3.02 hours – only a few minutes shorter. A great deal of time is invested in following what is on offer in the mass media because television offers something that people need. People choose to watch because news editors and television producers deliver products that meet the need for information and recreation. In this context, media providers make every effort to ensure that they employ the most efficient strategy for optimally matching supply with demand as distinct from ascertaining the genesis of viewer needs or the moral and cultural quality of viewer preferences.

The dominant model used by media providers to interpret their connectedness to the viewing public is the economic relationship between producers and consumers. It is a model that is perceived to be morally neutral, scientifically objective and in keeping with the ethos of a liberal culture. The contemporary liberal culture is premised upon the viewpoint that no authority can determine what someone should consider good or important. Subjective preferences ought not to be scrutinised in a manner that suggests that media providers are society's moral guardians. It is this cultural context that explains the reason for the success of the economic model of producers and consumers in becoming the standard language, not only when one speaks about the media, but also about culture, academic education, social security, health care and so on.

There are problems however with the economic model of producers and consumers that cannot easily be avoided. This model makes it possible to believe that everything is all right as long as a person's "natural" and personal needs and preferences are taken care of satisfactorily. The prevailing use of economic language seduces us, without our being aware of it, into forgetting that a human being can indeed be a frightening creature. It helps us to cover up the fact that *Dasein* (to draw on Heidegger) is a poignantly open question, a project in an incomprehensible world, in anticipation of an equally incomprehensible death. Speaking in terms of producers and consumers keeps this kind of dark speculation at a safe distance and maintains the illusion that, as a result of developments in science and technology, every consumer possesses a world of unforeseen possibilities and opportunities.

The language of consumers and producers forms a key element of our individualistic culture. In this paper I shall discuss some pessimistic presuppositions from Émile Durkheim, Gustave LeBon and Sigmund Freud. These authors confront us with anti-individualistic and unconventional views on human nature and offer a mass psychology for understanding the way in which the mass media dominate so much of our free time.

## Collective spheres of emotions

There is a tendency today to assume that personal decisions are, by definition, the result of independent reflection and consideration, and that choices are made on the basis of personal preference. Even when the motivation for our behaviour is attributed to "unconscious" processes, the "blame" is ascribed, more often than not, to our personal life history. When we reflect on the multiplicity of things that can happen to a person, it is the individual that we tend to place before our mind's eye. These perspectives reflect a movement to a more individualistic culture in "western" society. Individualism as a political doctrine argues that society only emerges as a consequence of agreement between autonomous individuals. This conceptual sequence implies that, in the first instance, there are individuals who, only in the second instance, form communities. The individual is thus considered to be the *arché* of society.

At the beginning of the twentieth century a number of researchers in France became convinced that this conceptual sequence needed to be turned on its head. They believed that the community had priority over the individual, and that an individual character developed only subsequently if at all. Such a point of departure implies that in our culture, individualism is a fairly recent development.[1] In the past, and to a certain extent still today, human life was and is regulated by a communal, "trans-individual" reality.

In every culture there exist phenomena that are not simply the result of what individual people desire, think or do. Such phenomena are "trans-individual", referring, for example, to concepts such as "group-sentiment", "mentality", "public opinion", "ambience", "current", "tendency", "trend", etc. In ancient communities, according to Émile Durkheim, this "trans-individual instance" made individual thinking unusual and unnecessary because the individual thought and did what would be considered proper for a community member to think and to do.[2] It rarely occurred to the individual to take a "personal" stand against the perceived wisdom of the community. Durkheim referred to this "trans-individual" reality as the "collective consciousness".

Durkheim's "collective consciousness" can best be understood in the context of "what people respect" and consider "worth the effort" being dependent upon something beyond the capacities of the individual. In contrast to what is often assumed, the respect we nurture for ourselves or for others, for customs or institutions, is not solely dictated by individual motives. It is dependent upon participation in something that transcends the individual. The individual does not have this collective consciousness at his or her "disposal". Furthermore, when the collective consciousness is dominant in a society, this does not necessarily imply a kind of undemocratic balance of power. The individual, as an autonomous entity, is in many situations, not really aware of his obedience to that which is expected of him. Similarly, in our culture today, the dominance of common presuppositions or commitments (the collective consciousness) is real, hidden and rarely questioned.

It is impossible to study ancient group sentiment directly, since sentiments and emotions can only be noticed by feeling them Therefore Durkheim analysed moral codes and civil law as expressions of the collective consciousness. In studying their evolution he concluded that the legal systems of ancient societies were geared towards the requiting of any violation of group sentiment with a punishment. Such punishment raised just as much emotion as that unleashed by the violation itself. The choice of terrible punishments such as quartering, beheading and torture was not the result of tyrannical whim, but was a response to necessity. Without some counterweight or response as impressive as the original transgression respect for order and authority, religion and government would vanish and society would disintegrate.

In modern societies, where internal cohesion is more a matter of economic dependence, the emotional connotation is no longer a part of the legal system. The purpose of a modern legal system is no longer atonement but rehabilitation. There is less talk of shame and disgrace. The degree of punishment is no longer necessarily equivalent to the degree of collective indignation.

Instead, punishment is measured in time and cost by objective facts and formal legal rules.

Collective emotions appear to play a much more restricted role in modern societies than Durkheim initially seems to have believed. It is possible that what was previously expressed in repressive jurisprudence now manifests itself in other ways, through the mass media for instance. It is undeniable that modern society is awash with collective feelings of emotion. Such feelings are broadcast and intensified by media reports. Examples include the collective mourning for the violent death of a prominent princess; collective indignation and gloating over the sexual delinquencies of a president; or collective enthusiasm or despair during the course of football's World Cup. All these types of reports have one thing in common; they affect the mood of the crowd.

## Sensation, honour, courage and trust

The sensational undoubtedly involves collective emotions. However, describing collective emotions and considering their impact on a person's motivation is a more difficult task. A collective emotion is usually conceived of as a sum of individual emotions. For instance, the emotion experienced by one person, in learning of the misadventures of a president, is strengthened by a similar emotion in other people. In this way, a collective emotional feeling arises that results in immense public interest.

The originality of Durkheim's theory of the collective con-sciousness can be seen in the way in which he develops his reasoning. As he perceptively recognised, the individual emotion of one person is not merely strengthened by the individual emotions of other people, but is also strengthened by the collective emotion as such. In other words, a self-strengthening movement arises that helps to give the collective emotion a life of its own. This implies that when an emotionally charged trend acquires a collective character, it cannot be said that any one individual shaped that trend. However, it may be said that an individual was shaped by that trend. An individual may not believe in or accept the authenticity of a certain atmosphere or tendency. However, the atmosphere still presents itself as an objective given, a *sui generis* reality. Durkheim stresses this by continually emphasising that the whole cannot be reduced to the sum of the parts. The person who frequents musical concerts or the theatre will know that musicians or actors, at certain privileged moments, are so inspired by a certain mood that takes over the concert-hall or theatre that they can give their music and words a new intensity. Looking back over their careers, many musicians and actors consider these experiences as their most gratifying, even though they cannot offer the slightest rational explanation for what happens to the audience and performers at such moments. Durkheim considered this sort of sacred, objective group emotion to be the source of religious feelings. Such practices and ideas were thought to permeate and transform every segment of social life. He also believed that, in modern societies, social institutions such as justice, politics and education derive their authority from this kind of collective emotion.

Durkheim's thesis also expounded the view that collective emotions generated courage and self-confidence. For instance, members of an energetic professional group, an enthusiastic family or a winning football team, discover growth in personal confidence. Alternatively, members of a family in which there is a painful disunity, or of a governmental department where things are dealt with slowly and bureaucratically or of a company where bankruptcy appears inevitable will undoubtedly experience difficulties in carrying out tasks. The feeling of "being someone", of "doing valuable work", of "counting for something", or of "being involved in something meaningful" is related to the atmosphere in which a person lives and works.

The groups in which a person participates, whether they be the family, the workplace, a neighbourhood, a religious community, a cultural association or a hobby club inspire ideals that transcend the individual's self-interest. When a person takes these ideals to heart, self-respect, courage and self-confidence increase. By participating in groups, individuals are capable of surpassing themselves. They take initiatives that would be foolish from a purely rational point of view. As long as there is an audience to give an individual the feeling that what is to be done is essential, there will be people who are capable of heroic acts. This phenomenon is evident in all aspects of life from family relations to work situations to theatre and sport. If one bears in mind this inspirational power, one can understand why human beings are indeed social animals.

The human soul (or *virtus*: self-respect, honour, courage and self-confidence) is the result of the individual's participation in the group rather than a natural need to be together. Similarly, people who exclude the outside world, friends and family will wither away unless they direct themselves to a virtual *alterité*, or an otherness that is not of this world. Interestingly, people are not very well aware of this kind of dependence because the prevailing individualistic ideology overshadows the importance of group feelings and attachments. A person's observable behaviour, however, clearly reveals those groups that affect his or her identity. The supporters of a football team are extremely interested in the latest achievements of their club; citizens, in the election results, and workers in the performance of their company. What is at stake here is group solidarity.

## Television viewing and group participation

Against the background of Durkheim's observations on the collective consciousness, I would like to return to the discussion of television's role in the modern world, a world that is often assumed to be dominated by an individualistic culture. According to Tocquevillee's definition, individualism is to be understood as a withdrawal from social life and a turning inwards towards family members and friends. Given that family life is so often fragmented in contemporary "western" culture, one might be led to conclude that individualism has never been so omnipresent as it is today.

It is true that in today's "western" culture people withdraw. However, in withdrawing, they do not completely separate themselves from the outside world. They keep an eye on what takes place in politics, in their neighbourhood and in the world at large. They have an informant, quite a good informant: one who tells them about the places where things happen, where decisions are taken, trends are set, films conceived, important matches played, the future created and riddles solved. This informant is television.

The role of television in our culture can be compared to that of

the court of Versailles in the France of Louis XIV. For the French
nobles, the closer the contact with the monarch, the more important
they felt. The nobles who were not at Versailles felt exiled; for
nothing important happened, if it happened outside the king's
court. Now, nothing happens unless it is reported on CNN.
Television broadcasts with large viewing audiences have a power
like Versailles. People watch television in the belief that they will
see what they have to see in order to be "in touch", in order to
belong to the world. Successful television gives citizens the feeling
that they will see what is going on at the very heart of the group
that affects their identity. So, news reports are devoted to mass
meetings, political events, shocking revelations concerning well-
known personalities. Similarly, entertainment programmes highlight
spectacular shows, soap operas and sporting events.

In recent years, the rise of commercial broadcasting has been a
significant development in the medium of television. Previously,
the public broadcasters had the lion's share of the viewing public.
However, many new broadcasters have now entered the arena in
Europe (from 21 TV channels in 1980 to 119 in 1997, each of
which serves only a fraction of the viewers). Given the wide variety
of broadcasters and television programmes, it would seem that
one can no longer claim that television keeps people uniformly
informed about what is going on in society. However, this view
must be qualified somewhat on the basis of market share statistics.
In each national state of the European Union, no more than two
broadcasters share half of the market per language. In light of the
enormous interest in the medium of television, these broadcasters
enjoy a very large audience out-reach.

The existence of a greater number of broadcasters does not
necessarily imply a completely different range of programming.
The difference of emphasis between reports from different
networks is usually minor. Network editors keep an eye on the
bulletins from rival networks and if the competition has some
interesting news, they will attempt to report the same news as
soon as possible. This is also true of entertainment. There is
usually little difference in the concept or in the formula with
which various successful amusement programmes and talk shows
are constructed. It is true that each broadcaster has his or her own

atmosphere and that people respond to what individual broadcasters are offering. In spite of the apparent diversity in television, viewers remain fascinated by programmes that involve a strong "us feeling", a feeling of "us against them". This feeling is strengthened by the idea that a large number of viewers are watching the same programmes. Therefore, television will always be a business with a few large broadcasters, even if they co-exist with many smaller specialised ones.

People spend a significant portion of their valuable time watching television because television provides them with information about the groups that affect their identity. Choosing to be on top of things, being alert to what is going on in society, is concerned with affective relations that people have with groups that they consider as their own. For an understanding of the affective relation between the individual and the group, the theoretical perspective that is most useful is undoubtedly the concept of "identification".

## Identification and the power of groups

The ability to attract others to identify with them gives power to persons, groups and institutions. This power can be a good thing if these persons, groups and institutions have good intentions like responsible parents and educators. However, it can also be terrifying. This is especially so, if the consequences of the process of identification remain hidden. We tend to use the term "identification" in an active sense. This creates the impression that during the process, the subject is in control. It suggests that the individual makes up his own mind about who or what he will or will not identify with and that he is able to give up previous engagements. This loose use of the term may cause us to forget how easily identification can turn people into accomplices to mass murder or similar horrors.

For historical reasons it is better to define identification as the semi-unconscious process of being seduced into identifying with someone or something. This is a process in which, once it has taken place, it is impossible to undo without leaving scars. One should bear in mind that identification is like "falling in love". Indeed, even without recognising it, people are aware that their self-respect is dependent on what their "identification models" value. Individuals are usually prepared to do foolish things to gain approval of the other. Even in the modern world people are extremely sensitive to what significant others think of them. In his treatment of the identification process Sigmund Freud often speaks of "self-respect". In his view self-respect relies on a reinvestment of energy in the self, a process that triggers the narcissistic associations of omnipotence. It is interesting that in this context he makes use of a metaphor that makes us attentive to those interpersonal processes that we tend to overlook in our individualistically oriented understanding.

In Freud's opinion it is as if energy, desire or love (the terms are frequently interchangeable) can flow from one person to another like some measurable quantity. A person loses the amount that has been invested in someone else and in consequence feels disconsolate, unsure and dependent, like someone in love. What the other person has "received" increases their personal energy, resulting in a feeling of pride, self-respect and omnipotence. Such a physical paradigm seems absurd because no one would accept that personal feelings can be quantitatively transferred from one to another. However, this metaphor seems less absurd when one realises that courage, resilience and vitality are closely allied with self-respect, self-assurance and even with a certain feeling of omnipotence, and that all these phenomena are linked with the support, love, encouragement and appreciation which has been shown, or is currently being shown to us, by those in our immediate environment.

If our initiatives are unappreciated, or if our requests for love go unanswered, then we feel shame. At such moments our self-respect and self-assurance have disappeared and we have the feeling that we no longer have any meaning. The conclusion here is the same: an individual's attitude to the people with whom he wishes to identify, is always ambivalent. Others can both encourage and destroy the motive and the meaning of what is personified.

What is crucial to our argument is the fact that people tend to misinterpret the existence of this ambivalence. Either they think that "to identify with something" is just a cognitive process with the same connotation as "to recognise something", or they are convinced that the people with whom they identify are just like friends and mean well. Usually they do both. Firstly, they have the impression that they can choose their own group of friends and fellow citizens, in the same way as they are convinced that they can rationally decide which values they want to follow. Secondly, they believe that they can participate in the groups with which they identify without provoking dissension. Freud investigated this kind of group in *Massenpsychologie und Ich-Analyse*. Before turning to a discussion of that book, it is necessary to say something about Gustave LeBon and his *Psychologie des foules*, a work that inspired *Massenpsychologie*.

Durkheim's views on group sentiment did not come into existence in a vacuum. A number of prominent researchers, with whom he would later engage in a dialogue, published material on the same topic around the same time. Three years prior to Durkheim's study, Gabriël Tarde's *Les lois de l'imitation*[3] appeared in 1890 and five years later Gustave LeBon published *Psychologie des foules*.[4] The latter publication was considered to be the most authoritative work on mass psychology for fifty years after its publication.

Concerned with the individuals who make up the masses LeBon wrote that individuals tended to experience a feeling of invincible power, losing their sense of responsibility in the anonymous crowd. Such individuals are quickly influenced or "infected" by the behaviour of the other individuals who constitute the masses, undergoing a sort of persuasion akin to hypnotic suggestion. The masses as such are impulsive, unstable, irritable, easily manipulated and gullible. Someone wanting to take advantage of the masses would do best not to employ reasonable arguments, but rather should offer fascinating visual images that they should repeat again and again. The masses, as such, shelter no doubts. For this reason they are able to offer blind faith in a particular authority and maintain a position of unlimited intolerance.

The only positive thing LeBon has to say is that the masses can raise the moral standards of the individual: "while the personal advantage of an isolated individual is more or less his or her only motivation, this is seldom the case where the masses are concerned."[5] The masses, however, do not elevate the moral standards of an individual by appealing to his or her capacity to reason, but rather on the basis of emotional influence. LeBon's denigrating choice of words goes back to his initial aversion to the socialist movements that he viewed, from his middle-class conservative standpoint, as a phenomenon of a counterfeit culture. The pessimistic tone of his work also stems from the delimitation of his topic: indeed, LeBon did not have in mind an organized society, but rather the ephemeral masses.

LeBon's *Psychologie des foules* was the point of departure for Sigmund Freud's *Massenpsychologie und Ich-Analyse*,[6] published in 1921. Fascinated by LeBon's observations, Freud asked himself how it is possible that people can be so strongly tied to one another despite the ambivalent nature of interpersonal relations and how it was possible that the intellectual capacity of the individual was so powerfully inhibited in a group situation. In an effort to answer these questions he proposed the following hypothesis: the masses emerge when individuals equate their ideals with the will of a single leader or with a single abstract system of ideas and thereby come to identify with one another. When the "ego ideal" became completely equated with the common ideal, then personal rationality tended to vanish.

The feeling of omnipotence experienced by the individual in a group context harks back to the narcissistic origin of his or her emotional capacity that has crossed over to the ideal of the group. In such a group every imperfection is projected onto people and institutions that are commonly believed to be "bad" and are situated outside the circle of "fellow feeling". When conformity comes under threat, the individual is affected at a level that constitutes his or her personal identity, namely his or her "ego ideal". Given the fact that the "ego ideal" is charged with narcissistic willfulness, the emotions released by the threat to the "ego ideal" are akin to the impulse of self-preservation. In this regard, Freud wrote: "in the undisguised antipathies and aversions which people feel towards strangers with whom they have to do we may recognise the expression of self-love, of narcissism. This self-love works for the preservation of the individual, and behaves as though the occurrence of any divergence from his own particular lines of development involved a criticism of them and a demand for their alteration ... it is unmistakable that in this whole connection men give evidence of a readiness for hatred, an aggressiveness, the source of which is unknown, and to which one is tempted to ascribe an elementary character."[7]

Like LeBon, Freud also had the ephemeral masses in mind. He was well aware that "the collective masses" that completely absorbed the individual were rather rare phenomena. "Each individual is a component part of numerous groups, he is bound by ties of identification in many directions, and he has built up his ego ideal upon the most various models."[8] With this theoretical background in mind, we will now return to our earlier analysis and see if it will open some other perspectives on why people devote so much time to television.

## Freedom and the attraction of the mass media

Freedom is normally defined as the ability to do what one wants. However, it seems unlikely that people feel free only to the extent that they have the means to do what they wish. Someone in financial need has the feeling of being fixated on material concerns, of course, but how is it that some people in the same dire circumstances feel more free and less worried than others? What is it then that leads to the feeling of not being free? The feeling that one is trapped is undoubtedly connected to the awareness that one is not able to take part fully in social life. People can feel quite free, even when they are suffering under all sorts of unbearable demands, if they feel they are participating in something that is at the core of the group life of which they are a part. Apparently what works in a liberating manner is the "we feeling". The need for involvement explains why people are so keenly interested in what happens to the groups that affirm their identity.

It is from this perspective that we must now re-examine the need for information discussed at the beginning of this paper. People do not watch television in order to acquire just any kind of information. The sort of information that people need primarily deals with news about events that affect the group of which they are a part. This kind of knowledge is only a very small segment of what is taken to be information. In this context, television functions not only as a provider of news about what affects the group, but also as a generator and intensifier of facts that affect the "we feeling". News on television forms the nucleus of a virtual popular stampede. Its affective significance does not only derive from the facts themselves, but also from the size and scope of this virtual stampede.

What can be said about the need for information can also be said about the need for entertainment. The success of soaps, game shows and films is often related to the fact that they are viewed *en masse*. There is always something or someone who succeeds in finding a tone that releases a specific emotion or appeals to a "we feeling". Once interest increases through increased media coverage the trend becomes self-fulfilling, until the masses are sated. The whole process resembles what LeBon described when he discussed the suggestibility of the masses.

The link between using the mass media and the feeling of freedom becomes exceptionally clear when people are asked to imagine a life without television. It appears that they can scarcely imagine how to live a televisionless life without becoming alienated from "reality". Television is no longer spontaneously considered a leisure activity. Leisure is associated with things like hobbies, gardening, going out, etc, while the media are considered to be on the same level as sleeping, eating, drinking and maintaining social contacts.

## Ethical consequences

For the purposes of this paper, I do not have to go into great detail concerning the ethical consequences of the group dynamic paradigm for which I have cited evidence. It seems sufficiently clear to me that such a perspective sheds a completely different light on the success of television as a medium than the consumer-producer paradigm. Yet I would like to show in what direction ethical evaluation is pointing. It should be remarked that the fundamental hypothesis for which theoretical evidence has been sought will have to be empirically founded. Can empirical observations be made which show us that television's success is primarily due to involvement in groups, whether real or virtual, that affect a person's identity? Is it true that people experience television as an instrument for breaking out of their closed existence by bringing them into contact with social life, whether it be the social life of the local, national or international community? And if that is true, is this instrument effective?

The ethical consequences opened up by the group dynamic paradigm point in two directions, one positive and one negative. From a positive perspective the medium of television can be considered as a relief for old, sick and isolated people. Empirical data shows, for example, that old people who watch a lot of television are more alert than those who do not. Television involves people in their community, and they feel less abandoned or excluded. The negative aspects are closely related to the evolution of social life in general.

Europe is witnessing a reduction of participation and interest in many groups. For instance the number of active members of religious communities has declined sharply, as well as the number of active participants in political parties, and the strength of European trade unions is waning. Similarly, membership of cultural organisations seems to be on the decline. In any case, the fraction of time invested by people in this sort of social involvement is quite small compared with the number of hours spent in front of the television. A consequence of this might be that the group dynamic generated by the media resembles that of an ephemeral mass.

If Freud is correct in saying that people owe their critical powers to the fact that they are members of various groups, then the reduction of social participation as a result of television will have negative aspects. Already one can observe that people with insufficient social capital and who do not participate in an interactive social life will more easily be tempted to believe what they see in sensational news reports. Such an audience is more receptive to undemocratic propaganda.

At the same time, the mass media have come more and more under the control of powerful financial groups. Such monopoly positions, combined with the increasing suggestibility of the viewing public, have resulted in a degree of concentration of power that has never before been seen. The entry of some media personalities into the world of politics is a foretaste of a future in which powers such as the political, the legal, the commercial or the journalistic may fuse into a single domain. In the interest of democracy, one can only be opposed to such a development.

## Notes

1 The best-known contribution to this debate is undoubtedly that of Marcel Mauss, "Une catégorie de l'esprit humain: la notion de personne, celle de 'moi'", reprinted in M. Mauss, *Sociologie et antropologie*. Paris, Quadrige-PUF, 1991.
2 Durkheim developed the idea that the community is completely dominated at the start by the trans-individual "collective consciousness" in *De la division du travail social*, Paris, Alcan, 1893-Paris, Quadrige-PUF, 1991, although it continued to play a fundamental role in his later work.
3 G. TARDE, *Les lois de l'imitation. Étude sociologique*, Paris, Alcan, 1895.
4 G. LEBON, *Psychologie des foules*, Paris, Alcan, 1895, 1926; (Quadrige, 14), Paris, PUF, 1983.
5 Id., op. cit., 1926: 42.
6 S. FREUD, Gesammelte Werke, Vol. 13: 71-161; Eng. Trans. Standard Edition, Vol. 18: 67-143.
7 Standard Edition, Vol. 18:102.
8 Ibid., p. 129.

## Bibliography

Canetti, E., *Masse und Mach*, Hamburg, Claasen Verlag, 1960.
Durkheim, E., *De la division du travail social*, Paris, Alcan, 1893.
Freud, S., "Massenspychologie und Ich-Analyse" (1921), *Gesammelte Werke*, Vol. 13, p. 71-161; Eng. Trans. Standard Edition, Vol. 18, p. 67-143.
LeBon, G., *Psychologie des foules*, Paris, Alcan, 1895.
Moscovici, S., *L'âge des foules*, Paris, Fayard, 1981.
Tarde, G., *Les lois de l'imitation. Étude sociologique*, Paris, Alcan, 1895.

# CHAPTER 8

# Narrativity, Ethics and the Media

## Paul van Tongeren

*The mass media have become the dominant storyteller in contemporary culture. Ethical questions emerge concerning what stories are told, and not told, by whom, to whom and in what context. These concerns can be clarified by examining the nature of narrative. Of particular importance are Ricoeur's notions of prefiguration, configuration and refiguration. These are considered within the context of a distinction between an ethical reflection on narrativity and narrative ethics:*

> *Our lives are ceaselessly intertwined with narrative, with the stories that we tell and hear told, those we dream or imagine or would like to tell, all of which are reworked in that story of our own lives that we narrate to ourselves in an episodic, sometimes semi-conscious, but virtually uninterrupted monologue. We live immersed in narrative, recounting and reassessing the meaning of our past actions, anticipating the outcome of our future projects, situating ourselves at the intersection of several stories not yet completed.*[1]

Story, or narrative, shapes human culture and identity. We are who we are because of the stories that we hold in common. Stories are the stuff of communication; the young child is immersed in a world of narrative. In contemporary western societies the mass media have become a dominant storyteller, determining what stories are told, and not told, to whom, and in what context. The narrative character of mass media, both journalistic and electronic, is strikingly evident. Advertisements frequently adopt a narrative structure by which products are situated in the context of the life-style of a particular target group of consumers. Television "soaps" create virtual communities based upon the stories of daily life. Film, drama and "docu-dramas" have an obvious narrative character. The news story forms the basis of local, national and international news reporting. Tabloid newspapers are filled with the life stories of the famous. Not only does the content of media reflect a narrative structure, but also media usage is often a determining factor in the personal life-story of the individual media user, shaping topics of conversation, the daily schedule and personal preferences.

Storytelling is an affair of the imagination allowing us to construct reality and explore our individual role within it. In this context, the relationship between mass media and narrative is fundamentally an ethical concern. This ethical concern can be articulated by means of a focus upon a number of elements: the relationship between an event and a narrative of that event; the relationship between the narrative and personal identity; the relationship between the storyteller and the story hearer; the relationship between narrative and the visibility of minority groups or members of other cultures, and the interplay between the medium of storytelling and the narrative.

## The structure of the narrative

By crafting and telling stories we seek to articulate and define our personal, social, global and cosmic reality. Our identity is largely constituted by the stories that are told about us, either by ourselves or by others. Our knowledge of the reality outside of ourselves is also mostly based on stories. This is the case for each of us personally, not only during childhood but also throughout life. It is also the case at a societal level; from the beginning of time human groups have sought to articulate the mysterious dimension of being human by telling stories, the great myths of every culture,[2] be they the myths of the great religious traditions or the sagas which shape tribal or national identity. Even in contemporary society science has not taken over the role of story as a vehicle for exploring depth identity. It is through narrative that each human culture transmits its tradition and knowledge to each new generation that is, in its turn, entrusted with preserving and telling the story to the next generation.

To understand the notion of a narrative structure it is first necessary to make the fundamental distinction between an event and the story of that event. It is immediately evident that there are numerous stories that can be told about a single event both by the same person and by other participants or observers. Stories exist by being told. Even the same person will tell the story in a different way depending upon to whom the story is being told and the purpose of its telling. Story telling therefore immediately introduces plurality, a range of possible interpretations and multiple perspective taking. Access to the reality of the underlying event is therefore never immediate but mediated through narrative.

Despite such narrative plurality, narrative also possesses a unity. Both the storyteller and the listeners recognise a story as an organisational whole. Every story is an organisation in which the different elements of the told event are brought together in a certain order with a certain sense of direction. Such unity and order are both necessary and unnecessary. They are necessary because this is the only way the story can be told. Without a beginning and an end, and an ordering and connecting of the intervening elements, there can be no story, and maybe – in so far as the event only comes about through its being told – no event itself. However while such order is necessary, none of the possible orders is strictly necessary on its own. Stories can be originated in many different ways and existing stories can evolve in new ways.

The order or organisation that characterises a story presumes and limits the heterogeneity of the elements of the story. Nevertheless without some heterogeneity there can be no story-telling, certainly no sense of suspense, but only repetition. Telling a story consists in the connecting of different elements with each other within the realm of the possible. That which is too strange is dropped – and possibly forms the seed for a new, different organisation of (partially) new elements, a new story.

Narrative is intrinsically related to time and temporality in a number of ways. Fundamentally a story exists in time. Not only does the reading or telling of a story take time, but there also is always a "history" in a story, an evolution from beginning to end. There are earlier and later elements that get their meaning by the order in which they are placed. Further a story is usually concerned to situate itself in a timeframe. The opening of a story normally gives the situation, even if this is not always as explicit as the famous examples of "in the time of ...", "once upon a time ..." or "in the beginning ...". One often notices how difficult it is to locate the precise moment at which a story begins, that is to draw a line somewhere in time that functions as a precise starting point for a series of events. Furthermore, different historical periods tell a story in different ways using different media (a fairy tale is a different kind of story to an epic or contemporary news reportage with accompanying video-clips). Each of these different narrative forms or styles is dynamic, they have accompanying conventions and traditions that have evolved over time and continue to evolve.

## Narrativity and ethics

Thus story telling is a creative activity, an action by which a person creates reality by giving order and meaning to the elements of an event. This creation is not a *creatio ex nihilo* and while the creative power is limited it nevertheless remains very large. Not only does the story exercise power over what is told, it also affects future possibilities. In this context Paul Ricoeur's (1988) three-fold distinction between prefiguration, configuration and refiguration is of interest. Here the focus is not just on the story in isolation but on the wider narrative reality encompassing the selection of what is told, how it is told, and the consequent narrative of our actions by which the story continues to be told.

Stories are prefigured in the sense that events occur which are suited to being the subject of a human narrative. Prefiguration is the structure that makes events suited to be told. As MacIntyre[3] writes "stories are lived before they are told". Human life has an implicit narrative structure because it is not only a biological fact but also and most importantly an event of meaning. A friend who dies, an accident that happens to us, a personal success, a war that breaks out, a political change, or a natural disaster we experience, all such "circumstances" demand to be given meaning by the act of telling a story. The search for meaning in such events demands the interpretation that is found in stories. Reality therefore has a prefigurative structure that asks to be made explicit in stories, makes such explication possible and guides it as well. In this sense a story already exists before it has been told.

Prefiguration points to the offer of meaning that is given with the world as the place where humans live. Our own experience, and the lives of other living beings around us, invite us to be story-tellers in order to explore the moral dilemmas within human experience. All morality begins with the search for meaning in terms of the "right" which must be done.[4] But such ethical inquiry immediately demands narrative. It has a basic moral quality because it testifies to the manner in which we are open to the potential meaning that announces itself in events.

Being told in an actual story configures the prefigured events. "Configuration" is the term for the story as it is actually told. The configured story is held in tension between prefiguration and refiguration. It can't be separated from the prefiguration which it makes explicit or from ongoing refiguration because every story is just the starting point for other narrative retelling. Refiguration constitutes a domain of continuing action that is invoked by the telling of a story. Thus the storyteller who speaks of a failure thereby forms the intention to make a new beginning or the one who tells of a violation or denial of rights begins a protest, etc. In those resultant actions the "told" is "retold" anew; the story is not finished, it gets a new direction and the earlier ending is given a new destination and meaning.

Prefiguration forces us into configuration, to an interpretation of events by structuring them in narrative, a structuring which involves taking a stand concerning which events are of significance and choosing a perspective from which to narrate. By the way we tell who we are, who the other is, how the world is made up, what happens and why, we accept the offer of prefigured meaning and fulfill our responsibility. Every story has a moral dimension in the sense that through the story we order the diversity of events and experiences into a "whole" with a certain coherence. Through the story we also preserve what has happened in the event and connect the past to the future. The story makes it possible to take responsibility for and to bear the consequences of our actions. Thus even the holocaust must be told.[5]

The philosopher Hanna Arendt identifies the actions of "promising" and "forgiving" as two of the characteristics that constitute distinctive human reality in the true sense of the word.[6] Both of these actions presume a narrative context. Promising is the bringing forth of a plan implying continuity in what would otherwise be just a series of coincidences. Forgiving implies that one doesn't regard a past human action as a definitive fixed fact, but that one puts it in a story, thereby allowing it to be told and retold in a way which is capable of generating new relationships. Such a retelling is a refiguration which exists primarily in the new action embedded in the continuation of the narrative. Refiguration flows from our understanding of the moral quest embedded in the story and how we shape and reshape ourselves accordingly. Primarily it is our moral reaction to the story, the way in which we do justice through action to the meaning we have articulated.

The moral task has an essential narrative dimension because human life is always itself a story and is contained in related stories. Every human is born into a web of stories about humankind in general, about certain people and himself or herself in particular. The task of each person is to assimilate these stories into his or her own story, a story that he or she can personally sign. Thus each human person is a story that he or she must learn to tell in the first person, or as Ricoeur notes "a story in search of its narrator". It is here that the essential moral task of humankind is located. This task is not to be fulfilled alone but together in dialogue with other storytellers, it is "only in fantasy do we live what story we please. In life, as both Aristotle and Engels noted, we are always under certain constraints. We enter upon a stage which we did not design and we find ourselves part of an action that was not of our making. Each of us being a main character in his own drama plays subordinate parts in the dramas of others, and each drama constraints the others."[7] As narrators of our own story we make an appeal to others who, at the same time, limit our freedom of narrating. Narrative self-interpretation stands under the demands of mutual recognition and reciprocity. But these demands are not some "mute reality", but a human reality that wants to be understood as part of the story that seeks its narrator and its destination.

## Narrative ethics

Narrative ethics draws upon philosophical or theological reflection. It has two complementary foci: on the one hand it is concerned with the moral aspects of the narrative structure of the human reality; on the other hand it is concerned with the narrative aspects of moral phenomena and ethical theories.

The first concern, reflection on the moral aspects of narrativity, has been dealt with above, especially in the discussion concerning the prefigurative narrative structure of reality as human reality, the manner in which human self-becoming is a matter of autobiographical configuration, and the way in which the possibility of refiguration exists in general moral actions but especially in the freeing practice of forgiving. The work of Nussbaum (1990 and 1995) is also helpful here. Using many examples, she illustrates how the reading of stories acts as a kind of moral education. Literature makes it possible for us to engage with moral experiences to a much greater extent than is possible in actual life, and therefore refines and sharpens our moral sensibilities.[8]

We turn now to the second focus of narrative ethics, the reflection on the narrative aspects of morals and ethics. Refiguration makes it possible to explain how a single event can receive a new meaning by being inserted into a new story or by giving the existing story a new twist. Once again this can be clearly illustrated by reference to the distinctively human act of forgiveness that refigures a previous configuration of a shared narrative of injury. Thus, in forgiving, an event or action can be forgotten as well as remembered. Forgiving or forgiveness can be explained as a virtue in the sense of an (Aristotelian) middle between two failed kinds of stories — on the one hand an obsessional repeating of the same static story of injury and on the other hand a discontinuous narrating of separated future stories.

We can go further. Ethics are not possible without narrative. How would it be possible to explain an ethical theory or ethical point of view, and to understand it, without making an appeal to stories? It is possible to take Kant's analysis of the moral experience of duty and reconstruct it in purely abstract terms. But to understand Kant's analysis presumes that it can be contained in stories, for example those of Heinrich Heine where he tries to explain German philosophy to his French friends. One can rationally reconstruct the derivation of the categorical imperative that forbids the reduction of a person to a means, but to understand this categorical imperative, and to make its normative force also motivating, one will have to tell stories, like that of Primo Levi (1958) of his experiences in Auschwitz. Ethics is a reflection on the obligation associated with human action; human action is both recorded and sustained by narrative.

## Ethical considerations concerning the mass media and narrative

With the above observations in mind we can return to our consideration of the ethical dimensions of the relationship between the mass media and narrative, bearing in mind that contemporary mass media have a definitive role articulating the story that society tells about itself and by which it becomes itself.

An initial concern relates to the narratives which the media choose to tell and those which they choose to ignore. Embedded within human experience are numerous narrative prefigurations, however the media only configure a small section of these. This is immediately evident when we examine the narratives related to news reportage. What stories are presented as the most important in the selection made by the news media and by the way in which they are presented? It is often claimed that contemporary mass media shape us into citizens of the global village, but on what stories is our interest in the extended human family focused? What for instance do we really learn about Africa or Latin America from media reports concerning these continents? And which ways of life are presented as being normal, desirable and ideal, or alternatively as being suspicious and problematic, through the selection of news topics as well as the manner of reporting them? It could be argued that the coverage of Islamic culture and countries in western media provides a thought-provoking illustration of this problem.

The media have for the most part taken over the role that the poets preformed for the ancient Greeks. The Greeks recognised that nothing actually happens without the mediating role of the poets; to have really happened, something must be told and sung about. Like the poets of the past, the mass media today have the power to let things be recognised as having happened or ignored as if they never happened. The eagerness with which all sorts of organisations and action groups ask for media attention for all their activities is nothing new, but a contemporary form of what humankind has always known: in order to exist, something must be narrated. The way in which the Dutch media focussed attention on refugees seeking asylum is an illustrative example of this. Around Christmas 1998 there was a lot of media attention for a group of asylum seekers who were in awful circumstances; while it was cold and wet, they were housed in leaking tents. Media attention led to immediate action by responsible politicians. However after the success of this media offensive, the asylum seekers disappeared from the public view rather quickly. While just about everybody remembers the leaking tents, hardly anyone knows what subsequently happened to this group of people.

A narrative media-ethic should also focus on an ethical analysis of actual patterns and characteristics of storytelling in modern media. If it is true that reading literature can function in the formation of moral sense, and if the mass media can be thought of as types of or analogues to literature, it is of great importance to analyse the way they shape the moral imagination. Concern should be wider than that which is presented or depicted but also include the manner of its presentation or depiction. What is told in a society about what is happening in and to that society forms society's story of itself. By what is told, and by the way in which it is told, a society forms itself. For instance, the heroic epic is not only the effect of, but also the producer of, a different type of society to the one that is expressed in tragedies. The nineteenth century newspaper forms a different society to the global society formed in the twentieth century by television, or the virtual society formed at the start of the twenty-first century by the "World Wide Web". The various media shape the stories that are told[9] and therefore affect the society that narrates itself in these stories.

Media not only choose which of the prefigured narratives to configure, they also configure them in terms of the characteristics of the medium involved.

Increasing technological sophistication is serving to sharpen further the question of narrative visibility and invisibility as an ethical concern. Through satellite and digital broadcasting the individual viewer or listener will be able to choose from a previously unimaginable number of media channels. The explosion of the Internet is also making vast amounts of information available. The argument is often made that such developments are personalising media usage and increasing personal control and selectivity. But do such instruments for selection have their own moral meaning? Is the selection of broadcast channels and "web-sites" only a matter for the individual user or do the providers bear some moral responsibility? Is the expansion of the possibilities for choice indeed a form of pluralism and an expansion of the range of (moral) experience? Or is the possibility of enhanced moral sensitivity and solidarity threatened by increasing personal selectivity since too large a choice makes it possible that someone can always satisfy his or her one-sided needs in a narrow way?

Finally narrative media-ethics should focus on the moral capacity of the media. The media can contribute to the refiguration or retelling of stories that historically or culturally have been configured in a manner which is blinding or choking of future growth. In deeply rooted conflicts (such as Northern Ireland or the Balkans) the media as storyteller can make a contribution to the refiguration of a complex history. Of course such retelling can be either a stereotypical confirmation of past prejudices or be a liberating refiguration which works towards forgiveness and reconciliation. Research is needed into which narrative media techniques prevent stereotyping. However the mass media enable a community to take ownership of its story; to configure it in a certain way, to tell it as they see it and, by interacting with the configured stories of others, to refigure their own story. Thus the media can play a vital part in the way in which a divided or minority community takes responsibility for what it makes of itself and its world.

## Notes

1 Brooks, 1984: 3.
2 cf. Stevens, 1985: 95ff.
3 MacIntyre, 1981: 197.
4 cf. Van Tongeren, 1994a: 203ff.
5 cf. Kearny, 1999, p. 27ff.
6 Arendt, 1989: 236ff.
7 MacIntyre, 1981: 213.
8 cf. Nussbaum, 1990 and 1995.
9 Postman, 1985.

## Bibliography

Arendt, H., *The Human Condition*, Chicago, The University of Chicago Press, 1989 (First edition, 1958).

Brooks, P., *Reading for the Plot; Design and Intention in Narrative*, New York, Vintage, 1984.

Heine, H., *Zur Geschichte der Religion und Philosophie in Deutschland*, Leipzig, Reclam, 1945.

Kearney, R., "Narrative and the ethics of remembrance", in R. Kearney and M. Dooley (eds.), *Questioning Ethics: Contemporary Debates in Philosophy*, London, Routledge, 1999, 18-33.

Kemp, P., "Towards a narrative ethics. A bridge between ethics and the narrative reflection of Ricoeur", in P. Kemp and D. Rasmussen (eds.), *The narrative path, the later works of P. Ricoeur*, Cambridge, MIT Press, 1989.

Levi, P., *Se questo e un uomo*, Torino, Giulio Einaudi, 1958.

MacIntyre, A., *After Virtue*, University of Notre Dame Press, 1981.

Nussbaum, M., *Love's Knowledge: Essays on philosophy and literature*, Oxford, Oxford University Press, 1990.

Nussbaum, M., *Poetic Justice: the literary imagination and public life*, Boston, Beacon Press, 1995.

Postman, N., *Amusing ourselves to death: public discourse in the age of show business*, New York, Viking, 1985.

Ricoeur, P., *From Text to Action. Essays in Hermeneutics II*, London, 1991.

Ricoeur, P., "Life: a story in search of a narrator", in M.C. Doeser and J.N. Kraay (eds.), *Facts and Values.* Dordrecht, Nijhoff, 1986.

Ricoeur, P., *Time and Narrative*, Chicago, University of Chicago Press, 1988.

Stevens, B., "Action et narrativité chez Paul Ricoeur et Hannah Arendt", in *Études Phénoménologiques* 1985, nr. 2, 93-109.

van Tongeren, P. (1994a), "Moral philosophy as a hermeneutics of moral experience", in *International Philosophical Quarterly* 34 (1994) 2, 199-214.

van Tongeren, P., (1994b), "The relation of narrativity and hermeneutics to an adequate practical ethics", in *Ethical Perspectives* 1(1994) 2, 57-70.

─────────── CHAPTER 9 ───────────

# Cultural Ecology and Media Ethics: a Perspective From a Christian Philosophy of Communication

*Andrew G.McGrady*

*The mass media either shape or constitute culture and the quality of a culture can be judged by the way in which, within each act of communicating, human spiritual well-being is either nurtured or inhibited. This paper proposes the notion of "cultural ecology" as a shared ethical focus between religious faith and media practice. The background to this concept is to be found in the Roman Catholic philosophy of "inculturation". The way in which we create and use our cultural environment is as much an ethical concern as our relationship with the physical environment. It is suggested that media professionals approach culture with an "ethic of care". The invitation to all involved in the media is to consider the effects of the decisions they make, and the products they produce and disseminate, upon the wider human cultural environment, particularly as this relates to the spiritual and imaginative aspects of culture that underpin human social and inter-personal communication.*

## Introduction

When considering ethical issues relating to mass media there is a tendency to look at micro-issues relating to the content of media productions and the effect of these on the worldview and behaviour of media users. Such an ethical emphasis is important, but there is also a need to stress structural or what we might call meta-ethical issues.[1] Media technologies transform the societies in which they are located, and they both condition our way of knowing and provide the interpretative paradigm which we use to negotiate meaning. The fundamental ethical issue which ought to be addressed – the meta-ethical issue – is the relationship between mass media and human culture. It is this relationship and our response to it which I wish to consider.

## Mass media, religion and culture

Contemporary western society is characterised by rapid cultural transformation, the replacement of a mono-cultural environment by cultural plurality, and the marginalisation of institutionalised religion from the cultural mainstream. Developments in commu-nications technologies and the emergence of the global market, along with increased personal mobility provided by cheap and regular international air travel, have provided the stimulus for this rapid cultural change.

In the popular imagination culture is associated with what we might call cultural artefacts – the physical incarnations of culture – a famous painting, a classical text such as a work of literature or a musical composition, a style of architecture or a particular consumer item. But such artefacts are only the tip of an iceberg; culture is deeper and more central to human endeavour. There are many differing opinions as to what constitutes culture,[2] however what they hold in common is their recognition that culture is a socially constructed environment which, using symbols, presents, often unconsciously, a dominant worldview, coherent or otherwise, within which individuals locate their identity and generate meanings. Just as the quality of the physical environment (the quality of the air we breath, the water we drink, the food we eat) has a direct effect upon our physical well-being, so the quality of our cultural environment has a direct influence upon our spiritual well-being, our self identity, our interaction as social beings, and the exercise of our imagination. Concern for culture is therefore an ethical concern that has a spiritual dimension.

An ongoing debate is that of whether the mass media simply reflects culture (or a variety of cultures) or in effect constitutes a culture (or set of cultures). In this context it is useful to acknowledge that the relationship between the mass media and culture is diverse, differing between different media forms, in different societies, and within different generations in those societies. This relationship can be conceptualised along a dimension; at one extreme the mass media simply reflect a broader culture, at another point along the dimension they actually shape culture, and at the other extreme, in a growing number of instances, they present so pervasive a world-view that they function as a cultural environment providing a mediated alternative to direct first-hand primary experience. Either as a culture in its own right, or a central factor shaping popular culture, the mass media have influenced the way in which people, especially the young, throughout the western world learn, form values, and express their identities. All perception and learning are determined and mediated by culture and popular culture, shaped by the media, provides the primary language of meaning for people. Media promoted products such as McDonald's fast food, Levi jeans, Nike shoes, Asics clothes and the music of pop groups provide the shared cultural icons of the international market place. They provide common points of reference for status and identity, determining what is of value and establishing themselves as loci of meaning. The media proclaim repeatedly that there is one of these products "for everyone in the audience", and invite consumers to recreate themselves in the image and likeness of the promoted products.

As the processes of individualism, consumerism and secularisation proceed unabated the mass media function as a cultural alternative to religion by creating the categories with which we perceive the world.[3] The mass media have also become the great mythmakers of our time, creating and sustaining myths about society in general, including the myth that happiness consists of limitless material consumption; that consumption is inherently good, and that property, wealth and power are more important than people. Further the media create the common rituals by which we order our lives, in a way similar to the manner in which the regular celebration of the divine office ordered the day in medieval monasticism. We rise in the morning to the sense of order and stability provided by the news on the early morning radio; we finish the working day by watching the scheduled news broadcasts; our primary sense of community is provided by catching up with the gossip provided by the virtual community of the soaps which we watch so religiously. Such media products provide us with an awareness of origins and a sense of destiny, and they offer models for personal and social integration.

How then should a religion such as Christianity seek to enter into dialogue with the media-centred culture of contemporary western society? Too often the response of the church is one of antagonism and suspicion, usually expressed by the view that the media is anti-church and is promoting a secular agenda. Another unacceptable response is to believe that no real dialogue is possible between religion and media-culture.[4] But religious belief cannot isolate itself from any dominant culture in which it finds itself.

## Towards a Christian philosophy of communication – inculturation

The emerging theology of inculturation in Roman Catholic circles provides a firm and acceptable basis for a dialogue with media culture. In several key texts the Second Vatican Council called for a dialogue between faith and culture.[5] The council saw the gospel as renewing and purifying human culture. *Gaudium et Spes* (para. 48) states that "the Church ... can enter into communion with the various cultures, to their enrichment and the enrichment of the Church herself". One of the initiatives of Pope John Paul II was the establishment in 1982 of the Pontifical Council for Culture. In this context he noted that the synthesis between faith and culture "is not just a demand of culture, but also of faith. A faith which does not become culture is a faith which has not been fully received, not thoroughly thought through, not fully lived out."[6] The concept of inculturation is also prominent in the recent (1998) papal encyclical *Fides et Ratio* which acknowledges that "from the time the Gospel was first preached, the Church has known the process of encounter and engagement with cultures".[7]

There are several key propositions of the emerging Catholic approach of inculturation. Firstly, the expression of the revelation upon which a religious faith is based reflects a particular historical culture. An ongoing task of evangelisation is that of continually re-expressing faith in the context of a plurality of cultures. Faith cannot be dependent upon any single culture but must be re-born in every age and culture. Further "culture itself has an intrinsic capacity to receive divine revelation" and "no one culture can ever become the criterion of judgement, much less the ultimate criterion of truth, with regard to God's revelation".[8]

Secondly, cultures are not static. "Cultures share the dynamics which the human experience of life reveals. They change and advance because people meet in new ways and share with each other their ways of life".[9] Human agency is the factor which shapes and reshapes culture: "all people are part of a culture, depend upon it and shape it. Human beings are both child and parent of the culture in which they are immersed".[10]

Finally, the encounter between faith and culture is one which brings about transformation. Christianity should embrace the "modern world in a spirit that is constructive and yet critical, that announces and denounces at one and the same time".[11] This is an interactive process of faith "entering into communion" with a culture, a process in which each culture is purified by the religious tradition, and the religious tradition itself is purified by the new culture.

The focus of inculturation is usually that of the evangelisation of a foreign, non-European culture within a missionary context. However the recognition that in many essential respects the mass media now constitute a culture allows the emerging theology of inculturation to be utilised as the general framework for dialogue. There is a need for a commitment to treat media products seriously as cultural mediations of contemporary human experience. This commitment should include a rejection of any stance which regards the electronic media as inherently less worthy a cultural expression than print, or of an approach which seeks to withdraw from media culture and create a religious subculture divorced from the cultural mainstream. Moreover, a recognition is needed that media products are human constructions rather than descriptions of actual reality, the camera does lie; it is possible to offer different constructions of reality. It must be recognised that media products present a world-view and associated value system. They often set the agenda for public discourse and determine what is visible and invisible within a society; and their producers and editors act as gate-keepers controlling access to public discourse within a society.

There is need for a balanced approach which includes a willingness to affirm, appreciate and celebrate those positive aspects of media culture as well as to challenge that which needs to be transformed. As Baum[12] notes the mass media of communication are often an exciting development at the heart of modern society, embodying human intelligence, artistic talent and technological innovation. Dialogue should be based on an abiding belief in the power of human agency, that is in the power of individuals to interpret and shape the media culture in which they are immersed and to be agents of cultural transformation. The mass media are not only the products of a deterministic political, economic and commercial supra-structure, they are human productions that are offered to human consumers. Each generation has the possibility of reshaping human media culture. It is possible to develop the critical faculties of media-users and to develop the ethical sensibilities of media-producers.

If the dialogue between faith and media culture is to be one that is mutually enriching then Christians must seriously ask what can be valued in media culture? There is of course much to be appreciated in the media concerning the explicitly religious. But at a deeper level there is also the need to appreciate other features of contemporary media culture, specifically the appeal to concrete experience, the celebration of the human creativity, the raising of a global consciousness, and the use of storytelling as a basic mode of communication. Further a dialogue based upon inculturation poses distinctive challenges to theology: specifically the manner in which the media dominate leisure-time activity suggests that what might be called a "theology of entertainment" needs to be articulated.

## Cultural ecology: preserving social communication

Whereas a philosophy of inculturation provides a basis for, and the imperative for, the dialogue between culture, religion and the media, it does not provide a clear neutral ethical focus for the dialogue. What is needed to facilitate dialogue with media producers and media users is an ethical concept which, while open to religious belief, does not presume or depend upon it. I wish to suggest that the notion of "cultural ecology" has considerable potential to provide such an ethical focus.

Ecology first emerged in the nineteenth century as a branch of biology dealing with the relations between organisms and their physical environment. The term is derived from the Greek *oikos* referring to "home" or "a place to live". During the mid 1960s (as the images provided by the Apollo space missions of the colourful, life-filled, warm earth floating like a bubble in the dead, inky blackness of space, captured the popular imagination) people became intensely conscious of the interdependence of all life forms, including human life, on the planet. Ecological issues became vital ethical issues as people recognised that the quality of the earth's physical environment determined the quality, and in some cases the very possibility, of human life.

More recently the concept of ecology has also been extended into the area of communications as "information ecology", or "media ecology". These refer to the actual and prospective, direct and indirect economic, cultural, social and environmental impacts of information technology. The *Recommendations for Actions and Commitments* at the Second Earth Summit held in June 1997 included a section on "information ecology" and called for:

> A major commitment to analyse and explore the opportunities and implications of the rapidly evolving 'information and communication ecosystem' and to identify critical information ecology issues.[13]

While the emergence of information and media ecologies is to be welcomed, I believe these are but an aspect of the more inclusive concept – "cultural ecology". Foundational to the proposed concept of "cultural ecology" is the recognition and acceptance that human social communication depends primarily upon the relational and spiritual quality of human culture and only secondarily upon technological systems. Thus the essential function of a culture is to provide an environment that nurtures and sustains human well-being and inter-relatedness.

Human spiritual well-being and the spiritual dimension of culture are interdependent. Human spiritual well-being depends upon an equilibrium which, alongside the satisfaction of basic human needs, acknowledges the imaginative and the aesthetic dimensions to human flourishing. It also signifies a movement away from personal egocentricity towards the recognition of the irreducible "otherness" of the other (Levinas) as a basis for both the acknowledgement of a transcendent dimension to human existence and the acceptance of its relational character. The recognition of a spiritual dimension to culture gives voice to the belief that culture is not exclusively a self-enclosed human system, but that there is a "giveness", or an "otherness" to which human society must be attentive. Reflection upon the dynamic of cultural evolution reveals a striving towards a *telos* (a goal, a greater good, an ideal). Thus, it is the presence of "the other" outside of the self, who invites the self to a relationship, that both constitutes human spiritual well-being and provides the spiritual foundation for culture

In summary, the way in which we create and use our cultural environment is as much an ethical concern as our relationship with the physical environment. The mass media either shape or constitute culture and the quality of a culture can be judged by the way in which, within each act of communicating, human spiritual well-being is either nurtured or inhibited.

To develop this concept of cultural ecology further I wish to consider several features of the ethical focus of biological ecology and use them analogously to explore cultural ecology.

*Ecological concern is an ethical imperative that is global in its scope. Preserving the environment is the task of all: while legislation and codes of practice are necessary to establish broad outlines governing behaviour, each individual ultimately needs to take personal responsibility.* It is generally recognised that solving the problems associated with the ecology of the physical environment requires a multi-layered approach combining inter-governmental and national legislation, codes of practice and enhanced personal awareness and acceptance of responsibility. This principle applies to cultural ecology. There is a need to develop a sense of ethical responsibility towards culture that transcends the requirements of legal frameworks and codes of practice. The parameters used within the media to make ethical decisions need to be set more broadly than a simple consideration of what may offend advertisers or avoid litigation. Each act of communication within a culture either enhances or restricts the capacity of that culture to support authentic human communication, that is to promote human spiritual as well as physical well-being. Just as each act on the part of individuals with respect to the way in which they interact with the physical environment influences the ecology of the whole of that physical environment, so too each act of communication within a cultural environment has a global impact. The truthfulness, honesty and integrity of each act of communication through the mass media influences the whole cultural environment for better or worse. Further, this is not just the responsibility of journalists and broadcasters. The issue of media usage (how messages are received and interpreted) is at least as important as issues of media production. Thus cultural ecology, as an ethical imperative, must be the concern of all.

*The environment has a delicate balance which can easily be upset, and which therefore must be understood and respected and protected.* Concern for the delicate balance of the ecosystems of the physical environment is now widely appreciated. It is recognised that this balance can easily be brought out of equilibrium by careless interventions and that such disequilibrium is detrimental to all. A careless intervention with respect to one element of the physical environment can have a profound "knock-on" effect throughout the whole system. The same applies to the ecology of culture. Many factors can upset this cultural balance and sensitivity towards them is needed. Thus there is a need for a balance between immediate and mediated experience, and between the real and the virtual. In this context a 1999 TV advertisement for Sony Play-station is of particular interest. A series of video clips depict a succession of young people of various nationalities against backgrounds of seeming social deprivation or physical handicap declaring that, despite the limitations of their environment, they have really lived and fearlessly faced the limits of human endeavour. It is then implied that they have achieved this by interacting with their games consoles. While fantasy has always been part of the human imagination, intense marketing of the virtual computer world runs the risk of removing young people from immediate experience. Further, preserving the balance of culture requires preserving the link between the spiritual and the physical dimensions of human needs. By way of example I wish to draw attention to the link between food and sexuality which is a persistent theme of contemporary advertising. Thus the consumption of ice cream and chocolate are increasingly marketed as a safe substitute for satisfying the sexual appetite and a range of explicit and suggestive imagery including masturbation, penetration and oral sex are used as marketing devices. Such constant association between intimacy and the consumption of food is reductionist. In denying the spiritual dimension of sexual intimacy such advertising ultimately devalues the human person. An over-emphasis on materialism for short-term gains upsets the balance of the cultural environment.

*Short-term exploitative human interventions have a serious long-term impact upon the environment to the detriment of all life. Limits must be placed upon technological systems to exploit resources for profit.* It is widely recognised that no producer or manufacturer has the right to exploit the limited or non-renewable resources of the physical environment for profit. Once again this principle applies to the ecology of culture. The most serious threat to the spiritual character of culture occurs when the link between market capitalism and mass media becomes all-pervasive. In many respects this is impacting upon the very nature of human communication itself since the basic human interaction has become that of the economic transaction between the producer and the consumer. The primary role of the human person is presented as being to consume and consume and consume, and money is worshipped unconditionally. Christian tradition will always be uneasy with such a reductionist view of the human person. In this context it is also of note that marketing is increasingly seeing culture itself as a commodity to be bought and sold. Everywhere one turns thousands of years of human endeavour and culture are simply seen as a resource to be exploited for the requirements of the market, rather like the way in which the earth's physical resources, such as Amazonian rainforests, are exploited for profit. Like a rainforest, culture can be permanently deformed by such intense market exploitation; it can become "imaginatively deforested". When it does so, human spirituality is deprived of the oxygen it needs to flourish.

## Conclusion

Underpinning each of the above aspects of cultural ecology is an *ethic of care*. The invitation to all involved in the media, both print and electronic, is to consider the effects of the decisions they make, and the products they produce and disseminate, upon the wider human cultural environment, particularly as this relates to the spiritual and imaginative aspects of culture which underpin human social and inter-personal communication. The invitation is to transcend legal requirements and to act in a personally aware, responsible and caring way that preserves and enhances culture rather than manipulating it for profit.

## Notes

1 Such a focus is not of course new – as early as the1960s Marshal McLuhan reminded us that the medium itself is the message. More recently researchers such as Postman (1987) have emphasised that media have an embedded epistemology.

2 Anthropology and sociology view culture as constituting all the learned behaviour acquired by an individual as a member of a social group or groups, (that is, non-genetically endowed behaviour). Aylward Shorter, a theologian, defines culture as a transmitted pattern of meanings embodied in symbols, a pattern capable of development and change. Culture comes into existence through collective processes, and involves sets of symbols and conceptions, interpretations of experience, and sets of social identities, which are communicated both formally and informally, consciously and unconsciously. He suggests the rather neat analogy that culture is the grammar of a society. Dermot A. Lane notes that culture includes ways of life, value systems, the rights of people, beliefs, and traditions shaping human identity.

3 See for instance Fore (1993), Gerbner (1979), Baum (1993), Geothals (1981, 1993, 1997), White (1997) and Fore (1987, 1990, 1993).

4 Postman (1987) for instance argues that to engage with mass media at all ultimately trivialises religion and denies its essence.

5 See especially *Lumen Gentium* (the Dogmatic Constitution on the Church), especially para.17, *Gaudium et Spes* (the Pastoral Constitution on the Church in the Modern World) which devoted a whole chapter to

132     *Media and the Marketplace: Ethical Perspectives*

culture (and in which paragraphs 44, 58 and 59 are often highlighted), and *Ad Gentes*, (which is concerned with evangelisation).

6 Letter from John Paul II to Cardinal Casaroli appointing him as president of the Pontifical Council for Culture; quoted in *L'Osservatore Romano*, 28 June 1982, pp.1-8.

7 *Fides et Ratio*, para. 70.

8 *Fides et Ratio*, para. 71.

9 *Fides et Ratio*, para. 71.

10 *Fides et Ratio*, para. 71.

11 Lane states that "inculturation brings out what is best in culture, or equally it can enable culture to realise creatively its full potential". Lane, 1993: 23, 35.

12 Baum, 1993: 65.

13 *Recommendations for Actions and Commitments*, section 4.4, Second Earth Summit, June 1997.

## Bibliography

Baum, G., *The Church and the Mass Media*, Concilium 1993:6, pp. 63-70.

Fore, W.F., *Television and Religion: The shaping of Faith, Values and Culture*, Minneapolis, Augsburg, 1987.

Fore, W.F., *Mythmakers: Gospel, Culture and the Media*, New York, Friendship Press, 1990.

Fore, W.F., "The Religious Relevance of Television", in Arthur, C. (ed.), *Religion and the Media*, Cardiff, University of Wales Press, 1993.

Gerbner, G. and Gross, L., "Living with Television: The Violence Profile", in *Television: The Critical View*, New York, Oxford University Press, 1979.

Goethals, G., *The TV Ritual: Worship at the Video Altar*, Boston, Beacon Press, 1981.

Goethals, G., *The Electronic Golden Calf: Images, Religion and the Making of Meaning*, Cambridge MA, Cowley, 1990.

Goethals, G., "Media Mythologies", in Arthur, C., (ed.), *Religion and the Media*, Cardiff, University of Wales Press, 1993.

Goethals, G., "Escape from Time: Ritual Dimensions of Popular Culture", in Hoover, S.M., and Lundby, K. (eds.), *Rethinking Media, Religion, and Culture*, London, Sage, 1997.

Lane, D.A., "Faith and Culture: The Challenge of Inculturation", in Lane, D.A. (ed.), *Religion and Culture in Dialogue*, Dublin, Columba, 1993.

Levinas, E., *Totality and Infinity: an essay on Exteriority*, The Hague, Martinus Nijhoff Publishers, 1979.

McLuhan, M., *Understanding Media*, New York, 1964.

Postman, N., *Amusing Ourselves to Death*, London, Methuen, 1987.

Shorter, A., *Towards a Theology of Inculturation*, Maryknoll, NY, Orbis Books, 1988.

Soukup, P.A., *Church Documents and the Media*, Concilium 1993:6, pp.71-79.

Williams, R., *The Sociology of Culture*, New York, 1982.

White, R.A., "Religion and Media in the Construction of Cultures", in Hoover, S.M. and Lundby, K. (eds.), *Rethinking Media, Religion, and Culture*, London, Sage, 1997.

Section 3

Media Ethics and the Dynamics of the Marketplace

———————— Chapter 10 ————————

# Must a Good Journalist be Morally Good?
## Media Ethics in a Liberal Culture

*Eoin G. Cassidy*

*It is argued that the ethics of the free market achieves a balance between opposing forces. However, it is a balance whose pragmatism ultimately destroys the very foundations of an ethical commitment to virtues such as truthfulness, fairness or honesty. I wish to suggest that if the values of the market come to dominate the ethical thinking of the media, the very foundations upon which liberal democracy rests will be in danger of being undermined. The codes of media ethics testify to an alternative vision of the media than that reflected in the maxim of neo-classicism, that the business of the media is profit.*

Operating without fraud; adhering to conventions regarding fair competition; operating in line with existing laws; recognising the given rights of employees and investors; seeking to maximise consumer satisfactions; and acting in ways that allow for the free choices of the individuals involved. This impressive list of principles reflects a generally accepted ethical core to the neo-classicist economic paradigm. Nevertheless, one of the principal architects of neo-classicism, Milton Friedman, would be the first to acknowledge that from a neo-classicist perspective the primary purpose of business is profit. Business leaders have no special authority to use resources entrusted to their care to save civilisation or to transform human nature according to their personal social convictions.[1] Rather, Friedman holds that the common good is best served when businesses pursue competitive goals. Morality, responsibility and conscience reside in the invisible hand of the free market system rather than in the hands of corporations and/or individuals within the system. Undoubtedly he would accept that there is a sense in which social or ethical issues ought to be part of the corporate remit, but it is the need for business to be attentive to the law and public relations rather than ethics that will provide the context within which these issues arise. From a neo-classical view point, the attempts to integrate ethical concerns with corporate strategy is seen as both inefficient, arrogant and an illegitimate use of corporate power.

The neo-classical economic paradigm that is both utilitarian and individualist would scarcely deserve mention if it were not that it has exercised and continues to exercise an enormous influence in the "western" world. It finds its roots and sustenance in the cultural climate of liberal individualism, and its importance today is in no small measure a reflection of the dominant position held by liberal individualism in contemporary "western" society. From a neo-classicist perspective, the business of the media is profit, a goal that it ignores at its peril, and the primary role of media providers – journalists, photographers, etc, is to serve the business that employs them. It is not the task of journalists to be the moral guardians of society or to promote desirable social ends. Unlike judges, politicians, teachers or bishops, a journalist's job is to report facts rather than to impart values or make ethical judgements.

The thesis that I wish to propose in this paper is that the idea of a media ethics will only be sustained in a culture that is prepared to critically contest the validity of the ethical paradigm of the market espoused by neo-classicism. Whereas the ethics of the market does achieve a balance between opposing forces, it is a balance whose pragmatism ultimately destroys the very foundations of an ethical commitment to virtues such as truthfulness, fairness or honesty. Furthermore, I shall argue that codes of media ethics that espouse these virtues are a powerful reminder of the reluctance of media providers to fully embrace the ethics of the market.

## A liberal ethic for a liberal society

The history of the rise of the culture of liberalism in the eighteenth and nineteenth centuries is the history of the emergence of the individual *qua* individual. In marked contrast to the whole of classical and medieval culture where the individual was consistently defined in the context of a recognition of the social character of human nature, the liberalism of the Enlightenment celebrated the birth, not just of the individual, but also of a culture marked by individualism. The causes of this movement in culture are complex, but the struggle to break free from the legacy of political authoritarianism and economic feudalism undoubtedly played no small part in the emergence of a culture that gave birth to both liberal democracy and economic capitalism. The twentieth century witnessed the flowering of this individualist culture in ways that could scarcely have been imagined by the founders of the Enlightenment. At least in theory, the freedom of the individual is seen as the *sine qua non* of a civilised society.[2]

The rise of liberal individualism is the cultural context within which the press as we know it today has emerged. Furthermore, liberal individualism provides the essential cultural context within which any study of contemporary media ethics must be situated. Most people are aware of the epic struggle for freedom of the press that spanned much of the last two centuries. It was a struggle that not only emerged out of a liberal culture but also was a critical factor in the very possibility of the emergence of liberalism. Even today the freedom of the press is still almost universally regarded as the single most important guarantor of the political expression of liberalism, namely liberal democracy.

The other cultural factor that can help explain the phenomenal development of the media is the emergence in the early nineteenth century of modern capitalism. What must be recognised is that capitalism needs the media every bit as much as liberal democracy and that the rise of capitalism in no small way facilitated the development of the media.

Despite the seemingly cosy alliance between capitalism and liberal democracy, they carry with them very different cultural and ethical imperatives. Inasmuch as it is premised upon the idea of free competition, a consumer and capitalist orientated society flourishes in an individualist culture. The values promoted are those of the market, namely self-sufficiency, freedom of choice and fair rules governing competition. Unlike its classical antecedent, liberal democracy also flourishes in an individualist society, but the values that it espouses differ significantly and, in some cases, might even be perceived to be incompatible with those of market capitalism. Alongside the values of tolerance, pluralism, equality and fair play, a liberal democratic culture also promotes the idea of the civil society. If the values of the market come to dominate the ethical thinking of the media there is the real danger that the ideals underpinning a liberal democratic culture will be undermined.

## Codes of media ethics and the practice of journalism

Even if it were to be confined to the European continent, an analytical study of the diverse media codes of ethics and press councils would be a daunting task. Fortunately much of this work has recently been undertaken by a group of Finnish researchers. In her comparative study of thirty-one European codes of ethics Tiina Laitila states that

> It turns out that the most common functions of the European codes are accountability to the public, accountability to the sources and subjects of inquiry and the protection of journalist's professional integrity. The principles corresponding to these three functions cover eighty-five percent of all the principles in all the national codes studied.[3]

Under the heading of "Accountability" she observes that, with almost no exception, the codes stress both the importance of a commitment to truthfulness, and the responsibilities attached to journalists owing to their influence in moulding public opinion. One can also see evidence of the importance that the codes attach to accountability to sources and the subjects of inquiry, particularly in the area of gathering and presenting information and in protecting the integrity of sources or subjects of inquiry. Under the heading of "Professional Integrity" Laitilla shows evidence of the importance that the codes attach to both the protection of the journalists' professional integrity and the protection of the status and unity of the profession.

It is interesting to observe that neither "accountability" nor "professional identity" easily fit into the cultural paradigm of liberal individualism that underpins neo-classicism. Rather, they presuppose the self-understanding of the journalist as a member of a community whose work can be evaluated in terms of the good of that community. This idea contrasts markedly with the culture of liberal individualism, where the community is simply an arena in which individuals each pursue their own self-chosen conception of the good life. Furthermore, the principles contained under the heading of professional identity presuppose that journalism is a profession with its own standard of excellence that should be pursued irrespective of how its pursuit might affect the attainment of individual goals such as money, fame and honour. Once again this understanding of journalism fits uneasily into a culture that has embraced the ethic of the marketplace. If Laitilla's analysis of European codes of ethics is accurate, these codes suggest a reluctance on the part of the journalist profession to embrace the ethics of liberal individualism. Rather it suggests an alternative ethical vision of the place of the journalist in society that is worth exploring.

## Questioning the appropriateness of codes of ethics

There are those in the media who would argue that the presence of no less than sixty-one ethical principles in thirty-one codes promotes an ideal of journalistic practice that is not only arrogant, unnecessary and unworkable but also constitutes an unacceptable intrusion into the freedom of the press. Arrogance is reflected in the presumption that the press has the equivalent of a divine mandate to be a watchdog in defence of human rights. Unlike the civic guards whose job it is to protect citizens, or the politicians who are elected to govern in a manner that promotes the rights of citizens, journalists are neither elected nor employed to be societies guardians.

The same critics of codes of media ethics might suggest that they are unnecessary because there are two perfectly adequate societal constraints on unethical behaviour, namely the market and the law. Media as a business is not immune to market forces. Where there is evidence that, in some restricted areas of media practice, market forces have proved ineffective in curbing unethical behaviour, society introduces laws that are specifically designed to act as a constraint on abuses of press freedom.

Perhaps the most telling criticism of media codes of ethics is not that they are arrogant or unnecessary but that they are unworkable. Firstly, they do not take account of the pressures under which the media has to operate. Apart from the particular time pressures within which a news media daily operates there is also pressure from advertisers, circulation numbers, ratings etc. Furthermore, in the light of contemporary findings in the science of hermeneutics, it could be argued that codes of media ethics are also unworkable at a much more foundational level. The ideals of truthfulness, fairness, objectivity and even the requirement to separate facts from opinion are lofty but essentially unrealisable ideals. Prejudice in the literal sense of pre-judgement is an inescapable part of the human condition and the pretence of objectivity is just that – pretence. It could even be argued that the call to separate fact from opinion is unrealisable because the very choice of facts depends upon a prior opinion or judgement as to what is of significance and what is not.

Finally, there are those who would argue that codes of media ethics represent an unacceptable intrusion into press freedom, which the media fought long and hard to establish. Furthermore, they have the effect of distorting the freedom of the market to promote the checks and balances within which businesses can flourish.

## Is the media a business?

There are many who would stress the importance of codes of media ethics in providing a counter balance to the vision of the media implicit in the neo-classical economic paradigm. However, in the light of this detailed list of criticisms, are there any persuasive arguments that can be made in favour of codes of media ethics? One could begin by questioning the rather over-confident assumptions of those who would hold that the media is simply a business and that the ethical parameters within which it operates should be similar to any other business.

What is manifestly obvious is that, unlike most businesses, the power of the media cannot simply or even primarily be measured in terms of its ability to generate wealth or profitability. The power of the media today is much more a factor of its enormous influence in forming or shaping public opinion. The extraordinary advances in recent media technology, the omnipresence of organs of the media in almost every home give credence to the viewpoint that, rather than reflecting the mores of society, the media actually shapes public opinion in its image. Furthermore, the media's influence on society is heightened by the contemporary suspicion of at least two other traditional moulders of public opinion, namely religion and politics. Finally, it must be recognised that it is not only public opinion that is shaped by the concerns of the media but also culture. Many would argue that the media has the power to either protect cultural diversity or to obliterate difference. What is indisputable is that the media today is not just a source of news or entertainment but is actually a source of identity. It possesses the power to create or at least to reshape the cultural parameters within which the public define themselves both individually and as members of society.

How important is it to be able to trust the media? While acknowledging that business only survives in a trustworthy atmosphere or environment, nevertheless the importance of the relationship of trust between media providers and the public is of an altogether different order. The importance of this issue in terms of the relationship between the public and the media would make one wary of an over simplified assumption that the media can be simply categorised under the rubric of a business. In the course of this century Europeans have witnessed at first hand the ways in which the organs of the media have been successfully used both to undermine democracies and to promote terrifying forms of racial and religious prejudice. There are salutary lessons to be learnt from these tragic episodes in the history of the media, not the least of which is the power of the media to abuse the public's trust by manipulating public opinion. The public has every right to be sensitive to the obligations on the media to adhere to an ethical code that will foster a relationship of trust with society.

Even if one were to simply treat the media as a business it would not be possible to accept the opinion expressed above that a journalist's job is simply to report facts rather than either to impart values or to make ethical judgements. Anyone who is even marginally aware of current major news stories in the Irish media would quickly recognise that ethics is the stock in trade of investigative journalism. In this respect at least, the media stands apart from any other business. On a daily basis investigative journalists are required to make ethical judgements, often of a most sophisticated nature. Not only have they to reflect on the ethical character of their own news gathering methods, but in many cases their daily work is devoted to bringing into the public domain abuses springing from unethical behaviour. From both perspectives, journalists need to possess a finely tuned sense of what constitutes ethical behaviour. Thus it is not possible to escape the conclusion that the making of ethical judgements is an inescapable dimension of news reporting.

Apart from the above there are good reasons to hold the view that the role of the media transcends that of a business because of its unique place in a democratic society. As a medium that both provides the public with a forum to engage in public debate and that also has the ability to uncover and investigate abuses of power, the media provides an essential service in ensuring the existence of the checks and balances necessary for a healthy society. Furthermore, few would deny that it has a privileged role in combating all forms of prejudice, in promoting universal human rights, and in fostering a sense of universal solidarity that has the potential to transcend narrow national or sectional interests. For better or worse, the media cannot lightly disengage itself from the task of promoting desirable social ends.

## Aristotle or Nietzsche

The thesis that I outlined at the outset of this paper is that media ethics will only be sustainable in a culture that is prepared to critically contest the validity of the neo-classical economic paradigm. This in turn is only possible if one is prepared to question the dominant position of liberal individualism in today's culture. It also suggests an alternative vision of the place of the journalist in society that is worth exploring.

The Scottish philosopher Alastair McIntyre is indisputably one of the most influential commentators on the culture of modernity. In his highly acclaimed book, *After Virtue,* he argues persuasively that liberal individualism is unable to sustain an ethic other than one that is based on power.[4] In his opinion, contemporary "western" culture possesses only the language of rights, duties and the good life. It is a language that is shorn of its essential supports, namely the shared vision of both the social and teleological or purposeful character of human nature. According to McIntyre, the ideal of the good life and the acceptance of universal rights and duties is inexplicable in the absence of any sense of ourselves as social beings who belong in a community with rights and responsibilities that flow from the community. Furthermore, these ideals are also untenable in the absence of any shared vision of the good or goal of human nature, or even a belief that there is a *telos* or goal to human nature. In the absence of these supports, one is left ultimately without any basis for ethics other than choice, an ethic which, as Nietzsche perceptively recognised, cannot avoid the logic of power.

It is McIntyre's view that, in the last analysis, there are only two possible ethical positions, both of which find their clearest expression respectively in the writings of the classical Greek philosopher Aristotle, and the nineteenth-century German philosopher Nietzsche. Aristotle's ethics is founded on the belief that one can offer a rational justification for the practice of ethics because human beings are social beings and human nature is oriented to the good. It is Nietzsche's view that all attempts to provide a rational justification for ethics are doomed to failure because there is neither an objective nor a transcendent source of meaning and order to human existence. In his opinion the pretence that it is possible to construct an ethic on any basis other than arbitrary choice is simply that – a pretence that is designed to obscure the harsh truth that there is only one ethic, namely that might is right. McIntyre argues that our contemporary liberal individualist culture is living with this pretence. It attempts to avoid the inexorable logic of Nietzsche's argument and continues to believe that, in the context of providing a rational foundation for ethics, it is unnecessary to address the core issue of whether there is an objective source of meaning that is accessible to human reason. The Nietzschean ethic divides the world into winners and losers, a persuasive logic that the capitalism of the nineteenth and twentieth century was not slow to embrace. Despite the ethical constraints that the neo-classicist version of contemporary capitalism builds into its economic paradigm, I remain to be convinced that it does not ultimately accept the logic of this Nietzschean worldview.

Is McIntyre's rather stark thesis sustainable? Even if one were to discount as inadequate the various relativist theories of ethics which uphold subjectivist and emotivist positions, it could be argued that there are at least two other ethical theories that adequately provide contemporary society with a basis upon which to frame ethical principles. For instance, there is large-scale recognition of the value of ethical theories that are based upon theories of human rights. Consequentialism is the most commonly accepted contemporary alternative to these deontological theories, and it also has received widespread acceptance in the various forms of Utilitarianism operative in society today.

## Human rights in a liberal culture

The increasing consciousness of the importance of human rights is one of the distinguishing features of contemporary society. This is evidenced by the importance attached to the various human rights conventions that provide an important source for the protection of citizens in a global context. However, a problem arises when one seeks to establish the basis upon which one constructs a comprehensive list of human rights. As is obvious, universal human rights are not free standing principles. They depend for their justification upon some theory of the good or some accepted understanding of human nature.[5] Our contemporary liberal culture however is premised precisely on the belief that, even if there is a goal to human progress that is expressed in the concept of the good, there is no possibility of achieving agreement on what constitutes the good. From such a perspective it is simply impossible to distinguish genuine human rights from those that are spurious. What is often forgotten is that the commonly accepted list of human rights, which finds expression in media codes of ethics, has its roots in a vision of the dignity of human beings that is largely inherited from Christianity. In the absence of some such shared vision of human nature, ethics based upon human rights rests upon a very dubious foundation.

The importance of this issue for those concerned with supporting the idea of a rights based ethics for journalism is obvious. There must be a recognition that such a system is not philosophically neutral in respect of foundational questions that touch upon the nature and purpose of human life. Few would deny that it is difficult if not impossible to argue coherently for a universal theory of human rights if one denies that life has any meaning or purpose. In the absence of any theory of the good one can undoubtedly understand the need to invent an idea of universal human rights as an alternative to a Nietzschean ethic of power. However, arbitrary sets of rights codified in law are apt to appear as an unacceptable restriction on the freedom of the journalist.

## Questioning the excellence of a utilitarian ethic

The most commonly practised alternative to a rights based ethics is Utilitarianism. Although this system bases its judgement of ethical behaviour on a theory of the good, one does not find in a utilitarian ethic any sensitivity to the value of pursuing the good for its own sake. The good is both defined in terms of, and pursued for the sake of, pleasure or utility. While not disputing the importance of both pleasure and utility in judging the value of an action, they do not nonetheless provide an adequate foundation for ethical behaviour. As anyone engaged in the media could testify, the practice of virtues such as truthfulness, fairness or a respect for the privacy of the individual could hardly be justified solely on the basis of either pleasure or utility. The practice of these virtues by a journalist is not guaranteed to facilitate the pursuit of either fame or fortune. What must be recognised is that Utilitarianism differs from the classical understanding of ethics in at least one respect: for the utilitarian an action is good because it is useful, for a philosopher such as Aristotle an action is useful because it is good. The difference is crucial because it touches on the core issue of why one ought to be moral.

Neo-classical theorists argue for the importance of observing quite a detailed set of ethical guidelines. But the question is why? With practically no exceptions they argue that, given the importance of the relationship of trust between producers and consumers, it makes good business sense to conduct one's business in an ethical manner. That is classical utilitarian reasoning which has little to do with ethics and all too much to do with shrewdness. It is a type of reasoning that is concerned with promoting the pragmatic ideal of efficiency rather than the ethical ideal of excellence. From a neo-classical point of view it is simply more efficient for a business to behave ethically than to behave unethically. The key difference between Aristotelianism and Utilitarianism can be summed up in the answer to the following question: is an action efficient because it is excellent, or is it excellent because it is efficient? Or again, in deciding upon a course of action which should we pursue: excellence or efficiency? Any system of ethics that resonates with Aristotelianism would stress the former, whereas any form of Utilitarianism such as that espoused by neo-classical business theorists would choose the latter. In the last analysis the only answer to the question "why be moral" which respects the ethical character of the question is to say, "we ought to be moral because that is what it is to be a human being". In this context, it is hard to avoid the conclusion that the absence of any commitment to a theory of the good for its own sake robs liberal individualism of any foundation upon which to rationally justify ethical behaviour other than the pragmatic considerations of usefulness or pleasure. When faced with the commercial pressures of contemporary business, codes of media ethics justified on these pragmatic grounds alone would have a very short shelf life.

## Journalism as a practice: a role for the virtues

Alastair McIntyre argues that, in terms of ethics, the key loss in our contemporary liberal culture is the loss of recognition of the role of the virtues in promoting an ethical culture. His view is that, in a liberal culture, the virtues serve no function because they have no place in a culture that replaces discussion of the good for society with what could best be described as preference bargaining among individuals. In proposing an alternative to individual liberalism that would be hospitable to the fostering of the virtues, McIntyre introduces the concept of a practice.[6] In the classical world of Greek culture the virtues were situated in the context of clearly defined social practices together with their own standards of excellence. He gives the following as an example of the context within which practices were understood in Greek culture:

> In the ancient and medieval worlds the creation and sustaining of human communities – of households, cities, and nation – is generally taken to be a practice in the sense in which I have defined it. Thus the range of practices is wide: arts, sciences, games, politics in the Aristotelian sense, the making and sustaining of family life, all fall under the concept.[7]

As explained by McIntyre, a practice is not reducible to a set of technical skills; rather it includes the acceptance of the good of the practice in so far as it contributes to the larger social vision of the good of society. A practice involves standards of excellence and obedience to rules as well as the achievement of goods. Furthermore, to enter into a practice is to accept the authority of those standards that currently define the practice. In a classical culture the virtues have their place primarily, although not exclusively, in the context of their role in promoting those goods that are internal to a particular practice.

The idea of a practice affords us an insight into that which separates a business from a profession. It is only in the latter case that one can speak meaningfully of goods that are internal to a practice as distinct from a good such as monetary profit that is external to all practices. Furthermore, in the context of media ethics, the idea of a practice allows one to understand what it means to treat of journalism as a profession rather than simply as a business. Under the rubric of a profession one can envisage the practice of journalism with its own standards of excellence that are internal to that practice. In this context, it makes sense to foster virtues such as truthfulness, fairness and honesty because these virtues further the goals that are aspired to by the profession of journalism. For those who understand journalism and the media exclusively as a business it is hard to justify the desire for any goals other than those such as money, honour or fame etc, which are external to the practice of any profession. The simple truth is that, unless one acknowledges one's place either in the larger human community or the smaller community defined by a particular practice or profession, it is difficult to find a reason to practise any virtue for its own sake.

In the light of this understanding of journalism as a profession one can see the significance of the codes of media ethics. It is precisely these codes that attempt to suggest guidelines within which a standard of excellence or best practice can be conceived. Furthermore, in this context it is not surprising that, as we have seen, the European codes of media ethics are grounded upon the twin principles of accountability and professional identity, because they give recognition to the existence of two overlapping moral communities within which the practice of journalism is situated. The principle of accountability reminds us of the larger human community, whereas the principle of professional identity speaks to us of the importance of the smaller community constituted by the profession of journalism. Media ethics like any other form of applied ethics finds its place only within a community where there exist clearly recognised goals, which the community believes ought to be pursued for their own sake. Codes of media ethics remind journalists that as members of this profession they belong to a moral community, and that it is only by attending to the practice of the virtues that they can contribute to the well-being of this community.

## Must the good journalist be morally good?

I wish to conclude by briefly addressing the question that is contained in the title of the paper, one that would seem to ignore the generally accepted distinction between the public and the private sphere. However, the question is worthy of study if for no other reason than to raise the issue as to whether there is a place for the study of ethics, and specifically the virtues, in education programmes designed for those entering the world of the media.

A cardinal tenet of Aristotle is that the moral quality of an agent is in direct relationship to his or her ability to discern and observe the mean between excess and deficiency.[8] According to Aristotle, discernment or the virtue of *phronesis* is the axis around which morality revolves.[9] It would be hardly surprising if those who belong to the profession of journalism agreed with this Aristotelian insight because unquestionably they need to be people of discernment. In the course of their daily work journalists are required to make moral judgements that are often quite complex in nature, and every moral judgement of necessity includes a process of discernment.

How does one attain discernment? Can one learn to find the golden mean between excess and deficiency just as one learns any other skill? One of the most important and certainly one of the least understood philosophical insights of Aristotle is that discernment or *phronesis* is a virtue. In other words, it is only possible to understand the virtuous path of action if one is in the habit of acting virtuously. Given the atrocities that have scarred and continue to scar the historical landscape of the twentieth century, one is only too aware of the correctness of Aristotle's insight. It is all too obvious that human beings who commit atrocities have an extraordinary ability to de-sensitise themselves from any understanding or even minimal awareness of that which they are doing. Aristotle perceptively recognised that, within certain limits, one can not only lose the ability to act ethically, but one can lose the much more important ability to discern what it is to act ethically.

In the context of a journalist's ethical responsibility to report news in a fair and balanced manner, what is the implication of Aristotle's theory? If one were to accept the correctness of his insight one would be led to conclude that it is possible to de-sensitise oneself from even the awareness of what constitutes a fair and balanced report. Not only the ability to report fairly but even the ability to understand what it is to report fairly presupposes that the journalist is to some extent a virtuous person. Discernment needs to be constantly re-gained. In Aristotle's view this can only be achieved by encouraging a culture that possesses the ethos or habit of the virtues. Unfortunately, our contemporary liberal ethos is not one that readily accepts the Aristotelian emphasis on the virtues. In this context, I would suggest that it is important for all with an interest in upholding ethical standards in the media to create space to encourage a dialogue that is open to recognising the place of the virtues in the practice of ethics. The challenge is also to find an appropriate place in the education of journalists for a course in ethics that both recognises that journalism is a profession and one which is dedicated to promoting discernment as a legitimate goal for that profession.

## Notes

1 The following quotation from Milton Friedman offers a good example of the rationale underpinning Neo-classicism: "When I hear businessmen speak eloquently about the 'social responsibilities of business in a free-enterprise system,' I am reminded of the wonderful line about the Frenchman who discovered at the age of 70 that he had been speaking prose all his life. The businessmen believe that they are defending free enterprise when they declaim that business is not concerned 'merely' with profit but also with promoting desirable 'social' ends; that business has a 'social conscience' and takes seriously its responsibilities for providing employment, eliminating discrimination, avoiding pollution and whatever else may be the catchwords of the contemporary crop of reformers. In fact they are – or would be if they or anyone else took them seriously – preaching pure and unadulterated socialism. Businessmen who talk this way are unwitting puppets of the intellectual forces that have been undermining the basis of a free society these past decades". Milton Friedman, *The Social Responsibility of Business is to increase its Profits* (1970), Reprinted (1993), 162.

2 For an important contemporary study of the making of the modern identity and the rise of individualism, see Charles Taylor, *Sources of the Self*, (1989). See also Charles Taylor, *The Ethics of Authenticity* (1995).

3 T. Laitila, "Codes of Ethics in Europe", in K. Nordenstreng (1995): 56. For a more general overview of codes of ethics in a global context see: K. Nordenstreng and H. Topuz (eds.), *Journalist: Status, Rights and Responsibilities*, 1989.

4 A. MacIntyre, *After Virtue*, London, Duckworth Press (1981), 2nd Ed. 1985, 109-120, 256-263.

5 Note that even John Rawls would admit the necessity of some theory of the Good. See Rawls, 1972: 395-492.

6 McIntyre, 1985: 187-203.
7 MacIntyre, 1985:188.
8 The most sustained treatment of this theme is to be seen in book two of *Aristotle's Ethics*. For an accessible edition, see: J. Thompson (trans.), (1965): 55-75.
9 See *Aristotle's Ethics*, book six, J. Thompson, (trans.), (1965): 171-192. For an excellent short treatment of this theme see Alastair McIntyre 1985: 146-164.

## Bibliography

Aristotle, *Ethics*, J. Thompson (trans.), London, Penguin, 1965

Belsey, A. and Chadwick, R., *Ethical Issues in Journalism and the Media* (1992) Reprinted, London, Routledge, 1995.

Christians, C., Fackler, M. and Rotzoll, D., *Media Ethics: Cases and Moral Reasoning* (1987), Reprinted, New York, Longman, 1992.

Cohen, E., *Philosophical Issues in Journalism*, Oxford, Oxford University Press, 1992.

Friedman, M., *The Social Responsibility of Business is to increase its Profits* (1970), Reprinted in White, T. (ed.), *Business Ethics: A Philosophical Reader*, New Jersey, Prentice Hall, 1993, pp. 162-167.

MacIntyre, A., *After Virtue: A Study in Moral Theory* (1981), 2nd Ed., London, Duckworth, 1985.

Nordenstreng K., *Reports on Media Ethics in Europe*, Tampere, Julkaisuja Publications, 1995.

Nordenstreng, K. and Topuz, H., *Journalist: Status, Rights and Responsibilities*, Prague, International Organisation of Journalists, 1989.

Rawls, J., *A Theory of Justice* (1972), Reprinted, Oxford, Oxford University Press, 1990.

Taylor, C., *Sources of the Self: The Making of the Modern Identity*, Cambridge Ma., Harvard University Press, 1989.

Taylor, C., *The Ethics of Authenticity*, (1991) Reprinted, Cambridge Ma., Harvard University Press, 1995.

Thompson, J., *The Media and Modernity*, Cambridge, Polity Press, 1995.

———————— CHAPTER 11 ————————

# The Impact of Law and Ethics on the Practice of Journalism in Ireland

## *Damien Kiberd*

*Is journalism a trade or a profession? Which exerts the most impact on journalistic practice, codes of ethics or legal requirements? At what point does the public interest cease to vindicate the work of a journalist? And where does intrusion into the private life of an individual begin? This paper considers, at a practical level, the whole question of discharge of duty and the achievement of balance, within some workable ethical framework in a media organisation.*

## Introduction

Nowadays, a lot of journalists can claim to have undertaken a special course in media studies. The schools of journalism and media studies at Dublin City University, Dublin Institute of Technology, University College Galway and elsewhere have grown in scale and confidence. More gifted academics have been hired, and the range of courses on offer has improved. Newspapers and broadcasting organisations too have begun to appreciate the value of investment in staff training and further education.

Yet journalism also continues to attract practitioners from all walks of life: financial executives who develop a taste for business journalism, professional sports-players who go on to write about sport, politicians who retire from the field of political battle. As conventional wisdom and the diktats of the marketing department promote a culture of commentary (at the expense of old-style factual reporting) and as the media business grows apace, the mode of development could at best be described as haphazard.

## Journalism as a trade

I have always regarded journalism as a trade, not a profession. Unlike doctors we don't train at a professional school for seven years. Unlike well-organised trades, there are no formal rules for entry to this walk of life. And no august bodies exist which might serve to regulate the business of journalism or even call to account those who are perceived to have erred in their work (as The Law Society or the Medical Council do elsewhere). In the context of the Celtic Tiger economy however, there are some similarities between journalism and plumbing. Good plumbers are scarce and so are good journalists. It's very hard to find to good journalist, and it's even harder to get him or her to address the job on hand in a focused way

But the absence of structures which might regulate the trade of journalism is just one unusual aspect of our calling in life. There are others too. Unlike almost all other vocational groups we do not plan for the long term, or even the medium term. We are entirely caught up in short-term issues and in fire fighting: seeking to assemble the news of the day or to beat a competitor to the draw on an important story. The nature of our trade develops and changes over the medium term, but it does so in an unplanned way.

We also face significant levels of competition, not just domestically but from overseas newspapers, TV and radio channels. There is no language barrier to insulate our media organisations from Anglo-American competition. In a sense the standards to which some or all of our media must operate will be externally determined. If the British newspapers decide that they should alter the rules whereby the game of journalism is played in this jurisdiction, we may do so as well. If they decide that certain unwritten rules should be broken, we may break them too – simply in the belief that this will keep us "in the game".

We have also failed to "think through" the long-term consequences of the switch from factual reporting to universal commentary.

When you had (in the past) newspapers which concentrated almost exclusively on the reporting of established fact, no third party could obstruct or distort that reportage in any significant way (though clearly bias was always present). But when newspapers give themselves over almost exclusively to commentary then it is clearly open to "like minded cabals" or ideologically motivated persons to seek to subvert the medium to their own ends.

It is clear therefore that – as a trade with an important role in society – we have a lot of problems. We prosper for the moment and our organisations expand. But there is very little long-term consideration being given to the consequences of what we are doing or to the direction in which we are heading.

I have referred above to the issue of education for journalism. It seems to me that other countries – such as the US – have adopted a much more systematic and thorough approach in this area. I admire their efforts in this regard. But at the back of my mind I cannot help wondering if it is really possible to teach new journalists in any college about the true nature of their chosen trade. Journalists learn their best and most bitter lessons only when they produce good newspapers or make good radio and TV programmes. They learn primarily by doing. Imaginary case studies, given to students on journalism courses, can encourage young would-be journalists to examine important legal, social and ethical issues. But the best training ground is the newsroom or the TV studio.

## Law rather than ethics

Talk of journalistic ethics is fine. But for many journalists and editors it is law, rather than ethics, which will ultimately inform their decision taking. When a newspaper editor reviews the proof of a page late in the evening, trying to decide whether or not to publish an article, his or her foremost consideration is legal rather than ethical. Will the newspaper be sued? If it is sued, what forms of defence will be open to it? If those defences fail, how serious will the consequences be and are the risks of publication justified?

Even in the small Irish media market some newspapers and/or newspaper groups are spending millions of pounds each year on what are called "legal expenses". These monies are paid, in the main, not to wronged plaintiffs or complainants, but to solicitors and barristers in the form of legal fees. It could be argued that such people make journalists accountable in a practical or painful way, though the reality is that many actions taken are drummed-up by law firms or plaintiffs or are simply vexatious.

But the point I would like to make is that whereas a newspaper or broadcasting company is willing to spend millions of pounds on litigation or on warding off threatened litigation, it will spend little or nothing on ensuring that it operates to a defined system of ethical standards.

Laws seek to protect and vindicate individual rights, and in some cases they seek to restrict the exercise of those rights. They also seek to define duties and responsibilities. Where the perceived right of one person clashes with the perceived right of another, law is used to find an acceptable accommodation. Ethical systems operate in the same way as the law in some respects. They seek to ensure the protection of individual rights (the right to privacy or the right to dignity, for example). They agree to the curtailment of those rights in certain defined circumstances. Where two perceived rights collide, they seek a harmonisation of those rights. If a journalist behaves in a way which contravenes the law (say of defamation or of contempt), he or she is likely to be brought to account quickly and directly. But the breaching of unwritten ethical codes will frequently not attract any direct sanction: indeed in the prevailing culture the discarding of ethical standards may sometimes be applauded.

## The private and the public

There has been a perceptible change in approach in recent times to the coverage of the private lives of those in public life. Many journalists are personally uncomfortable about covering this area. It's not just that their newspapers or radio shows may be asking people in public life to observe higher standards than might be observed by journalists and producers themselves. It is because it is very hard to determine what is justified by considerations of the public interest.

At what point does the public interest cease to vindicate the work of a journalist? And where does intrusion into the private life of an individual begin? Ten years ago in Ireland newspaper and other media organisations would not have covered the private life of a public figure at all. Today, that has changed. The ground rules have changed, with the change in some cases being pushed along by newspapers which are owned by overseas corporations. We have seen rather intrusive coverage concerning the marriage and personal life of the current Taoiseach (Bertie Ahern). We have seen the publication of the Terry Keane memoirs. We have seen a number of lurid stories published about the personal lives of a number of opposition politicians. It's not just politicians who are seen as suitable targets. Rock stars, broadcasters even sportsmen and women are also not immune.

We know that a right to privacy exists, not just in unwritten ethical codes but also in law. There is just such a right set out in our Constitution (and sooner or later someone whose private life is dragged through the gossip columns is going to make use of that provision to vindicate his or her legal rights). But equally it is true that the private space of someone who elects to take part in public life is less than the private space of someone who is a wholly private person. Where is the line to be drawn between what is acceptable and what is not in terms of coverage?

Journalists frequently argue that where the private behaviour of a public figure clearly contravenes ethical standards which he demands in his public life, then that hypocrisy justifies journalistic investigation which might otherwise be seen as intrusive (the cases of Bishop Casey and Fr Michael Cleary spring to mind). But even in such cases, the argument is by no means conclusive. For where the private space of an individual is explored, inevitably there is collateral damage. The lives of uninvolved third parties are affected, sometimes wrecked. Children read about their parents' infidelities in newspapers. Sometimes those children are photographed by the media. A politician is outed by the media as being a homosexual: his wife must still face neighbours and friends the following day. Clearly the public interest is served by exposing hypocrisy, or indeed by pointing-up the dangers that may exist when a person is acting in a way which contravenes his/her own publicly professed beliefs. But who is to determine the point at which commercially driven intrusion and affected prurience take over from the service of the public interest?

The case of Taoiseach Bertie Ahern's private life shows just how difficult it can be for the media to deal with such sensitive matters. What might be described by some as intrusive commentary on this matter first appeared in the newspaper, *Ireland on Sunday,* and a robust debate ensued concerning the propriety of such publication. Now because the Taoiseach has confirmed publicly that he has separated from his wife and because he has an open and long-established relationship with a new partner, there is no "public interest" justification for publishing material pertaining to his private life

Most newspapers did not follow up the story about the Taoiseach. I suspect that many editors similarly felt that no public interest might be served by writing about such matters. Yet to my amazement the Leader of the Opposition, Mr Bruton, went on television and drew a distinction between the issue of intrusion into the private life of a sitting Taoiseach on the one hand and the issue of whether or not the Taoiseach should be accompanied on trips overseas by his partner (the protocol issue). I was similarly amazed when a Church of Ireland newspaper sought to criticise the Taoiseach in an editorial, and when a number of so-called liberal commentators stepped in to defend the right of that newspaper to criticise the Taoiseach in relation to his private life. Three senior commentators employed by *The Irish Times* attempted to justify the attitude of the Church of Ireland's newspaper. Were the same commentators alive in the 1890s Mr Parnell would not have got much of a hearing in the columns of *The Irish Times* in relation to his involvement with Mrs O'Shea.

More recently we have seen a quite lurid example of three tabloid newspapers and a radio programme directly reporting in a prurient fashion on an alleged sexual encounter by a respected senior opposition politician. It must be absolutely clear to the journalists producing such stories that this politician cannot be accused of hypocrisy and that the matters being reported can have no effect on the performances of his official duties. It appears to me that no matter how hard they tried they could not plausibly advance any "public interest" defence for their reports, or indeed any defence at all. The process of reporting this story in the press (it had been known for weeks in journalistic circles) began in a British based tabloid paper. When the story was subsequently carried in an Irish title, the British publication was used to justify the second publication of the story on the rather tendentious grounds that "it is now a matter of public debate and controversy". This argument, however spurious, would indicate that the standards to which Irish newspapers operate can now to a significant extent be determined by newspapers whose headquarters are outside the country.

Significantly the vast majority of newspaper titles in Ireland (whether Irish or English owned) refrained from publishing details of this story in subsequent editions, even after the story had been fully covered by the three tabloids. It is unlikely that such forbearance would have been shown in Britain, where the flood-gates tend to open in such circumstances. Does this mean that the Irish media possesses some sort of residual ethical system which might serve as a point of departure in developing considered responses to the handling of such situations? It's hard to tell at this stage. What is clear however is that various bridges are being crossed in a haphazard and unplanned way. This story would not have been published at all a decade ago: now sub-editors and desk editors whose names are unknown to the public and who are personally unaccountable (except in the legal sense) are taking decisions which significantly alter the nature of what is deemed fit to publish.

**Other ethical issues**

Turning away from the whole question of the right to privacy of a person in public life, let us look at other ethical issues. I will raise a number of possible scenarios, each of which throws up specific ethical questions: the answers in each case may not be simple, and may indeed be complex. Journalists may disagree as to the correct approach to adopt in each case. This is a most complex area.

Is the consumer of news and information always entitled to know how that news and information has been gathered? If a concealed camera has been used to take pictures, should the viewer be informed of that fact? If an interview subject has been taped without notice being given, should the reader or viewer be so informed?

Similarly, if the legal rules which form the parameters within which journalists function permit the reporting of certain facts, should those facts properly be published in all cases. In one recent bizarre case the DUP leader Dr Paisley stood up in the House of Commons and named twenty people who, he claimed, had been involved in criminal acts along the border. Legally speaking, parliamentary privilege meant that newspapers, radio and TV could all safely publish those names, linking those named with outrageous acts of criminality. Most newspapers elected not to publish the names, thereby exercising what might be termed an ethical choice. It was obvious to editors, if not to the Good Doctor, that the "naming" might jeopardise the lives of those named and of their families. What standard of proof did Dr Paisley impose upon himself in drawing up the list of those whom he decided to name under the cloak of parliamentary privilege?

If a newspaper or broadcasting firm decides to investigate crime or terrorism, and if as a result of its investigations it is subsequently sued by alleged criminals or terrorists, what rules should it observe in setting out to defend itself against such litigation? Does it have the right to pay witnesses to come forward or are such payments unethical? Such witnesses might otherwise be afraid or unwilling to testify. If it has a right to pay witnesses, then how much should it be allowed to spend? Some media organisations have enormous resources at their disposal and may deploy them massively against a plaintiff (who may genuinely have been wronged). How is a proper balance to be struck in such a situation? The newspaper could claim it had a right, or even a duty, to use whatever means were at its disposal to fight alleged crime. Meanwhile the person accused of wrongdoing could claim a right to vindicate his or her good name without having to overcome oppressive odds.

If a doctor or a psychiatrist decided to disregard the normal conventions of his or her calling and to speak openly to the media about a patient, should a journalist facilitate the doctor or the psychiatrist in such a case? If the journalist agreed to reproduce the medical professional's comments, then where should a line be drawn in relation to the extent of the coverage? This is no simple matter. Medical professionals may behave in unusual ways. The case in which a doctor who cared for the late Francois Mitterrand subsequently offered for sale pictures of the dying man is by no means an isolated case.

I do not pretend to be able to supply absolute answers to the questions enumerated above. In each case, however, a journalist or editor may have to deal with such problems, and deal with them quickly.

Frequently the toughest journalistic choices have to be made where the journalist or the editor has to reconcile (as part of the preparation of a story) two conflicting rights or sets of rights. Frequently we witness in the media the cannibalisation of rights. In order to vindicate one perceived right, it seems that journalists opt to destroy another. Good journalism will strive to allow both rights to co-exist, to achieve a process of "harmonisation of rights", in so far as that is possible.

One problem I have noticed in the course of my work within Irish journalism over a period of two decades is that journalists have developed a somewhat negative or cynical frame of mind (not without justification perhaps given the scale of recent scandals). They tend to proceed from a presumption of guilt, unlike a court of law which will proceed from a presumption of innocence. Add to that the tendency of headline writers and reporters to dramatise their work and to exaggerate its more unusual aspects and you have a recipe for protracted and rather lurid finger pointing. Where does one draw the line between legitimate and admirable investigative journalism on the one hand and serial finger pointing on the other? I cannot give you the answer to this question. What is true is that a great body of investigative journalism has been vindicated in recent times as the Tribunals of Inquiry and Dáil Committees follow up on "exclusive" stories. But equally an almost Pavlovian tendency to point the finger has developed in some quarters, provoking a similarly Pavlovian "need" for such finger pointing among readers, listeners and viewers.

## Ethical frameworks

What we are discussing here, of course, is the whole question of discharge of duty, and of the achievement of balance, within some workable ethical framework in a media organisation. There is the further question: whose duty is it to create the ethical framework within which journalists work and to refine that framework over time?

It seems to me that the individual journalist and editor can develop a workable system of dealing with complex issues in a fair and ethical way simply by dealing with those issues thoroughly from day to day, by being careful to ensure that various rights are vindicated, including of course the right of the pubic to know what is going on in its society. But is there not a parallel obligation on those who manage and own media organisations to assist in the process whereby a workable set of ethical guidelines can evolve? As each media organisation has its own distinct characteristics, and as each must appeal to its own target market, it seems to the author that such ethical systems aimed at creating a new form of "media accountability" will vary from one organisation to another. Be that as it may, provided an honest effort is made to set and uphold decent standards, this should offer a great improvement when compared to the current situation of drift, whereby ethical standards are being invented and reinvented in an entirely unplanned and un-co-ordinated way.

# CHAPTER 12

# Market Forces and Mass Media: Competing for an Audience of Consumers

*Geert Demuijnck*

*The media industry, especially television, has become big business, run by private companies. It is steadily growing in financial importance. It is therefore useful to ask what influence the market mechanism might have on the content of the information processed by the media. Some observers are worried and argue that the growing pressure of the market on the media might threaten our democratic political system. Recently the French sociologist Pierre Bourdieu has denounced the negative influence of the media's commercial logic on political and cultural life. In this contribution I will briefly sketch Bourdieu's main assertions and relate them to other interpretations of the way television and the media in general function. I will also pay some attention to the solutions proposed by the different authors in the debate.*

## Introduction

In January 1998, one of the weekly television supplements of the French newspaper *Le Monde* published a detailed analysis of how the two main French TV stations, *TF1* and *France 2,* produce their evening news. The analysis revealed that, during the programme, the news presenter of *France 2* could see a monitor showing the news from *TF1*. Furthermore, in the case of *TF1*, all newscasts from the rival channel are systematically analysed with a view to reshaping the presentation of their own news bulletins. In other words, the choice of the topics to be presented is determined as much by a desire to upstage the rival network as by the intrinsic news-worthiness of the topic.[1] The reason for this is obvious. Prime time is commercially so precious that the most important aim of the news editorial team is to prevent spectators from channel surfing.

This story illustrates the influence of market forces on the mass media, and particularly on television. The following three questions form the background of my discussion in this paper of the influence of market forces on the media. Firstly, does the growing pressure of the market on the media pose a threat to our democratic political system? Secondly, are the media exerting a negative influence on the way in which culture and science function in our society? And thirdly, if the answer to both questions turns out to be affirmative, how should society respond to these challenges posed by market forces?

## Bourdieu's discussion of the journalistic field: the impact of the market forces

Recently, the well-known French sociologist, Pierre Bourdieu, has highlighted the influence of the media's commercial logic on political and cultural life.[2] In particular, he suggests that the influence of market forces on television leads, via indirect and invisible mechanisms, to a uniformity of media output which creates a kind of censorship of journalists' work. The effect of this influence is that television contributes to a depoliticisation of public life. Furthermore, the dependence of journalism on market forces subverts cultural life. The autonomy of art, literature, philosophy and the social sciences is threatened by the influence of a "best-seller" logic.[3]

According to Pierre Bourdieu, the journalistic field has one typical characteristic: it is much more dependent on external forces than other fields of cultural production such as mathematics, science, literature etc. The ever-present influence of the logic of market forces is key to understanding the workings of the journalistic field, especially the television medium. The high cost of television programming ensures that even publicly funded television must be particularly sensitive to the laws of supply and demand. Furthermore, the ever-present imperative of audience ratings in regard to television content has effects that transcend this medium.[4] Bourdieu's structural analysis of the field of journalism shows clear evidence of the growth of both symbolic and economic capital that is in the hands of television journalists (p. 45). The implications of this growth in the power of the television media are already evident. As Bourdeiu observes, competition between television networks is changing the work ethic of journalists. For instance the distinction between reporting and analysis is no longer clear-cut and we see that even the most independent papers (like *le Monde*) are influenced by the choices made by television journalists.[5] Furthermore, the impact of the television medium on the whole field of journalism flows from the way television is organised.

In their quest for market share television journalists seek to avoid "hard" topics that might divide or exclude. Hence the relatively long time that is spent on "soft" material such as the weather forecast. Within the area of television, the most "successful" journalists are those who report sensational news that is not divisive, such as natural disasters or accidents. These are always apt to arouse curiosity and are therefore of importance in the race for a "scoop". Similarly, much attention is given to reporting incidents that can evoke universal sympathy or outrage, such as the kidnapping of children. Finally, every effort is made to broadcast topics that have the widest possible audience. For example no matter what has happened in the world on a given day, more and more often the evening news either begins with, or is interrupted by, the French soccer scores or the results of some other sporting event. (p. 51).

One of Bourdieu's most telling criticisms of television is that it contributes to the depoliticisation of society. This is particularly evident in the way that political stories are treated in an anecdotal fashion. For example when a French hostage is liberated in Chechnya, one sees a reporter interviewing the hostage's grand-mother, asking what her feelings are. By reducing what happens in the world to the level of anecdote, these human-interest stories can have the effect of creating a political vacuum.[6] The reasons for this approach to news coverage have to do with structural constraints. Firstly, because television time is precious, the longer one devotes to one particular topic the less time remains to transmit another. Human-interest stories thus have a crowding-out effect on other items of news. Secondly, because journalists are so afraid of being boring, they seek to impose a particular vision of the political field: political conflicts are reduced to rivalries between people. These same concerns explain journalists' preference for talk shows that feature popular public figures, entertainers and well-known panellists. (Bourdieu calls them "television intellectuals" or "fast thinkers").

Finally, Bourdieu highlights a form of symbolic violence that is typical of programmes in which politically or socially sensitive issues are debated. This violence is exerted by an almost invisible mechanism: for example by the way people are permitted to talk in a debate. Time pressure is usually so strong that people unskilled in the procedures of journalism rarely succeed in receiving a fair hearing. Moreover, debates are frequently biased by an excessive use of social categories (e.g. Mr X is a professor) which gives more or less symbolic weight to certain people's opinions.

## Private ownership of the media and the protection of democracy

In the light of the above it seems clear that market pressure can exert a negative influence on the media, and may contribute to the depoliticisation of society. Paradoxically, private ownership of the media has always been justified on the ground of its beneficial effect on democracy. It has been argued that a minimum requirement of the media in a democracy is that it should foster diversity. Independence from the government thereby seems to be desirable and private ownership is seen as important in achieving such diversity. It could also be argued that the market addresses the concerns of the consumers and thus protects the public from the bias of state-run media. It is not immediately obvious what might be undemocratic in a competitive market in which the people choose their television station and the kind of amusement that they desire. Indeed, it could be suggested that government control of the media is paternalistic.

In a short essay highlighting the threats to the health of democratic society of a purely commercially run media, the late philosopher Karl Popper rejected the argument that commercial television gives the people what they want and is therefore an agent of democracy. According to Popper, democracy consists in protecting society against dictatorship. Democracy presupposes a well-educated people. Consequently, the aspiration of democrats ought to be to raise the level of education among citizens. In pursuing this goal television has an obvious role to play. But this role is not on the agenda of commercial television, which promotes trivial amusement and sensational news reporting. According to Popper, commercial television ought therefore to be controlled in the service of democracy.[7]

Bourdieu agrees with Popper in arguing that private ownership of the media could be a threat to democracy. His main contention is that private ownership of the media merely gives the allusion of competition.[8] The fact is that media providers are, for the most part, private monopolies with high entrance barriers to new competitors. Furthermore, the major world media firms are not restricted to any one sector. Companies such as Time Warner, Disney, Bertelsmann, CLT control major outlets in the television, radio, press and cinema sectors of the media. Consequently, media firms are also each other's best customers. In short, the media market is so non-competitive that a few firms have enough market power to impose media content globally. They have the power to choose content that lends itself to advertising and merchandising: programmes for children are saturated with commercials and there is a general levelling down of the content of programmes in order to attract large audiences.

Several recommendations have been made to reverse this trend towards privatisation of the media. Some authors have argued in favour of "civic journalism" in which journalists themselves try to reduce sensationalism.[9] However, the proponents of this reform neglect the role of economic incentives in determining media priorities. Others suggest focusing on education, so that people become media conscious. However, a weak point of this "media literacy" approach is that it implicitly accepts the idea that the media give people what they want. Stronger proposals for reform stress the necessity to create more publicly funded media providers such as the BBC and/or a strict regulation of advertising. Above all, there is widespread recognition of the need to shift control from suppliers to consumers in the media market by way of anti-trust measures. Finally, Karl Popper suggested the creation of a professional board of media people which could award or refuse a professional licence to work in the media business, not only for producers but also for all people working in the business. Rather than external pressure, Popper believed in self-policing professional consciences. He compared the possible working of this board to that of the (British) Medical Association.

## Media and the subversion of cultural and intellectual life

Bourdieu argues that the media are not only threatening democracy but that they are also a danger to our highest cultural disciplines such as literature, art and philosophy. His argument is that the journalists exert particular pressure on these domains which need complete autonomy in order to produce high quality. In particular Bourdieu deplores the fact that journalists, by means of their role in the media, exercise an undue influence on the choice of "experts" in the social sciences who will be offered research contracts. The media give prominence to those who court popularity. However, he also admits that this is possible only because some academics collaborate in this selection process. How times have changed. Raymond Aron was intellectually suspect twenty-five years ago because he wrote for the right-wing journal *Le Figaro*. Now the opposite is true: the press gives authority. According to Bourdieu, the overall effect is that media pressure has a detrimental influence on the way in which expertise is measured across a range of autonomous disciplines.

All this has, according to Bourdieu, nothing to do with elitism. It has to do with defending conditions of production, with diffusion of the greatest human creations, and with the obligation to diffuse knowledge. However, it could be argued that Bourdieu is mistaken in accusing the media in this matter. If the official research institution (the CNRS) takes media popularity into consideration, then it is the CNRS that is to be blamed and not the media.

Bourdieu's remarks on the subversion of cultural life clearly echo the analysis of the "mass media" by the early Frankfurt School in the 1950s. The philosopher T.W. Adorno published very early on in the history of television some negative essays about the way television influences cultural life. Adorno's concern was not journalism but the hidden ideological content of television serials. One of his claims is that television, like the whole culture industry, seriously diminishes the already very limited access of the socially disadvantaged segment of the population to the world of art and culture. In order to grasp this process, one should take into account the technical, economic and artistic aspects of television. Despite the greater technical possibilities for the distribution of art today, the subjective conditions for achieving this are not fulfilled.[10] The commercial logic that underlies television programming does not aim at educating the mind but merely at distraction. The result is serials based on stereotype psychology. Their hidden messages are directly conservative and, in many cases, reinforce both sexist and racist prejudices.

In a sense, Adorno's vision is less pessimistic than Bourdieu's. In a surprising conclusion he expressed some optimism about German state television in the sixties. The situation as he saw it was not hopeless; since the ideological manner in which television functions, is neither intended nor the result of producers' incompetence. It is the result of the economic and structural mechanisms of a modern capitalist society. To counterbalance these factors Adorno proposed a board of social scientists that would study the effect of television and criticise and reject the use of stereotypes. If we are to believe Bourdieu, the commercial logic driving the agenda of media providers has been so influential that it has turned social scientists into television stereotypes.

## Conclusion

This presentation of some philosophers' reactions to the growing influence of market pressure on television and the media in general has shown that philosophers from very different ideological backgrounds argue in favour of different forms of state intervention in the media.

However, from a normative viewpoint, their arguments can be distinguished according to their proximity to traditional economic logic. Some arguments follow this economic logic very closely, in the sense that they justify public intervention because it remedies market failures. Other arguments, such as Popper's insistence on the need for education in a democracy, or Adorno's rejection of stereotype psychology, start from the standpoint of a radical separation between the rationality of the market and that of a political forum. They are to be considered against the background of a much larger debate about the nature and aims of democracy. The two forms of argument are clearly complementary, but of a very different nature. Strangely, by focusing on the description of the typical disposition of journalists and the structures of the media, Bourdieu somehow eludes the normative debate, which weakens the ethical basis of his criticism.

## Notes

1 This is not always so. The article mentioned as an exception the fact that TF1 spent a relatively large amount of time on sailing races. The reason for that was simply that Patrick Poivre d'Arvor, the TF1 anchorman (so popular that people and newspapers christened him PPDA) liked sailing very much.

2 A scandal in France at the time led to the denunciation of a few spectacular reports in the programme 'Envoyé spécial', which turned out to be fakes: so-called drug-dealers were policemen who acted out the important scenes in the report. In another programme, policemen had played the part of careless skiers.

3 Unless indicated otherwise, this section draws on the first part of "On television and journalism" (p. 13-38). Page numbers refer to the English translation.

4 Of the six French stations that broadcast over the whole territory, three are privately owned (TF1, Canal Plus and M6), the others (France 2, France 3 and Arte) are state-owned. Arte is fully subsidised, but France 2 and France 3 depend partially on advertising and, generally, tend to copy TF1 which dominates the market.

5 Having been a subscriber to Le Monde for a couple of years, I have observed that this trend did not pass unnoticed. Regularly, after publishing long articles about Lady Di, or the French popular singer Johnny Halliday, the "letters to the editor" section was filled with indignant reactions.

6 Bourdieu, 1998b: 51.

7 Popper, 1995.

8 These arguments draw on McChesney (1998).

9 For references about these different reform proposals, see McChesney (1998) and his comments in the same issue of the Boston Review.

10 Adorno, 1963

# Bibliography

Adorno, T. W., "Fernsehen als Ideologie", in *Eingriffe. Neun kritische Modelle*, Frankfurt am Main, Suhrkamp, 1963, pp. 81-98.

Bourdieu, P., *La distinction. Critique sociale du jugement*, Paris, Les éditions du minuit, 1979.

Bourdieu, P., *Raisons pratiques: Sur la théorie de l'action*, Paris, Editions du Seuil, 1994. (English translation: Practical Reason: On the Theory of Action, Stanford, Stanford University Press, 1998a.)

Bourdieu, P., *Sur la télévision*, Paris, Liber, 1996. (English translation: *On television and journalism*, London, Pluto Press, 1998b.)

Bourdieu, P., *Contre-feux. Propos pour servir à la résistance contre l'invasion néo-libérale*. Paris, Liber, 1998c.

Bourdieu, P. and J.C. Passeron, "Sociologues des mythologies et mytologies des sociologues", in *Les Temps Modernes*, 1963, pp. 998-1021.

Bourdieu, P. and L. Wacquant, *Réponses. Pour une anthropologie réflexive*. Paris, Editions du Seuil, 1992.

Elster, J., "Snobs. Review of La Distinction", *London Review of Books*, 1981, 5-18 November, pp. 10-12.

Ferry, L. and A. Renaut, *La pensée 68. Essai sur l'anti-humanisme contemporain*. Paris, Gallimard, 1985.

McChesney, R., "Making Media Democratic", *The Boston Review*, Summer 1998.

Mongin, O. and J. Roman, "Le populisme version Bourdieu ou la tentation du mépris", in *Esprit*, Juillet 1998, pp. 158-175.

Popper, K., "Une loi pour la télévision", in K. Popper and John Condry, *La télévision: un danger pour la démocratie*, Paris, Anatolia, 1995.

Schneidermann, D., *Du journalisme après Bourdieu*, Paris, Fayard, 1999.

Taylor, C., "To follow a rule", in Mette Hjort (ed.), *Rules and Conventions*, Baltimore, The John Hopkins University Press, 1992.

——————— CHAPTER 13 ———————

# What's Wrong with Advertising? An Ethical Perspective on Communication in Advertising

*Bert van de Ven*

*Does advertising induce an uncritical acceptance of a consumer lifestyle? And, if it does, should it be criticised for furthering materialism, or rather for the way it often does this, or both? In a word, what is wrong with advertising? The purpose of this paper is to answer these questions and, in doing so, to develop tentatively some features of a critical approach to advertising which should enable an assessment of the moral qualities of adverts. The argument draws on two influential pragmatic theories of communication, Jürgen Habermas' theory of communicative action, and Dan Sperber's and Deirdre Wilson's relevance theory.*

## Introduction

Advertising has always had its passionate defenders and critics. It has been praised for its ability to "transcend nature in the raw", and to "augment what nature has so crudely fashioned", much in the same way as the artist and the priest influence their audience "by creating symbols that promise more than that which is observable."[1] According to Levitt (1970), adverts, like art, satisfy the basic human need to modify, transform, embellish, enrich, and reconstruct the world in which we live. For instance, people do not want to buy a car as just a means of transportation; they want to believe in the illusion of status, adventure, and sex appeal associated with it through the power of advertising. In so far as advertising succeeds in defining the social meaning of a specific brand of cars, one could contend that it is not illusory at all to think that the possession of a product can give you a certain desired status (Arrington 1982).

Advertising creates social meaning and gives social guidance to consumers who want to know what messages they communicate to others by their choice of products. It is this social guidance function that so troubles some of its critics. Many see a pollution of our psychological and social ecology as an unintended consequence of advertising (Pollay 1986). They think that advertising leads to uncritical acceptance of a consumer lifestyle, which is considered detrimental to one's autonomy (Lippke 1988) or to the cultivation of virtues. (Waide 1987). This uncritical acceptance of the consumer lifestyle, which is also referred to as "consumerism" and "materialism," seems to be the primary object of criticism. "But does advertising really induce such uncritical acceptance of consumerism and materialism? And, if it does, should it be criticised for furthering materialism, or rather for the way it often does this, or both? In a word, what is wrong with advertising?

To answer such questions it is necessary to develop a critical approach to advertising which facilitates an assessment of the moral qualities of adverts. In the first section of this paper the informative function of advertising is examined using Jürgen Habermas theory of communicative action. The discussion centres on why truth and truthfulness are important criteria in the international code of advertising. In the second section, the persuasive function of advertising is discussed with reference to Dan Sperber's and Deirdre Wilson's[2] relevance theory. This clarifies how advertising succeeds in furthering consumerism, often in a rather covert way in spite of the fact that many of us think we are nearly immune to its influence. In the final section it is argued that business corporations should take responsibility for the moral quality of the adverts that are communicated on their behalf.

## The informative function of advertising: truth and trust

Two main functions of advertising can be distinguished: informing and persuading. Both functions should serve the commercial goal of selling the product.[3] However, the advertiser does not inform potential consumers to teach them something about the world, but rather to sell a product. That is why persuading the audience is more important than informing it. In this section, the informing function is examined with the help of the theory of communicative action as proposed by the Critical Theorist, Jürgan Habermas.

Habermas' theory considers the performance of a speech act by an actor who is trying to reach a shared understanding with his audience. According to Habermas, "reaching an understanding functions as a mechanism for co-ordinating actions only through the participants in interaction coming to an agreement concerning the validity of their utterances, that is, through inter-subjectively recognising the validity claims they reciprocally raise."[4] An actor who wishes to be understood in this fashion must satisfy all of the following three validity claims: that the statement made is true, that the speech act is right with respect to the existing normative context and that the speaker means what he says. Thus, the speaker claims truth for statements, rightness for legitimately regulated actions and truthfulness for subjective experiences.

The free acceptance or rejection of validity claims is the rational basis for the co-ordination of action. If one accepts a speech act freely then one is rationally motivated to act in accordance with the content of what is said. In this context, the validity claims of truth and rightness can be assessed by rational discourse. However, the validity claim of truthfulness cannot be redeemed solely by arguments. Truthfulness must be apparent from the actual behaviour of an individual in the course of time.

When considering advertising, several features of Habermas' theory should be clarified. Firstly, not all agreements involve rational motivation on the grounds of a mutual understanding of a situation. For instance, the exercise of power can empirically motivate or force someone to accept a point of view. However, "what comes to pass manifestly through outside influence or the use of violence cannot count subjectively as agreement. Agreement rests on common convictions".[5] If, for instance, someone holds a gun to your head and orders you to fill a bag with money, you are not in a position to freely accept the request. You do what is asked of you because of the negative consequences that you will face if you refuse to co-operate. Rational motivation always refers to the free acceptance of validity claims.

Secondly, both speaker and hearer are responsible for raising and accepting or rejecting validity claims, they hold each other responsible for what is being said. They engage in a social relationship with each other by performing speech acts. Consider the following example: someone is smoking a cigarette in a non-smoking area, a non-smoker is irritated and utters:

(1) Do you know that you are not allowed to smoke here?

The smoker answers:

(2) No, I did not know that, but I see the signs now.

The acceptance of (1) by the smoker by her utterance of (2) creates the expectation on the part of the non-smoker that the smoker will act accordingly and will put out her cigarette. If the smoker knows that it is forbidden for her to smoke in this place, and if she does not reject the validity of the prohibition itself (the validity claim of rightness), it is normal to expect that she will act in accordance with the valid norm.

The possibility of a free co-ordination of action and of an open discussion (a discussion where only the force of the better argument counts) carries with it the promise of solving conflicts of interests in a non-violent way. Furthermore, it holds a promise of gaining better insight into one's own subjective experiences in terms of cultural values and of developing one's own identity in relation to the legitimate norms of society. Communicative action is crucial for becoming an autonomous individual, one who is able to live according to his own conscience and who is able to enhance his own well-being by drafting the main lines of his plan of life.[6]

Before applying the theory of communicative action to adverts, it should be acknowledged that Habermas himself thinks that communicative action does not play a role in commercial transactions. He thinks that the medium of money suffices to co-ordinate such transactions and that money uncouples these transactions from the burden of reaching understanding communicatively. Although it is true that, to a certain extent, money indeed lessens the burden of reaching understanding, Habermas is mistaken in contending that money is the only mechanism of co-ordination in the marketplace. To the extent that assertions, questions, imperatives and other kinds of speech acts are used in marketing activities such as adverts, the advertiser cannot avoid raising validity claims and is therefore to be held responsible for these claims. Insights from the theory of communicative action are therefore directly relevant to norms, such as the international code of advertising, which concern the truth and truthfulness of adverts.

Let us consider the following example of the assertions made by an advert for G-Shock watches:

> Before we designed the world's toughest watch, we designed the world's toughest tests. We've thrown them out of third-storey windows, strapped them to the tyres of mountain bikes, we've even hit them with ice hockey sticks. Not very scientific maybe, but effective all the same. Especially when your goal is to build the world's toughest watch. Only when a watch can survive a drop of 10 meters onto concrete, resist water pressure of at least 10 atmospheres (in fact all G-Shocks are now 200 meters/20 atmospheres resistant) and has been developed to last for a minimum of 10 years can it truly be called a G-Shock.

Three pictures of the G-Shock watch accompany the text of this advert

(i) falling out of a three- storey building

(ii) strapped to the tyre of a mountain bike

(iii) lying on what seems to be ice.

The message of the advert seems straightforward: G-Shock is the toughest watch of all time because it survived the world's toughest tests (validity claim on truth). Notice also the disclaimer concerning the scientific status of the tests. The advertiser is not saying that these tests are scientific, but he does claim that they are effective. The advertiser means that the tests are an effective means of proving that G-shock is the world's toughest watch because, although they are not scientific, they are the world's toughest tests. The audience does not have to agree with that, it can make up its own mind about the toughness of the tests. Because of the scientific disclaimer, the meaning of the qualification "the world's toughest tests" can be brought up for discussion. The advertiser carefully avoids creating the false appearance of scientific objectivity, thereby turning the qualification "world's toughest tests" into a judgement based on some normative criteria concerning "toughness". If the advertiser is believed to be sincere (third validity claim), a dispute about this qualification could, therefore, concern the rightness of these normative criteria (second validity claim). Apart from the claim of toughness, the advert also contains other assertions in which the validity claim of truth is most important. The advertiser claims that all G-Shock watches "are now 200 meters/20 atmospheres resistant". This, of course, must be true; if not, the advert would be misleading.

In general, if the advertiser wants to inform the audience about certain features of the product he has to make sure that the message is taken seriously. Since audiences generally do not trust advertising to be truthful this poses a problem for the advertiser who really means some of the things he is seeking to communicate. In order to motivate the audience to accept the claims he has to make sure that the part of the message that has an informative function is presented in a serious, unambiguous and trustworthy manner. It should be clear to the audience that the information given is the serious part of the advertising message, that is the part for which the advertiser is prepared to be accountable for the validity claims. In the example given above, the advertiser seems to believe that the written text is seriously meant; the advertiser seems sincere in claiming that the G-Shock watch is the toughest watch in the world.

The following regulations in the International Code on Advertising confirm the viewpoint that both truthfulness and trust are important issues for advertisers.

> Article 2. Advertisements are to be set up in such a way that the consumer cannot be taken advantage of in terms of trust or lack of knowledge or experience.

Article 4.1. Advertisements may not contain assertions or pictures that could mislead the consumer, either directly, or indirectly through omission, ambiguities, or overstatement ...

Article 2 contains a stipulation concerning the relationship of trust that should exist between advertiser and consumer. This stipulation is important if advertising is not to fall into disrepute. Where there is a lack of trust, the addressee will only accept the advertiser's message on the basis of her own knowledge of the relevant facts. If, however she trusts the advertiser, it is possible that she will accept his claims because she finds him trustworthy (acceptance of the validity claim on sincerity).

If an advertiser does not want to take advantage of the trust of the consumer, he should avoid misleading him by saying things that do not correspond with reality (validity claim on truth). In this context, article 4.1 is closely related to article 2. Although the intention of these articles is not to prohibit persuasion they seem to conflict with existing advertising practice where the use of puns, ambiguities, metaphor and the like are commonplace. It is clear that the articles are directed at that part of the message that has an informative function or that could be understood to be informative by the audience. Only if an audience believes that the advertiser means what he says it is open to being deceived. Advertisers, however, often make use of assertions, questions, imperatives and other kinds of speech acts that raise validity claims in a manner that does not correspond with the facts. Our example of the G-Shock watch clearly illustrates such a communicative attempt: the advertiser wants his audience to believe that the G-Shock watch is really the toughest watch in the world. Since it is a general feature of communicative action that both speaker and hearer consider themselves to be responsible for validity claims, it is understandable that the International Code on Advertising holds advertisers accountable for the truthfulness of their adverts and for not abusing the trust of the audience.

There are many ways to suggest something, without actually saying it or saying it in so many words. In addition to the linguistic message, adverts usually contain a visual component that can help clarify the meaning of the linguistic message.[7] From the perspective of the theory of communicative action, one can understand why it is so attractive for advertisers to avoid raising validity claims overtly. If they do so, they are responsible for backing up the validity claims with arguments, and can be held accountable for the social and cultural impact of their claims. For instance, it is not attractive for a tobacco company to simply claim the following: "If you're looking for adventure, smoke *brand X*". Furthermore, this would not have the desired effect because it makes an appeal to a conscious desire that we do not have, or one that we know smoking cannot fulfill. It would probably only trigger criticism and distrust on the part of the audience. The desired association between *brand X* and adventure can only take root in the consciousness of the audience if it succeeds in evading the reality test of the conscious self. The worst way to attempt this would be to explicitly claim what is so apparently false.

## The persuasive function of advertising: covert communication

In the previous section it was shown how adverts use speech acts directed towards reaching understanding (communicative action) to inform the audience about features of the product. More often, however, the accompanying text is not geared to reaching an understanding on the basis of an acceptance of validity claims. In such cases the information given by the visual component is necessary to limit the possible set of interpretations of the text. As Forceville (1996) has shown, linguistic and pictorial information can complement each other in many different ways. This complementary relation between pictorial and linguistic information is used to indulge in what has been called "covert communication" (Tanaka 1994).

Tanaka distinguishes "covert communication" from "ostensive communication" as follows:

> Ostensive communication: an overt form of communication where there is, on the part of the speaker, an intention to

alter the mutual cognitive environment of the speaker and the hearer.

Covert communication: a case of communication where the intention of the speaker is to alter the cognitive environment of the hearer, i.e. to make a set of assumptions more manifest to her, without making this intention mutually manifest.[8]

Tanaka bases her distinction on the relevance theory developed by Sperber and Wilson (1986). In order to understand Tanaka's application, however, some theoretical concepts of relevance theory need to be explained.

Sperber's and Wilson's relevance theory provides a framework for utterance interpretation. Their framework is based on ostension, that is the communicator's intention to communicate and to publicise his intention, and the principle of relevance that rules communication. In the case of ostensive communication, the communicator wants to point out that the set of assumptions was deliberately made available to the addressee by the communicator. If, on the contrary, there is no attempt to make the informative attention mutually manifest, that communication is covert.

The principle of relevance states that whatever the nature of a stimulus its interpretation by the addressee will be constrained and guided by the latter's awareness that this interlocutor is trying to be relevant to him.[9] In order to be relevant, a message should both be easily accessible and capable of altering existing assumptions.

Two other important distinctions are those between strong and weak communication and between explicatures and implicatures.[10] Explicatures are assumptions that are explicitly communicated. In contrast, assumptions that are derivable from the proposition expressed by the utterance together with the context are called implicatures. In order to be relevant to the audience implicatures must be processed by the audience. As Forceville observes "the more strongly an assumption is communicated, the more the communicator takes responsibility for having it derived by the addressee; the weaker an assumption is communicated, the more the addressee takes responsibility for deriving it. Interestingly, certain utterances aim at triggering weak rather than strong implicatures."[11] Let us consider the following example of strong and weak implicatures in an exchange between Peter and Mary.[12] "Do you want some coffee?" Peter asks, and Mary replies, "Coffee would keep me awake." This answer is in itself insufficient for Peter to decide whether Mary wants coffee or not. In order to make sense of her reply he has to activate certain contextual assumptions. This is achieved through the introduction of the relevance principle. If Peter knows that Mary wishes to retire early, Mary's statement that "coffee would keep me awake" communicates the message that "I do not want coffee". It is important to realise that Mary's statement only becomes relevant if this implicature is processed. Mary's utterance however conveys more to Peter. He could interpret it as a statement that she is tired, that she has no energy for lengthy discussions or that she does not wish to be disturbed. It is possible that Mary has the above-mentioned assumptions in mind. However, Peter cannot be sure if this is the case. It cannot be said that Mary made any of these assumptions strongly manifest to Peter. However, she does wish that Peter would entertain some similar assumptions. These assumptions are thus made weakly since the validity of deriving them is not guaranteed as strongly as Mary's refusal to have coffee.[13]

One may wonder, however, why Mary does not simply answer "yes" or "no" to the question posed by Peter since that would cost less processing effort than the answer that she gave. According to Sperber and Wilson, the effort needed to comprehend Mary's answer is justified by the range of responses from Peter that could be prompted by her answer. It is enough that the hearer pays attention to some of these weaker implicatures for the relevance of the intended interpretation to become manifest. A simple affirmative answer to Peter's question would not have the range of (potential) effects that are triggered by Mary's answer.[14]

Forceville and Tanaka both apply insights from relevance theory to advertising. Tanaka's concept of covert communication is akin to the concept of weak communication. Tanaka focuses on the characteristic feature of covert communication: the opportunity it provides to shift responsibility for the derivation of certain assumptions from the communicator to the addressee. In a comment on Tanaka, Forceville points out that "This, of course, is precisely what happens in weak communication ... Covert communication necessarily makes ample use of the possibilities of weak communication, but not all weak communication is covert communication."[15] We need not concern ourselves here with the details of the conceptual relation between weak and covert communication, it suffices to note that it is assumed that in covert communication the communicator *has the intention* to alter the cognitive environment of the hearer, *without making this intention mutually manifest*. One important way of doing this is by triggering weak implicatures for which one cannot be accused of providing strong backing.

According to Tanaka and Forceville, advertisers have commercial motives for engaging in covert communication.[16] At a general level the advertisers want to make the addressee forget that they are trying to sell him something. The phenomenon of disguised advertising illustrates this point: "Disguised advertising messages are those that individuals may not perceive as being sponsored because the source of the message is unclear, or because they are presented as editorial material, rather than as adverts."[17] The second goal of covert communication is "to avoid taking responsibility for the social consequences of certain implications arising from adverts."[18] According to Tanaka, "advertisers wish to avoid negative social reactions which may arise in response to certain aspects of their adverts, such as the use of sex and the exploitation of the notion of snobbery". These problematic elements in their adverts appear to boost sales. Consequently, advertisers wish to continue using them but they also wish to avoid taking any responsibility for so doing.

Tanaka examines the exploitation of the possibilities of weak communication in some detail in his analysis of a number of Japanese adverts for a miniature television set.[19] The mutual manifest (ostensively communicated) message of a caption of one these adverts is (1) "If you go without watching what you want to watch, your personality will shrink". A picture of three young western people accompanies this caption: two girls holding each other intimately. While holding a miniature television set in one hand a boy grasps one of the girls from behind with the other.

There is a faint suggestion of illicit behaviour which is reinforced by some text that is attached to the caption, "the curiosity which drives a mob is the source of energy which has driven mankind to grow this far ..." Both the text and the caption encourage curiosity. Tanaka also notes that the Japanese word for "to shrink" is normally used to describe an inanimate object, and it is unusual to use the verb "to shrink" to describe a personality. The word thus hints at something physical that shrinks. Combined with the faint suggestion of an orgy, it is not far-fetched to say that this thing is a penis.

Tanaka suggests that the original caption (1) can be interpreted as follows: "if you refrain from having an orgy, your penis will shrink". There is another caption, in English, accompanying the advert, which pushes the interpretation in the same direction: "Anytime OK! Everywhere OK!" Tanaka notes that it is unclear what is "all right" any time and anywhere. Since this is an advert for a miniature television and the original caption (1) is apparently talking about being able to watch something, the following interpretation is possible: "With our television set you can watch television anywhere at any time". But, Tanaka argues that the phrase "if you refrain from having an orgy, your penis will shrink" occurring together with "Anytime OK! Everywhere OK!" can equally be interpreted to suggest that "you can have an orgy anywhere at any time".

In her final comments on this advert Tanaka concludes that there is an intuitive reluctance to say that the advertiser has *overtly* communicated this sexual interpretation, since it appears irrelevant to an advert for a miniature television set. "There seems to be no reason why the advertiser should encourage an orgy or a lesbian relationship, which are taboo in Japanese society."[20] She suspects that sex is used here to catch and retain attention and that such a discussion takes place at a "subliminal level". Tanaka's suggestion that covert communication, which makes use of this kind of weak implicature, is intended to influence the audience on a subliminal level seems very plausible. While one would expect the advertiser to think twice before saying such controversial things overtly, it is clear that a covertly communicated appeal to fulfill sexual desires "anytime, anywhere" will catch the attention of the audience and is therefore commercially attractive.

Apart from sexual images, advertisers also play on societal prejudices and stereotypes. Covert communication manipulates triggers to which the human mind is highly susceptible.[21] This influence works on a subliminal level because if the addressees were to be fully conscious of the content of the covertly communicated message advertisers would be subject to a lot of criticism. However, even if the audience is conscious of the covertly communicated elements in the advert, its influence on the subliminal level is not thereby negated. In fact, such general acknowledgement is likely to result in a less critical assessment of the content of adverts: we think that we are immune so we do not bother to check the content of what is being covertly communicated.

Is it then too far-fetched to suspect that people who listen to or watch commercials will come to uncritically accept a consumer lifestyle? Is it an exaggeration to say that advertising succeeds in reproducing and expanding over time the patterns of assumptions that are required for the continued growth of capitalism? According to Phillips, there is no doubt that this is the case (Phillips 1997; Leiss *et al.* 1986). She mentions and examines three negative collective effects that have been attributed to advertising and that can be grouped under the umbrella of increased materialism in society:

1 the elevation of consumption over other social values
2 the use of goods to satisfy social needs
3 general dissatisfaction with one's life.

According to Phillips, who cites Leiss *et al*, "the overarching problem with materialism is that 'commodities themselves and the income to purchase them are only weakly related to the things that make people happy: autonomy, self-esteem, family, felicity, tension-free leisure, friendship'. Capitalism obscures this fact and focuses consumers' attention on goods as the solution to *all* of their needs."[23] According to Phillips, advertising is just one tool that capitalism uses to reach its goals, and that "if advertising is stripped of its power to accomplish capitalist objectives, other tools will be used".[24] She concludes that, instead of blaming advertising for creating consumerism or materialism, capitalism itself should be held responsible: "our own capitalistic economic system directly causes the negative social conditions which lead to increased materialism. Advertising, as the mouthpiece for capitalism, presents values and assumptions that colour consumers' perceptions of reality. Therefore, advertising becomes a target for social criticism. However, advertising does not create the values it presents".[25]

Would capitalism remain so successful in furthering the reproduction of materialism without its most suggestive and seductive tool? As I have argued above, by exploiting the possibilities of covert communication and thereby evading the test of the conscious self, advertising succeeds in inducing an uncritical acceptance of materialism. This means that even individuals who consider themselves to be autonomous are subjected to an influence to which they cannot have a free and open relationship. If advertising were to be abolished it is doubtful whether a tool exists that has a comparable impact: that of reproducing the consumer lifestyle without provoking serious unease and criticism among consumers in so doing.

Advertisers try to let the public forget that they hope to sell them something. Furthermore, they also want to disguise how it is sold to them. In general, people like to think of themselves as autonomous and free from manipulation and advertising succeeds in undermining this autonomy without being noticed. In fact, phrases like "making your own choice", and "it's your life" (both of which refer to the integrity and autonomy of one's character) are often associated with a product that has become popular as a result of group pressures. What other tool could accomplish this? Of course advertising, in its present form, is a consequence of capitalism and the affluence it has created. Therefore, I agree with Phillips, that capitalism lies at the root of materialism. However, I do not agree that advertising is simply a tool that can be easily replaced. Moreover, and more importantly, it is not an innocent tool. It freely uses powerful images but avoids taking responsibility for the use made of them.

## The moral responsibility of business for the content of advertising

We have argued that advertisers use covert communication to hint at certain assumptions without taking responsibility for them. In this respect covert communication is the opposite of communicative action in which the advertiser cannot avoid raising validity claims for which he is held accountable. Communicative action is more akin to the concept of ostensive communication in which the intention to alter each other's cognitive environment is mutually manifest. By performing a speech act to reach an understanding, the communicator makes it overtly clear that he wishes to communicate something.

It was argued that, from the perspective of the theory of communicative action, one can understand why it is so attractive for advertisers to avoid overtly raising validity claims. If they were to raise validity claims they would be held accountable for backing up these claims with arguments. In addition, they would be responsible for assessing their social and cultural impact. Communicative action always involves entering into a social relationship in which one is held responsible for what one says. If we look at the weak assumptions that can be recovered in some cases, it becomes clear that it is not attractive to be held responsible for strongly backing them. Surely many corporations would not want to be accused of being prejudiced in relation to certain groups such as the elderly and blacks. Nevertheless it would probably not surprise anyone to find corporations that have explicitly formulated positive discrimination policies and rules of conduct regarding sexual harassment, covertly using obscene sexual triggers and sexual stereotypes in their advertising.

Is such a discrepancy morally acceptable? This is a question that must be asked by the various actors – the advertising agency, its clients and the media – who together are responsible for a commercial or an advertisement. In this respect, it is remarkable that Laczniak and Murphy found that almost none of the companies whose code of conduct was examined spelled out their ethical perspective on advertising.[26] This is illustrative of the lack of attention given to the moral quality of marketing communication.

There still seems to be a "buyer beware" attitude in the advertising business. In spite of its immense social and cultural influence, advertising has no explicit social goals or social responsibility (Pollary 1986). If, however, corporations are sincere in accepting their social responsibility I do not think that they can avoid formulating a policy that reflects their ethical perspective on advertising.

What, then, should the content of such a policy be? Should advertising refrain from covert communication altogether? Yes, if we agree that covertly hinting at assumptions for commercial purposes is morally unacceptable. That would mean that we can no longer allow advertising to tap the resources of our unconsciousness to promote a materialistic lifestyle. A consequence of this, however, might be that consumption would fall below the level needed for the continuous growth of the economy. It is not unthinkable that some societies with a capitalistic economic system would be capable of a cultural transition towards less materialism in terms of consumption, work and leisure time. In my opinion a profound change in that direction is required before demanding that advertisers stop covertly influencing people on a subliminal level.

At the same time, however, I do think that we should demand that advertisers take responsibility for the content of covert communication. The heart of the problem is that, in some cases, advertising persuades its audience by covertly communicating assumptions that they would refuse to back if challenged. This is a manipulative, opportunistic and irresponsible use of triggers to which the human mind is highly susceptible. If advertisers are not prepared to back the weak implicatures of what is covertly communicated, they behave irresponsibly. From a moral point of view, if one wishes to accept one's responsibility to society one must be prepared to account for one's actions and words. In the case of covert communication the advertiser tries to do the opposite, namely to avoid having to take responsibility for what is covertly communicated. Therefore, I conclude that the readiness to account for that which is covertly communicated is a suitable criterion for evaluating the moral quality of advertising. If applied by the actors who are involved in the creation of a commercial message, I suspect that this criterion would lessen the use of stereotypes in advertising. Advertisers should not fear that this would make their work less effective. An approach which utilises positive messages about women, human sexuality, and the differences between people, has the potential to sell products that would otherwise be unattractive.

## Notes

1 Levitt, 1970.
2 In this paper I will not treat the differences between these theories, nor will I examine whether they are compatible, although I do think that they are, to a large extent, even complementary.
3 Rossiter and Percy, 1987: 3.
4 Habermas, 1984: 99.
5 Habermas, 1984: 287.
6 Habermas, 1988: 222-223.
7 Forceville, 1996: 73.
8 Tanaka, 1994: 41.
9 Sperber and Wilson, 1986:158.
10 Tanaka, 1994: 26-27.
11 Forceville, 1996: 93.
12 From Sperber and Wilson, 1986: 34.
13 Forceville, 1996: 92-93.
14 Forceville, 1996: 91.
15 Forceville, 1996: 104 -107.
16 Tanaka, 1994: 43.
17 Nebenzahl and Jaffe, 1998: 805.
18 Tanaka, 1994: 44.
19 Tanaka, 1994: 47-51.
20 Tanaka, 1994: 51.
21 Tanaka, 1994: 54.
22 Leiss et al, 1986:252.
23 Phillips, 1997: 116.
24 Phillips, 1997: 117.
25 Phillips, 1997: 112.
26 Lacnziak and Murphy, 1993: 170.

## Bibliography

Arrington, R.L., "Advertising and Behaviour Control", in *Journal of Business Ethics*, 1, No.1, 3-12, 1982.

Forceville, C., *Pictorial Metaphor in Advertising*, Routledge, London /New York, 1996.

Habermas, J., *The Theory of Communicative Action, Volume 1, Reason and the Rationality of Society*, Heinemann, London, 1984.

Habermas, J., *The Theory of Communicative Action, Volume 2, Lifeworld and System: A Critique of Functionalist Reason*, Polity Press, Cambridge, 1987.

Habermas, J., *Nachmetaphysisches Denken. Philosophische Aufsätze*, Suhrkamp, Frankfurt am Main, 1988.

Laczniak, G.R., and Murphy, P.E., *Ethical Marketing Decisions. The Higher Road*, Allyn and Bacon, Boston,1993.

Leiss, W., Kline, S and Jhally, S., *Social Communication in Advertising: Persons, Products, and Images of Well-being*, Methuen Publications, New York, 1986.

Levitt, T, "The Morality of Advertising", in *Harvard Business Review*, 48, 84-92, 1970.

Lippke, R.L., "Advertising and the Social Conditions of Autonomy", *Business and Professional Ethics Journal*, 8, No.4, 35-58, 1989.

Nebenzahl, I.D., Jaffe, E.D., "Ethical Dimensions of Advertising Executions", *Journal of Business Ethics*, 17, 805-815, 1998.

Phillips, B.J., "In Defence of Advertising: a Social Perspective", *Journal of Business Ethics*, 16, 109-118, 1997.

Pollay, R.W., "The Distorted Mirror: Reflections on the Unintended Consequences of Advertising", *Journal of Marketing*, No. 19, April 1986.

Rossiter, J.R. and Percy, L., *Advertising and Promotion Management*, McGraw-Hill, New York, 1987.

Sperber, D. and Wilson, D., *Relevance: Communication and Cognition*, Blackwell, Oxford, 1986.

Tanaka, K., *Advertising Language. A Pragmatic Approach to Adverts in Britain and Japan*, Routledge, London/New York, 1994.

Waide, J., "The Making of Self and World in Advertising", *Journal of Business Ethics*, 6, 73-79, 1987.

──────── CHAPTER 14 ────────

# The Privacy of the Individual: An Ethical Challenge for Contemporary Journalism

## Marthe Lievens

*This paper focuses on the vexed question of the ethics of privacy and journalistic practice. It draws attention to a key moment in this ethical tension, i.e., that between the freedom of the journalist to engage in investigative journalism and the freedom of the individual to have his or her privacy respected. The paper argues for the need to provide an ethical as distinct from a purely legal foundation for a code of journalistic practice. It concludes by arguing persuasively for the need for ethics to be included in media and communication courses.*

It is arguable that no other issue in contemporary journalistic ethics has proven to be as troublesome as the invasion of privacy. A number of reasons can be given for this and they include the changing public perception of what is public or private, the conceptual difficulties concerning privacy and the growing public interest in and concern with privacy. Community and national ordinary standard practices are constantly changing: what is unacceptable or is taken grave exception to today is commonplace tomorrow. What was once strictly private is later regarded as common property. What constitutes an invasion of privacy and what used to be our own perception of what is private or public has changed and will continue to change. In fact there would seem to be widespread confusion surrounding the private versus public distinction. Because of this confusion, journalists are confronted with many varieties of ethical dilemmas in privacy issues and have no precise rules to guide them even though some broad guidelines have emerged.

A striking common theme in contemporary privacy literature is the impossibility of giving an exact definition of privacy. Furthermore, it seems that having regard to both legal decisions and philosophical discourse media ethicists are deeply divided about the meaning, value and grounds of protecting privacy. In this context, journalists frequently find themselves caught between what the law allows and what their consciences permit.

The public is increasingly expressing disquiet about what it regards as unethical behaviour by journalists. For example, journalists working within the law are frequently blamed for invading privacy and for pushing back the boundaries of privacy. The feeling of disquiet expressed by the public seems to suggest that the public expects journalists to be sensitive to ethical considerations which transcend what the law permits. It could even be argued that precisely this failure on the part of some journalists to avert to the ethical as well as the legal dimensions to their work has undermined their credibility in the eyes of the public. The well-published controversies surrounding the intrusion of reporters and photographers into the life and death of Princess Diana and the reporting of the relationship between US president Bill Clinton and Monica Lewinsky have not only generated a lot of public debate, but have also shown that privacy-intrusion is experienced as an ethical issue. Controversies such as the ones mentioned raise a number of questions that carry important moral dimensions. Where should the journalist draw the ethical boundaries of privacy? Can privacy-intrusion be legitimised? When does a private person become a public figure? Who decides the measure of privacy a public person can enjoy? Does it belong to the task of the journalist to follow closely those who occupy important positions in society? Is it in the public's interest to know so much about other people's lives?

The problem journalists face is how to reconcile ethics with a profession in which getting the news often necessitates intrusiveness. It is arguable that some invasion of privacy is essential to the news gathering process if the public is to be well informed. The ethical dilemma arises in deciding where to draw the line between professional and unprofessional journalistic conduct. The journalist who without justification frustrates or contravenes a person's desire for privacy is perceived to transgress the boundary of acceptable behaviour and to violate what has been perceived in contemporary liberal democracies as the principle of respect for persons. In the light of this I will seek to analyse the ethical challenges facing journalists as they endeavour to grapple with issues concerning respect for the privacy of the individual.

One consequence of the clear blurring of the public/private distinction by unscrupulous organs of the media is that there is a growing public concern at what is perceived as the lowering of ethical standards in the media. This has led to a situation in which privacy has become a major issue for those concerned with journalistic ethics. A forceful illustration of this growing concern was the establishment in the UK in 1990 of the Calcutt Committee. This committee was given the following terms of reference:

> In the light of the recent public concern about intrusions into the private lives of individuals by certain sections of the press, to consider what measures are needed to give further protection to individual privacy from the activities of the press.[1]

As is obvious from the terms of reference the government was acutely conscious of the need to protect individuals from unwanted intrusions into privacy. Most interestingly the major finding of the committee's concluding report affirmed that the influence of market forces has become an increasing factor in the invasion of privacy. This is clear in the following statement from the Calcutt Committee:

> The last two decades have seen huge changes in the character of the tabloid market characterised by a high degree of competition and this has led some tabloid editors to feel let off the leash and become too intrusive in pursuit of competitive advantage.[2]

On the recommendation of the committee, a Press Complaints Commission was established to supervise the drafting of a code of practice by the newspaper industry. Whilst it gave newspapers a first serious taste of self-regulation it also served as a final warning to the industry to raise its standards and eliminate intrusions into private lives. If the news media did not respond, statutory protection for privacy would be introduced. The British government published its response to the findings of the Calcutt Committee in 1995, entitled *Privacy and Media Intrusion*. It concluded that there was no compelling case for statutory regulation but recommended that a Protection of Privacy Bill should be introduced. This has remained a recommendation.

Whilst it is the assertion of this paper that one should look in the first place at ethics and self-regulation for the protection and enhancement of privacy, one cannot ignore the chorus of voices calling for the establishment of legislation in order to enshrine protection for the individual's privacy interests. It is to this that we now turn our attention.

## The limits of the law

Privacy law has its origins in the classic 1890 article by L. D. Brandeis and S. D. Warren, *The Right of Privacy*, which appeared in the Harvard Law Review.[3] The authors proposed a legal recognition for the right to be left alone. Offended by newspaper gossip and what they saw as violations of the standards of decency and propriety, both lawyers proposed monetary damages for citizens who had suffered from the prying and insatiable curiosity of an unrestrained and unrepentant press.

In the hundred years since the publication of the Harvard Law Review article, the right to privacy has been given protection in the legal systems of continental European countries by their constitutions and by the incorporation into their law of article eight of the *European Convention on Human Rights*. Article eight states:

> Everyone has the right to respect for his private life, his home and his correspondence and there shall be no

interference by a public authority with the exercise of this right except such as is in accordance with the law and is necessary in a democratic society in the interests of national security, public safety or the economic well-being of the country, for the prevention of disorders or crime, for the protection of health or morals or for the protection of the rights and freedom of others.[4]

In Ireland, the right to privacy does not exist as a monolith. There is a constitutional right to privacy and the Irish courts accept that the Constitution recognises such a right even though it is not spelled out in the text. The extent of the right to privacy is unclear and it remains for the Irish courts to identify the right and the particular aspects of it. There is also a complex of torts, supplemented both by the action for breach of confidence and by the protection of wards. Whilst there is no statutory right of privacy in Ireland, the individual has a reasonable measure of constitutional protection, including judicial review, as well as the ordinary laws relating to defamation, confidence, trespass, nuisance and provisions in the criminal law.[5]

The position in Ireland regarding the right to privacy can be viewed as intermediary between the United States and the United Kingdom. In the United States the right to privacy is explicitly legally recognised and protected. In US jurisprudence the right to privacy has actually developed into four separate and distinct torts and has been supplemented by some constitutional protection.[6]

The right to privacy is not legally recognised and protected in jurisdictions such as the United Kingdom.[7] English law provides no general protection in the form of a right to privacy against the disclosure of personal information. If people want to prevent such a disclosure they must bring their claim within another recognised remedy such as defamation, nuisance, confidence, etc. In criminal law the intentional interception of communications by post or the public telecommunications system, the watching or besetting of a place where a person resides or happens to be, harassment are all subject to penal sanctions. These remedies are not very useful in the context of privacy, because their primary concern is punishment by the state of certain forms of conduct and not the prevention of disclosing information. The civil remedies appear more effective in affording a measure of protection for individual privacy. They include trespass, private nuisance, defamation and malicious falsehood, confidence and court reporting.

It is questionable whether tougher privacy laws are the right mechanisms for protecting privacy interests. One obvious reason is that stricter legislation could have a chilling effect on press freedom. Legal restrictions on the press may prevent it from fulfilling its proper and democratic role. Tougher privacy laws could provide the additional cover for rich, powerful interest groups who should be accountable to public scrutiny. The investigation by the press of the use and abuse of power should never be regarded as an invasion of privacy because unaccountable power is the enemy of any democracy and thus needs to be targeted by a vigilant press. Furthermore, certain privacy and defamation laws already seriously hamper investigative journalism. In this context, it is not difficult to conceive of situations in which journalists refrain from giving a frank appraisal of someone's suitability for public office for fear of a libel action, or situations in which journalists are discouraged from pursuing what are in fact ethically correct forms of action for fear of legal consequences.

A second reason pointing to the limitations of the law in dealing with privacy interests lies in the fact that actually very few cases in which a private citizen's right to privacy is violated, make it to court. Papers like the German *Bildzeitung* or the British *Sun* do not hesitate to listen-in to the police radio in order to follow the family of a suicide victim to the hospital, funeral or to interview their neighbours. Whilst this is an obvious case of privacy intrusion, few private citizens will have the confidence or the money to take these papers to court. Furthermore, it is questionable whether these types of cases would stand up in court.

When a journalist intrudes upon an individual's privacy, whatever the legal remedies are, they are only available after the fact. Whilst a huge monetary award can make a plaintiff rich it can never return the individual's sense of control which the initial invasion took away. For this reason alone one could argue that the law provides an unsatisfactory solution and that ethical thinking prior to publication is preferable to a battle in court afterwards.

There are also many ways in which journalists can offend without straying beyond the law because the law permits many immoralities. What is legal is not necessarily ethical and thus legal principles are not a worthy foundation for journalists when making ethical judgements concerning the lives of others. The professional journalist will require a different tool for dealing with the complex issue of privacy-intrusion.

In the light of the above reasons the Canadian Professor Day observes:

> Whilst it is clear that our preoccupation with privacy and the legal protections against violations of our right to privacy have increased dramatically as we seek solitude and attempt to maintain some autonomy over our personal affairs, privacy law has not achieved the balance between public and private interests envisioned by media critics at the turn of the century.[8]

This would seem to confirm the need for an ethics of privacy that goes beyond the legal principles and provides a moral compass for journalists in fulfilling their obligations to society.

## The need for an ethics of privacy

Identifying convincing arguments for a system centred on an ethics of privacy, transcending legal considerations, is a daunting task for anyone to embark on. In what follows I shall draw on the writings of well-known media ethicists.[9]

The first argument, which these authors formulate in favour of an ethics of privacy, is that, in the eyes of the law, little about the lives of public people is sacred. The law seeks to protect individual privacy but excludes public people. The courts as a result have given the media extraordinary latitude in reporting on public people. The claim to privacy is thus different for different categories of people. This seems to suggest that because public people chose to throw themselves into the public arena, they are willing to undergo vigorous scrutiny and to suffer the consequences of embarrassing revelations. Ethically it is very suspect to imply that public people must sacrifice all privacy and relinquish all autonomy over their personal affairs. Obviously, they have to expect some fallout from the glare of publicity and their zone of privacy will be narrower than the average citizen, but the key question from the standpoint of ethics should be to what extent does the public information relate to the individual's public performance or image. The focus should be on the relationship of private concerns to matters of public interest.

Secondly, the press has been given great latitude in defining newsworthiness. One of the primary legal defenses of the publication of embarrassing private information seems to be newsworthiness. This very liberal approach can lead to the conclusion that anything disseminated by a news organisation can be considered news. More precise criteria are called for in an ethical context. The distinctions between the right to know, the need to know and the want to know need to be revisited. Whilst the right to know is a form of counterbalancing of government power and the need to know a way of providing information to citizens to help them go about their daily lives in society, the third concept is the least ethically compelling as a rationale for acquiring information. We all want to know a lot of things but we don't really need the information as such. It merely serves the purpose of gossip. An ethics of privacy would be concerned with the real public interest value of information rather than how much appeal to mere curiosity can be tolerated under the law.

Thirdly, the legal efforts to protect privacy have accorded substantial latitude for newsgathering in public places. It seems that anything taking place in public view can be reported upon. But we can all think of situations in public where we still want some degree of solitude. Moral sensitivity, good taste and compassion are required on the part of journalists in these circumstances, especially when they are reporting about victims of accidents or other tragedies.

Fourthly, the legal efforts beg many questions about the relationship between self and society. Very often the public's right to know has been used to cheapen the richness of the private/public relationship. The intellectual ethical debate has as a result been reduced and narrowed down in order to allow legal conclusions to be drawn. Thomas Emerson has recognised the richness of the private/public relationship. In his view, the concept of a right to privacy attempts to draw a line between the individual and the collective, between the self and society. It seeks to assure the individual a zone in which to be an individual, not a member of the community. In that zone he can think his own thoughts, have his own secrets, live his own life, reveal only what he wants to the outside world. The right of privacy thus establishes an area excluded from the collective life and not governed by the rules of collective living.[10]

Finally, three moral principles should underpin an ethics of privacy: decency and fairness, redeeming social value and respect for persons. These three moral values can provide the foundation for an ethics of privacy. Decency and fairness would be very important. They would automatically rule out falsehood, innuendo, recklessness and exaggeration. Law explicitly rules out none of the latter. The criterion for selecting which private information is worthy of disclosure could be redeeming social value. This would eliminate all appeals to prurient interests as devoid of news-worthiness. Respect for the unique dignity of the human person should be another key moral principle. Whilst all of these principles bring us beyond the scope of law they are very good guides from an ethical perspective. They would be the ideal tests to determine whether personal information is ethically justified.

## The treatment of privacy in various codes of ethics

Journalists have to operate within the parameters of the law and the market. Despite being widely regarded as a perfectly adequate societal constraint on unethical behaviour on the part of journalists the law is limited and the criteria behind the legal considerations are not always effective in safeguarding privacy interests. Journalists face real difficulties when constructing an ethics ot privacy in a climate where market strategies supercede ethical considerations. The factual economic market mechanisms which wield so much power and pressure upon the mass media, and the enormous influence of the neo-classical economic paradigm in contemporary society, form the background against which many intrusions into privacy take place. In spite of these difficulties I will argue that ethical thinking can transcend legal considerations and counter market-forces.

The physical embodiment of journalistic ethical principles manifests itself most clearly in journalists' codes of ethics. In this context, it is particularly rewarding to examine the trouble which journalists go to in constructing their codes of ethics. This illustrates that there already is a very noble tradition within journalism itself of reflecting upon the ethical core of its work.

The most common types of cases which press councils in Europe deal with relate to issues of privacy, accuracy and the right to reply. The Council of Europe's publication *Media and Democracy* confirms this by stating that most complaints handled by press councils in Europe concern violations of the right to privacy.[11] In the light of this information it is important to raise the question: How does the privacy-issue actually fare out in codes of ethics? In order to answer this question I will examine four of the most authoritative codes in Britain and Ireland at present. They are the *Broadcasting Guidelines* for personnel working in RTE (the national broadcasting station in Ireland), *the National Union of Journalists Code of Conduct* (UK and Ireland), the *Code of Professional Practices for Irish Times* journalists and the Press Complaints Commission's (UK) *Code of Practice*. These codes will be examined in relation to their treatment of privacy and whilst overlap is inevitable, the differences in approach will be clarified.

The *Broadcasting Guidelines* for RTE personnel are firmly based on existing legal frameworks. The section on privacy alone is three pages long and summarises the general legislation regarding privacy in a transparent manner. By referring to Article 40 of the *Irish Constitution*, the *European Convention on Human Rights* and the *Broadcasting Authority Act* of 1976, privacy as a legal concept is outlined. However the interpretation of the legal issues reflects a keen sensitivity to the ethical issues that have given rise to the legislation and to the ethical implications of that legislation. A clear illustration of this is RTÉ's interpretation of the *Broadcasting Authority Act* in relation to privacy. Whilst the Act states that

"The Authority shall not, in its programmes and in the means employed to make such programmes, unreasonably encroach on the privacy of an individual," RTÉ goes further when outlining the specific responsibilities of its personnel in this area:

> RTÉ must be concerned, therefore, with any encroachment on an individual's privacy, with unethical methods of obtaining material for broadcasting and unwanted broadcast publicity concerning private persons or private affairs.[12]

By including the ethical implications of this Act for its staff RTÉ demonstrates a keen awareness of the importance of a general attitude of respect for the privacy of an individual and a good understanding of the public/private distinction.

RTÉ's guidelines dealing with *Unwanted Broadcast Publicity* clearly reflect the need for ethical considerations when stating:

> The recording of what is clearly an uninvited attendance by a reporter at an individual's home for the purposes of obtaining an interview or comment and an attempt to interview or get comment from an unwilling individual at his office, as he enters his car or as he walks along the pavement all require sensitive consideration.[13]

This illustrates that RTÉ expects its personnel to use ethical considerations in deciding whether or not to seek consent or reveal the identity of an individual in obtaining information and not merely to operate within the constraints of the law.

RTÉ places particular emphasis upon the ethical means of obtaining information when stating that, "the problems of intrusion into personal privacy have become a major issue with the development of very sensitive surveillance and recording devices."[14] RTÉ then continues by restating the firm guidelines in place regarding this matter, for instance:

> The use of surreptitious recording and filming devices that would be altogether outside normal recording and filming

practice is ruled out, except in the most exceptional cases where compelling reasons may be advanced for suspending the general prohibition and where the means proposed to be employed would not, in the circumstances, be regarded as constituting unreasonable encroachment on privacy.[15]

Only in exceptional circumstances may this guideline be overruled and the actual criteria for determining such cases are included by RTÉ. By listing these criteria RTÉ prevents its staff from operating in an ethical vacuum and provides them with a framework for ethical reasoning. This contrasts with the *National Union of Journalists Code of Conduct* which provides no criteria to determine whether the use of other means is justified. It is to this code that we now turn our attention.

Ireland has no separate journalists' organisation and Irish journalists observe the *Code of Conduct* drawn up by the United Kingdom's National Union of Journalists. The code was written in 1936 and the initiative came from the journalists themselves. Additional guidelines were drawn up in 1976 and in 1987 the Annual Delegate Meeting of the National Union of Journalists of the United Kingdom and Ireland adopted a twelve-article code of professional conduct. Opening with the statement that, "a journalist has a duty to maintain the highest professional and ethical standards"[16] the remainder of the code contains a list of do's and don'ts for journalists. The brevity and lack of detail in the articles of the code compromise their overall effectiveness in dealing with the ethical dilemmas journalists face. Only articles five and six deal with privacy. Article five states:

A journalist shall obtain information, photographs and illustrations only by straightforward means. The use of other means can be justified only by overriding considerations of the public interest. The journalist is entitled to exercise a personal conscientious objection to the use of such means.[17]

Initially it seems that this article emphasises the straightforward means in which information, photographs and illustrations must be obtained in the same way as RTE's *Broadcasting Guidelines for Personnel*. However there is a major difference between the codes in the way they formulate their justification for using other means. Clearly this justification is not spelled out in the text of article five, as opposed to RTE's code which includes a detailed list of criteria for determining whether the use of other means is justified. Despite the inclusion of the phrase "overriding considerations of the public interest", as a possible criterion for justifying the use of other means, the concept public interest is nowhere explained in the code. Merely stating that the journalist is entitled to exercise his own conscientious objection to the use of other means is not exactly helpful when confronted with difficult ethical dilemmas and little time to reflect upon them. It could even be argued that such a personalist or subjective approach to decision-making can undercut the value of more structured models of ethical reasoning so emphasised in journalistic training today.

It is a pity that the concept of public interest has not been explained in greater detail in the NUJ Code, because it has proven to be a very useful tool in making ethical decisions. This is clearly illustrated in the *British Press Complaints Commission's Code of Practice* which has gone to great lengths in preserving and clarifying a proper understanding of this concept. The concept of public interest is repeated in article six of the NUJ *Code of Conduct* but no further clarification is given: "Subject to the justification by overriding considerations of the public interest, a journalist shall do nothing that entails intrusion into private grief and distress."[18]

This seems to be a rather minimalist requirement and one would hope that journalists demonstrate a heightened degree of moral sensitivity characterised by compassion and good taste when dealing with individuals in these unfortunate circumstances.

The *Code of Professional Practices for Irish Times journalists* takes as its departure point the previously examined *National Union of Journalists Code of Conduct*. Journalists of the *Irish Times* are not only expected to observe the requirements of the NUJ code but also to adhere to a set of guidelines regarding independence from advertisers, travel, gifts, entertainment, affiliation and income and sponsorship. Apart from the relevant articles in the NUJ code no other information about privacy is included in the code for journalists of the Irish Times.

The Code of Professional Practices for Irish Times Journalists was formulated with a two-fold aim in mind: to outline an ethical code for journalists of the *Irish Times* and to help remove the public perception of low ethical standards among journalists in general. It accepts that the vast majority of journalists already behave ethically in a manner that is wholly compatible with the code. This positive starting point helps to clarify the underlying rationale of the code. It does not intend to be a document for reprimanding journalists about unethical behaviour but rather aims to make clear to the general public and those seeking to influence journalists for their own vested interests that journalists in the Irish Times practice according to a set of ethical principles.

What is unique to the *Code of Professional Practices for Irish Times Journalists* is the information the code provides about its ethics committee:

> The ethics committee will make recommendations to the editor in marginal cases, interpreting the spirit of this document and, where necessary, setting down lines of definition. The committee will draw up the wording of the written undertaking to be given by journalists in specified posts that they will not use their positions for personal gain.[19]

The existence and the function of the ethics committee at the Irish Times reflect an awareness of the proper role and task of the journalist and an acknowledgement of the need to move beyond a mere following of a set of rules. It also stresses the importance attached to continuous assessment of the code and a proper articulation and definition of concepts contained in the code. The existence of the committee thus ensures that ethical reasoning is automatically part of any discussion of marginal cases and of the job descriptions of individual journalists.

The Press Complaints Commission's *Code of Practice* is widely regarded as the cornerstone of the system of self-regulation in

Britain. The Commission was set up in 1991 and in spite of being a non-statutory body with very limited powers of censorship it has been quite successful in dealing with privacy-intrusion. This is in no small way due to the detailed treatment of privacy in the code. Keeping in mind that violations of the right to privacy are the public's most common complaints the Commission has to deal with, almost half of the code is taken up with the privacy issue. Privacy is dealt with under the sections privacy, harassment, intrusion into grief or shock, children, children in sex cases, listening devices, hospitals and innocent relatives and friends. Some of these sections will be looked at more closely in order to do justice to the full spirit of the code.

The section on privacy begins by quoting article eight of the *European Convention on Human Rights* and ends with the following clause:

> The use of long-lens photography to take pictures of people in private places without their consent is unacceptable. Note that private places are public or private property where there is a reasonable expectation of privacy.[20]

Whilst the means of obtaining private information has also been an intrinsic part of other codes, this code outlines the concept of a private place. Undoubtedly this will help journalists when interpreting this section and avoid possible misunderstandings of its proper meaning. The section on harassment highlights that:

> Journalists must not photograph individuals in private places without their consent; must not persist in telephoning, questioning, pursuing or photographing individuals after having been asked to desist; must not remain on their property after having been asked to leave and must not follow them.[21]

At first this appears to be a very firm and straightforward commandment for journalists to obey. However, it is founded upon the ethical principle of respect for persons. As autonomous individuals we are all entitled to a certain amount of dignity and this should never be arbitrarily compromised. In this context the clause leaves no room for intimidating, harassing, pursuing, exposing or hindering individuals in the process of obtaining information. Section five entitled *Intrusion into Grief or Shock* urges the journalist to demonstrate a virtuous character:

> In cases involving grief or shock, enquiries must be carried out and approaches made with sympathy and discretion. Publication must be handled sensitively at such times, but this should not be interpreted as restricting the right to report judicial proceedings.[22]

By including words such as sympathy, discretion and sensitively the language of the code supports its central commitment towards respecting the rights of the individual.

The section on children stresses the importance of allowing young people to complete their time at school without unnecessary intrusion. In addition, it stresses that the publication of material about the private life of a child is not justified because of the fame, notoriety or position of the child's parents or guardians. Journalists might be able to answer the question of how much privacy their subjects really deserve by rendering judgement based upon the moral principle of justice.

Section eight forbids the practice of obtaining information through the use of clandestine listening devices or the interception of private telephone conversations. The section can thus be regarded as a further addition to the section dealing with privacy.

Finally there is the section on hospitals clearly reflecting the code's awareness of a place where individuals are particularly vulnerable to having their privacy intruded upon. Journalists should be careful not to take advantage in such situations and respect the privacy of those finding themselves in these unfortunate circumstances. Moral insensitivity displayed by journalists at this time can contribute towards an erosion of the journalist's respectability in the eyes of the public.

There are a number of reasons that make the *Code of Practice* from the Press Complaints Commission one of the most useful codes of ethics currently existing. Amongst these are the transparent, detailed, inspirational and personal nature of its sixteen sections, the unique definition of what is meant by the concept public interest, the open invitation to the public for comments or suggestions regarding the content of the *Code* and the image it holds up of a good professional journalist by describing clearly the virtuous character traits needed by journalists. In addition to this, the code illuminates precisely those aspects where stress and tension have been felt within the journalistic profession and emphasises positively the role of the press within a democratic society. The language throughout the code reflects ethical considerations and terms such as welfare, responsibility, freedom, moral obligation, sympathy, discretion and sensitivity.

## Conclusion: ethics as an educational foundation for journalists.

In Europe there is no standard educational prerequisite for becoming a journalist nor is there any necessity to join or be admitted to a professional body. This open system of admission to journalism ensures that any person can become a journalist simply by becoming employed as a journalist. However, there is ample evidence of the attractiveness of courses that provide an entry-route into journalism by means of a university qualification. In Ireland there are several such courses on offer.

The fact that with only one exception[23] these colleges do not include the study of ethics in their course content points to a possible deficiency in the educational training of journalists. If the existing curriculum of journalistic education does not provide a systematic study of media ethics, one can easily envisage situations where students emerge from their college experience untutored in ethical considerations and ill-prepared to cope with the ethical exigencies of contemporary journalism. A number of authors have addressed this issue and highlighted the need for bringing ethics into journalistic education and for allocating a rather special place to it.[24]

In this context it is interesting to observe the claim in the

Council of Europe's publication *Media and Democracy* that many training institutions fail to play a significant role in shaping the professional qualities of young journalists. Barely half of journalists surveyed counted the training process they received as a significant influence on their ethical development.[25] These concerns are not confined to the continent of Europe. In a carefully researched study the Canadian social philosopher L. A. Day argues that the rapidly expanding literature on media ethics reflects a widespread recognition that the need for a renewed emphasis on ethics in journalistic education has never been greater.[26] Journalism is a rapidly expanding course in many colleges throughout the USA and Canada, and only a proper educational structure, which allows students to develop their ethical skills, can respond to this need.

Gradually interest in ethics is reappearing in journalistic education programmes. Names of philosophers are slowly filtering into journalism classes and the growing insistence that more emphasis should be placed upon the ethical foundations of journalism has resulted in a rapid increase in textbooks for students considering the complexities of media ethics. The textbooks have developed different frameworks for making ethical judgements in journalism.[27] These frameworks illustrate that ethical theory and the practice of ethics can be combined in courses of media ethics. The models on which students can base their ethical decisions have been developed in the belief that good ethical decision-making in journalism is a craft and a skill comparable to good writing, good photography or good editing. This difficult skill, like all the other skills of journalism, takes training, time and effort in order to master it.

In order to ensure that students acquire this skill, a good course in media ethics must meet five educational requirements. It must stimulate the moral imagination of students and it must enable them to recognise ethical issues. Furthermore, it must develop their analytical skills, it must elicit a sense of moral obligation and personal responsibility and finally, it must help students to tolerate disagreement. A course which fulfills these five demands can promote moral conduct because it provides students of journalism with the means to make ethical judgements, defend them and then criticise the results of their choices.

In order to ensure that each journalist is provided with the opportunity to study ethics, the current educational training of journalists must be re-evaluated. Already new models of journalistic education which allocate a special place to the study of ethics are being debated in Canada and the United States.[28] One conceivable model requires that those interested in careers in journalism take a normal three-year arts degree first, with at least a minor in philosophy. The arts degree could be followed up by a number of years of practical training consisting of in-office experience as a working journalist. Such a model would have room to facilitate a comprehensive study of ethics which both bears upon the cultivation of skills and understanding that are useful in journalistic practice and is tailored to the problems that actually confront journalists.

Ongoing journalistic education is another area that requires urgent attention because it could play an important role in facilitating the study of ethics for working journalists. Perhaps journalists would benefit from a sabbatical pause during their high-pressure and deadline-oriented careers. The quiet of a college setting would be the ideal place for taking time out. It would provide them with the opportunity to systematically explore the many nuances of decision-making, revisit real but old case studies, ponder upon ethical judgements previously made and identify their ethical implications and the questions they raise. A study of ethics in this way would deepen their understanding of contemporary society, expand their horizons and increase their personal growth. More importantly it would equip them with the necessary tools for dealing with the complex ethical challenges of contemporary journalism, including the privacy of the individual.

## Notes

1 The National Heritage Committee's Fourth Report, *Privacy and Media Intrusions*, p. 8.
2 Browne, 1996: 144.
3 Rubin, 1978: 23.
4 McGonagle, 1997: 124-5.
5 For a critical evaluation of the current legal mechanisms to provide protection for privacy interests, this article proves to be particularly helpful. After having identified the intersection of privacy interests with media

speech rights O'Dell considers the legal doctrine most suited to the protection of privacy interests. See O'Dell's paper, "When Two Tribes go to War: Privacy Interests and Media Speech", in McGonagle, 1997: 181-256.

6 Day, 1991. He gives a detailed analysis of the torts of intrusion, publicity of embarrassing private facts, false light and appropriation within the framework of civil privacy law in the US.

7 There are those who claim that the British media are more restricted by the law than in most other countries of the democratic world. See Kieran 1998: 98-99.

8 Day, 1991: 108.

9 See Besley and Chadwick (1992) reprinted 1995. See also Christians, Rotzoll and Fackler (1987) reprinted 1991.

10 Emerson is quoted in Christians, Fackler and Rotzoll, 1991: 110-111.

11 Nordenstreng, 1995: 20.

12 RTÉ Broadcasting guidelines, 1989: 32.

13 Ibid: 33.

14 ibid: 32.

15 Ibid: 33.

16 NUJ code of conduct: Art. 1.

17 Ibid: Art. 5.

18 Ibid: Art. 6.

19 Irish Times Code: 4.

20 Press Complaints Commission 1998: 1.

21 Ibid: 1.

22 Ibid.

23 Griffith College, BA course in Journalism and Media Communications. In year two it offers a course in media ethics.

24 See A. Serafini, in Cohen, 1992: 256-263. See also Louis Hodges, 1996: 35

25 See Peters in Media and Democracy 1998: 74.

26 Day, 1991: XV.

27 See Fink, 1995: 8. See also Christians, Fackler and Rotzoll, 1991: 118-119. See also Day, 1991: 58. See also Merrill, "Ethics and Journalism", in Barney and Merrill: 1-16.

28 Rubin, 1978: 262.

## Bibliography

### Codes of Practice and Official Reports

*Broadcasting Guidelines for RTE Personnel*, Radio Telefís Éireann, Dublin, 1989.

*Code of Professional Practices of Irish Times Journalists*, Irish Times Publishing, Dublin.

*Media and Democracy*, Strasbourg, Council of Europe Publishing, 1998.

*National Union of Journalists Code of Conduct for Journalists*, NUJ, London.

*The National Heritage Committee's Fourth Report on Privacy and Media Intrusion*, London, 1995.

The Press Complaints Commission's *Code of Practice*, London, 1998.

### Secondary Sources

Barney, R. and Merrill, J., *Ethics and the Press, in Readings in Mass Media Morality*, Hastings House, New York, 1974.

Belsey, A. and Chadwick, R., *Ethical Issues in Journalism and the Media*, (1992), Reprinted, London, Routledge, 1995.

Christians C., Fackler M. and Rotzoll K., *Media Ethics: Cases and Moral Reasoning*, (1987), Reprinted, New York, Longman, 1991.

Cohen, E., *Philosophical Issues in Journalism*, Oxford, Oxford University Press, 1992.

Day, L. A., *Ethics in Media Communications: Cases and Controversies*, California, Wadsworth, 1991.

Dandekar, N., "Privacy: An Understanding for Embodied Persons", *The Philosophical Forum*, 24/4 (1993).

Fink, C., *Media Ethics*, Massachusetts, Allyn and Bacon, 1995.

Hodges, L., "The Journalist and Professionalism", *Journal of Mass Media Ethics*, 1/2 (1986).

Kieran, M., *Media Ethics*, London and New York, Routledge, 1998.

McGonagle, M., (ed.) *Law and the Media*, Dublin, Round Hall Sweet and Maxwell, 1997.

Nordenstreng, K., *Reports on Media Ethics in Europe*, Tampere, Julkaisuja Publications, 1995.

Rubin, B., *Questioning Media Ethics*, New York, Praeger, 1978.

Schoeman, F. (ed.), *Philosophical Dimensions of Privacy: An Anthology*, Cambridge, Cambridge University Press, 1994.

Thompson, J., *The Media and Modernity*, Cambridge, Polity Press, 1995.

———— CHAPTER 15 ————

# Between Clinton and Mitterand: on the Distinction between the Public and the Private in the Media

*Egidius E. Berns*

*This contribution analyses the distinction between "the public" and "the private" in relation to media coverage of individuals in the public eye. It discusses two situations covered by the media in late 1998 and early 1999, Monica-gate and the Mazarine-case, seeing them as opposing conceptions of the public-private distinction. The paper treats of the historical and cultural contexts within which these concepts have developed and examines their current meaning and significance for media ethics.*

## Introduction

The title of this contribution *Between Clinton and Mitterand* refers, on the one hand to Monica-gate (the extra-marital affair between USA President Bill Clinton and Monica Lewinsky) and, on the other hand, to the extra-marital affair of the late former French President, Francois Mitterand. The latter affair came into the public spotlight with the presence at his funeral of his extra-marital daughter Mazarine. The subtitle of this article, *On the distinction between the Public and the Private in the Media,* indicates my particular focus. I wish to reflect on the way in which we differentiate between the public sphere and the private sphere. The conduct of the protagonists referred to is not the focus of this contribution, but the tumults – especially in the media – which resulted from the news of their extra-marital relationships. Press and media coverage of these affairs focused attention on the distinction between the public and the private.[1] In this respect the Clinton and Mitterand cases are of particular interest because their coverage in the English and French language media clearly illustrates opposing conceptions of the distinction between "the private" and "the public". I shall argue for a middle position between these opposing viewpoints – the virtuous position is often in the middle of a tension.

## The press: accountability and the public space

Our concern with the Clinton and Mitterand affairs is the delimitation of the private and public spheres as they were articulated in the press. The press functioned in both cases as an important element of the *public space*. But what is the exact nature of the public space? How is it related to the idea and functioning of a *free market*? What has it to do with media and marketing techniques, with language, with economic interests? To what extent could the press be accused of creating both affairs? To what extend can and should the press be held accountable for its coverage? These are urgent questions. In late January 1999 the French newspaper Le Monde published a front page article entitled: *Affaires Clinton et Dumas: La presse coupable*? Another French newspaper, *Le Figaro*, spoke about *lynchage médiatique*. *The New York Magazine* had as its headline *Impeach the media!* *The Columbia Journalism Review* pointed to haste, sensationalism, and a too strong attention to rumours as characterising press coverage. In short, the media were accused of deliberately obscuring the distinction between news and entertainment.

To what extent can these charges against the media be regarded as valid? For instance there was much less inaccurate reporting in the case of Monica-gate than in Watergate. In fact there was only one major mistake: the assertion that there was a visual witness to the love affair between Clinton and Monica Lewinsky. Furthermore, in the light of possible impeachment proceedings and the political crisis attending such proceedings, the press could not easily be accused of providing disproportional coverage of Monica-gate. Like *Le Monde*, I conclude, *Non la presse n'est pas coupable.* Nevertheless, the way in which these scandals were reported raises fundamental questions regarding the manner in which the press respects both the presumption of innocence and an individual's right to privacy. Both of these issues draw attention to questions concerning the relationship between the public and private spheres of individuals in public office that need to be addressed.

Concerning the Mazarine case, a very brief statement from President Mitterrand expresses perfectly a classical conception of the private/public distinction. Questioned by a journalist as to whether he had an extra-marital daughter, Mitterrand answered: *Oui, et alors? Yes, and so what?* His non-answer expresses unambiguously the viewpoint that the question is a non-question to a person in public office. It is not a question that is validly in the public realm. If one accepts this standpoint the separation between the public and the private is absolute and is also a condition for the very existence of the public and political space.[2]

There are strong differences between Mitterrand's and the French public's reaction to the Mazarine case and the American reaction to Monica-gate, which suggest that in the USA the public space, is not accorded an autonomous existence apart from the private to the same extent as in France. However, one must not forget that the Republicans accused President Clinton not simply or even primarily because of his extra-marital affair, but because of subsequent perjury and obstruction of justice when the affair became public. Furthermore, those who opposed the President's impeachment did so not because they rejected the allegations of the Republicans against Clinton but because of the wish to maintain the distinction between public responsibility and private life. For the Americans, Monica-gate has become an extraordinary instrument of pedagogy, not only into the distinction between the public and the private, but also into the moral nature of this distinction. It has raised issues which clarify the nature of questions such as "what is a good President?" or "who should govern, what does it mean to govern? Is a person who is guilty of perjury a fit person to govern?"

## Classical and liberal conceptions of the public and the private

Mitterrand's "and so what?" is paradigmatic of the classical conception of politics. It goes back to the Greek opposition between the *oikos*, the house, and the *polis*, the sovereign city. Its contemporary form is liberalism (at least in its universalistic and deontological form which we find for instance in Rawl's *Theory of Justice*). However, there are fundamental differences between the Greek and the contemporary conceptions of the public and private spheres. For the Greeks the private space of the household is deprived of freedom; personal freedom can only be fulfilled in the public space. The opposition is between the private and the public rather than the personal and the public. Furthermore, the basis for the distinction between the private and the public lies in the economic and political dimension of human life. For us today, the distinctions are different. The private and the personal life are much closer to each other and personal and public life more distinct.

Despite the differences between these two conceptions of the public and private spheres, we share with the Greeks the idea that the public space has a strong normative character. We share the belief that the ethical "good life" can only be fulfilled in the public sphere of the *polis*. Even if the modern individual believes that freedom is achieved by acting in his or her own interest, nevertheless it is accepted that it is only as a good citizen acting for the common interest that he or she can fully express this freedom. Therefore, the concepts of the state and the common interest are moral as well as descriptive concepts. Furthermore, it is no accident that, within these conceptions of the state and the common interest, description and evaluation meet. It must be remembered that the concept of *polis* (for instance in Aristotle) or the state (for instance in Hegel or Hanna Arendt) signify entities that are self-referential and self-contained. They are autarchic, self-sufficient and self-evident. Furthermore, that is why they are supported primarily not by positive law but by natural law, i.e. the capacity of the law to refer to the right in itself.

If western thought has upheld from the beginning the normative character of the public space and the general interest or common good, there were nevertheless important changes and discontinuities that created ambiguities. This was already evident as early as the classical Greek culture. For instance, there are different emphases between Plato and Aristotle and even within the writings of Aristotle. Nevertheless, the main break came with the emergence of the culture of Modernity. According to Aristotle the *polis* is a *koinoonia politoon* (a community of citizens), these citizens being *meros poleoos* (parts of the city). Housekeeping and the household are private in the sense that they are deprived of publicity. The law of the housekeeping (the *nomos* of the *oikos*) *oikonomia* (economics) is self-interest, while the public sphere is that of common interest. The Ciceronean translation of *koinoonia politoon* into *societas civilis* already signified a move to a juridical concept of living together based on contracts. However, up until 1820 societas civilis remained the definition of the state. Nevertheless, it is not by accident that the Hegelean translation of *societas civilis* in *Bürgerliche Gesellschaft* became in 1820 the name for the non-political sphere of contractual relations between persons acting solely out of concern for their own interests. With the advent of modernity, it had become no longer possible to restrict private actions to those of the household. Thus a part of that which was for the Ancients a public space is incorporated in the private space and no longer ruled by common interest but by self-interest. This incorporation transformed the ancient economic conception of the household into the modern one characterised by intimacy and privacy, leaving economic activity outside the household. In this new context, the political community has to accept the need to share the public sphere with the private sphere of the market and the other institutions of the civil society such as unions, churches, and non-government organisations. Thus in the culture of modernity, society as a whole is increasingly perceived as a web of contractual relations. Furthermore, according to the German philosopher Hegel, it is the political economy that gives us a way of understanding the workings of this web of contractual relations. The consequence of this development is that Modernity has reversed the classical Aristotelian order: citizens are no longer *meros poleoos* (parts of the state). Rather, it is individuals who create the state. Emerging as a consequence of a contract by pre-existing individuals the state can only be understood as an expression of the contractual nature of living together.

Liberalism gives an explanation of this contractual nature of modern society. People act in self-interest. Furthermore, liberalism explains modern living primarily not only from a private point of view but also in terms of an economic paradigm (in so far as economics gives us the theory of social entities based on self-interest). But, and I would insist on this, liberalism is able to transcend this purely private economic perspective. By considering the juridical as well as the economic dimension of the social contract that constitutes the state, liberalism is able to incorporate the classical opposition of private and public. What must be recognised is that the contract instituting the state is not an ordinary contract (a contract between you and me), it is a contract *about* a contract. It is a contract that you and I shall honour our contract, that we are obliged to put into effect that which we have agreed upon even if this is no longer in accord with our personal interest. So living together, considered as a web of contracts between pre-existing individuals, ends up affirming a sphere of normative character that transcends the sphere of private relations. This is contemporary liberalism in its universalistic and deontological form. Even if we find it insufficient we cannot simply abandon liberalism, because as is obvious, liberalism accords with the contemporary "western" cultural ethos. Furthermore, through its strong opposition between the private and the public, liberalism does affirm the normative character of the latter and the universality of the law. In the context of the acceptance of contemporary liberalism, Mitterand's words *et alors?* remain for me among his finest and the manner in which the American House and Senate debated Monica-gate appears to be unacceptable. However, irrespective of whether or not one accepts liberalism, the question remains as to whether the relation between liberalism and truth is well thought out.

One must remember that the contract about the contract, which obliged me to keep my word, is still a contract between pre-existing individuals. Consequently, the transcending necessity of obligation depends on nothing more than the contingency of pre-existing individuals. However, there is a way of countering this objection: the individual is supposed to be rational in himself or herself, irrespective of any consideration of the community into which he or she was born. Therefore, the private point of view of the individual can, in principle, be in accordance with the public point of view. Furthermore, the individual is able to understand that the public obligation to execute a contract (even if it is not in his private interest) is in accordance with his interest as a rational being. This is the liberal solution and the reason why liberalism upholds the universality of human rights

From a communitarian perspective the arguments underpinning the rationale of liberalism are flawed. They point to the fact that individuals do not pre-exist before their insertion into the community whose normative dimension they are supposed to institute. Furthermore, if they are rational it is because of their insertion into the community, the education they receive and the public space they live in.

## Conclusion

While accepting the force of the communitarian critique of liberalism I nevertheless do not think that communitarian criticisms can allow us to forget the strength of the liberal argument. However, it does change the nature of the argument. The public sphere has no longer a self-evident character, sustained by natural law, fulfilling the highest human possibilities. Rather, it is an abstraction and therefore a historical and corruptible construct with which we can never fully identify and from which we will always remain separated. One should maintain the public space because it refers to the universality of the law. However, it alone cannot sustain morality. As the contemporary philosopher Emmanuel Levinas showed: the other possesses his or her singularity which transcends the public sphere reflected in positive law, even if one cannot meet his or her demands other than through the law. In the context of media ethics Levinas' philosophy alerts us to the need to be, attentive to the singularity of a demand. To say it in lesser normative terms, our fascination for the private life of politicians, sports-persons, royals, or even artists, writers or philosophers indicates that what counts in public life are their singularities which are always already covered up by public forms. To conclude, I find myself chartering a middle course that does not fully accept either the approach of Mitterrand to the Mazarine case or the way in which the American public reacted to Monica-gate. I would maintain the necessity of the public but not deny a place for the private.

## Notes

1 Many other illustrative examples could have been selected. In February 1999 when the Clinton and Mitterand situations were being covered in the media there were other instances for example the resignation of MEP Tom Spencer over drugs and pornography was widely covered, as was the "private belief" of English football coach Hoddle which led to his resignation from the national team management.

2 In fact things are much more complicated. The French also have a solid tradition of transgressing the rigorous distinction between public and private life. In the seventeenth century the French Catholic Church acted against Louis XIV in exactly the same way as the Republicans acted against Clinton. It fought against the king's policies by condemning his love affairs from the pulpit. Moreover, the French were proud of President Mitterrand because he was a president *qui aimaient les femmes*. This suggests that certain private actions, in French eyes, enhance public acceptability.

## Bibliography

Aristotle, "Politics", in *The Complete works of Aristotle*, The Revised Oxford Translation (Volume 2), New Jersey, Princeton University Press.

Levinas. E., *Totalite et Infinité: Essai sur l'Exteriorité*, La Haye, Nijhoff, 1961.

Hegel G.W., *Vorlesungen uber die Geschichte der Philosophie*, Jubilaumsausgabe, Vol.19, Stuttgart, Frommann Verlag, 1965.

Rawls, J., *A Theory of Justice*, (1972), Reprinted, Oxford, Oxford University Press, 1990.

———————— CHAPTER 16 ————————

# The Net, its Gatekeepers, their Bait and its Victims: Ethical Issues Relating to the Internet

*Paul Brian Campbell SJ and Michael J. Breen[1]*

*This paper examines the significance of the Internet as a growing phenomenon that continues to exert a significant influence on society. It looks at the media oligopoly that the Internet has now joined and considers the trend of recent Internet developments. Comparing the promise of the new medium with its reality, the paper examines some of the downsides of the Internet and the need for critical evaluation of its place in terms of social change and social equality.*

## Introduction

Writing about the introduction of television into American homes in the late 1940s and early 1950s, George Comstock noted its diffusion was so rapid, "that what occurred approximated a revolution, even though its effects on the whole were slow to evolve."[2] The arrival of Internet access to homes across the (mostly developed) world approximates the next revolution, and its effects may well be equally slow to evolve. Although it may not fit all the criteria of the existing mass media, it is nonetheless the fastest growing communications medium in the world today. Its widespread diffusion promises to have significant global consequences.

One especially noteworthy aspect of the Internet is that until now it has not been formally controlled by any public or private entity. The United States, with its enduring frontier mythology and history of gold rushes, has seen many of its citizens embrace the Internet as an opportunity to homestead on a virtual frontier. They are seizing the opportunity to map out new electronic territories and, increasingly, they dream of striking it rich through on-line commerce. The Clinton-Gore administration had a policy to hook up every elementary and secondary classroom to the Internet by the year 2000. Indeed, across the world there has been a growing consensus that schools without such access are in some sense depriving their students of a fundamental educational resource.

A variety of promises have been made, or at least implied, in relation to the Internet. Its proponents make much of its ability to deliver the latest research from a wide variety of disciplines to millions of users. It is seen by some as the saviour of democracy, the social weapon that will destroy hegemony and prevent the political manipulation of society. Claims are frequently made that it will create a new and powerful voice for the people. The promises, extensive and seemingly limitless, are however often made without reference to any of the costs involved in the delivery of such a system. No technology has ever been adopted without social cost, and it is certain that, whatever the benefits, a communications technology as powerful and as "revolutionary" as the Internet will exact a considerable cost from existing social structures.

There is no such thing as a free lunch. The goods promised by Internet development have to be paid for in hard cash. These costs are not only financial, but also social and cultural. A few commentators have begun to count the cost. Some caveats have been forthcoming from neo-Luddites, ranging from a concern about a loss of writing skills, already evident from the use of spell checking in word processors and a tendency to produce streams of ungrammatical prose in e-mail, to a range of social ills, up to and including an Orwellian nightmare of excessive social control.

## A growing phenomenon

Bruce Sterling, an Internet historian, describes "the seething, fungal development of the Internet."[3] As the 1990s progressed we became aware of just how big a phenomenon the Internet was going to be, although we still have no idea what its final shape will be. The year 1996 was a year when the Internet kept on growing, increasing by 50 percent or doubling its user base over 1995, depending on what surveys you believed. At the end of 1996, the best estimate is that there were approximately 45 million people using the Internet, with roughly 30 million of those in North America (USA/Canada), 9 million in Europe and 6 million in Asia/Pacific (Australia, Japan, etc.). The scale of change is evident from the 1997 figures seen below in Table 1. And by 1998 the worldwide figure had grown to 153 million users. Table 1 indicates the scale of change over the three-year timeframe.

*Table 1: Million Internet users by continent, 1996-1999*

|               | 1996 | 1997 | March 1999 |
|---------------|------|------|------------|
| Africa        | -    | 1    | 1.14       |
| Asia          | 6    | 14   | 26.55      |
| Europe        | 9    | 20   | 36.11      |
| Middle East   | -    | 0.5  | 0.78       |
| US/Canada     | 30   | 64   | 94.2       |
| South America | -    | 1.3  | 4.5        |

**The new media**

Each new communications medium is always hyped as it is being introduced. Adoption is encouraged by promises about the quality products that it will deliver. As usage becomes widespread however, there is little further incentive to maintain consistent levels of quality so that, in the end, programming tends to follow the formula for the lowest common denominator as junk overwhelms the quality material. This is evident, for example, in the case of television, with many commentators lamenting the demise of "the golden age of television" of the 1950s. The increase in available broadcast slots, on terrestrial, cable and satellite television has not been matched by an increase in quality materials, so much of what is used to fill the vacant spaces is of low quality, mass produced for a mass market with little attention to content or effect. It is the technological equivalent of Parkinson's law, that content expands to fill the broadcast time available. Given the incredibly large capacity of the Internet, in which each individual user is a potential publisher, it seems reasonable to expect that a certain amount of what is offered in this new medium will be of the high volume, low cost variety which offers little by way of quality.

At the same time it is important to indicate the enormous potential and actual benefits of Internet development. Despite the proliferation of material of dubious quality, the Internet has already proved itself a social boon. It allows for the easy communication between individuals and groups, from the one-to-one of personal e-mail to large-scale communications across corporations, academies, and multinational interest groups of all kinds. It makes available an enormous amount of documentation on a bewildering array of issues. It allows the swift transmission of information hitherto almost impossible.[4] The Internet also facilitates the transmission of software, in the form of programs or patches, which have made technical support vastly easier for both supplier and end-user.

The Internet, however, remains an infant medium, still in the early years of its adoption curve. It is still growing dramatically in terms of both its user base and its product offerings. But like most other media, the potential uses are probably largely unseen at this stage of development. A quick survey of previous adoption factors in relation to other mass media indicates some of the issues in connection with Internet development.

## Previous instances of hype

The telegraph made at least four important contributions to communications.[5] Firstly, by separating communication from transportation it allowed for instantaneous communication across vast distances; it allowed for the co-ordination and expansion of both military and commercial activities. With the rise of wire services the commodification of information began. The development of the telegraph in the United States in the hands of private enterprise served as a model for subsequent communication technologies.[6]

The telegraph was initially received with spontaneous gatherings of cheering crowds in New York and other American cities. People were excited at the possibility of being in closer contact with other parts of the United States and Europe. It did not take long, however, for Henry David Thoreau to come up with a critical insight:

> We are in great haste to construct a magnetic telegraph from Maine to Texas; but Maine and Texas, it may be, have nothing important to communicate. Either is in such a predicament as the man who was earnest to be introduced to a distinguished deaf woman, but when he was presented, and one end of her ear trumpet was put into his hand, had nothing to say. As if the main object were to talk fast and not to talk sensibly. We are eager to tunnel under the Atlantic and bring the Old World some weeks nearer to the New; but perchance the first news that will leak through into the broad, flapping American ear will be that the Princess Adelaide has the whooping cough.[7]

Just because a technology is available, it doesn't mean that it will provide an important benefit for society.

The telephone was "the first electric medium to enter the home and unsettle customary ways of dividing the private person and family from the more public setting of the community."[8] Although by any standards the telephone's diffusion was remarkably rapid, it began with business users, only gradually being adopted for residential use. As with the Internet now, claims were made that the telephone was a force for democracy because it enabled citizens to communicate across distances without being controlled by a central authority.[9] Although this is interesting speculation, the early history of the telephone, at least in the United States, is replete with efforts to keep the technology out of the hands of ordinary citizens.[10] In the same way that the telegraph spawned Western Union, the first of the huge communication conglomerates, so the telephone brought about the rise of AT&T.

AT&T was also an important force in the commercial development of radio. At first, radio was the domain of enthusiastic amateurs and later was promoted as an advertising-free service by the makers and retailers of radio receivers. In 1922, however, AT&T's New York City station began selling advertising time and American radio soon fell into a largely commercial format consisting mainly of popular music, dramas, sports and comedy. The ubiquity of radio broadcasting meant that it had little trouble establishing itself at the heart of American culture. Television would later adopt and retain the same basic format as radio. When television was first introduced, it was important to provide good children's programming and quality dramas for adults so that those who could afford the expensive TV sets would be persuaded to part with their money. As TV diffusion gathered pace, there was less need to provide non-revenue producing programming and so the quality of its offerings began to diminish.

Both radio and television in the United States, and increasingly in other countries, are not so much communications media as marketing channels. Their major goal is to gather audiences with popular and undemanding entertainment so that sponsors may advertise to them. We may well be experiencing the final days of the Internet's "golden age." There can be little doubt that many of the Internet's promoters see it as a "new and improved" means of selling goods and services and that their voices will increasingly dominate the bandwidth of the Internet.

**The history of the Internet**

Cold War military exigencies were behind the development of Internet technology. The goal was to enable command and control information to survive a nuclear attack by being sent along the multiple paths of a shared network. The initial hub of ArpaNET, the first wide area computer network, was established at UCLA (University of California at Los Angeles) in 1969. The following year hubs were added at Harvard and MIT (Massachusetts Institute of Technology). The goal was to experiment in reliable networking and to link together the US Department of Defense and its military research contractors, including universities doing military research. So many other academic institutions clamoured to be linked to the network, however, that military functions were given a linked but separate network. ArpaNET was replaced in 1990 by NSFNET, which was still dedicated only to education and research. Commercial users, however, are able to communicate with this or any other network. The result is called the Internet – a worldwide network of networks with no one person or group in control.

As initially conceived, the Internet was intended for high-level research functions involving the transfer and sharing of data files. After some time, however, researchers realised that it could be used to send personal messages back and forth and thus e-mail was born. A little later, the first entrepreneurs ventured on to the Internet and began offering various goods and services. The university researchers and other initial users of the Internet, however, did not have electronic commerce in mind when they talked about the benefits of the Internet, preferring to see it as a potential boon for democracy, an electronic town hall where all sorts of voices could be heard because the traditional hierarchies had no control over the use or content of the Internet. Enthusiasts like Howard Rheingold, who was one of the first to write about the Internet as a "virtual community",[11] saw it as a harbinger of freedom which would bring an end to the hegemony of the existing social and political elite.

It did not take long, however, for managers and other high-level officials to install filters into their e-mail programs so that only those messages they deemed as important could get through to them. Further, mindful of studies showing that up to a 60% reduction in office productivity occurs when e-mail and the Internet are introduced, companies are increasingly monitoring and in other ways restricting the Internet activities of their workers.

## Recent developments

As this is being written (in early 1999) survey data indicates that there are 43.2 million Internet hosts in the world. Sixty per cent of these are in the United States and more than 12 million of them are commercial sites (".com").[12] It should also be noted that both the backbone of the Internet and the registration of domain names have been privatised. A report from the Marketing Corporation of America states that $8.5 billion was generated through "e-commerce" during the 1998 Hanukkah and Christmas season.[13] US companies are plowing enormous sums into developing Web-based marketing. IDC Research indicates that American companies will spend $85 billion on the Internet in 1999 and other "first world" countries are also increasing their investments.[14] Increasingly the Internet is turning into an electronic shopping mall. Intelliquest's most recent study indicates that 60 percent of US users shop online, with 20 percent purchasing online. Books are the most popular product to buy online, while automobiles and computer products are the most popular products to shop for online.[15] ActiveMedia report that, in the past year, retail, entertainment, and other Websites catering to consumers (half of all online business sites) have been the fastest-growing category on the Web.

> Average monthly sales revenue (among retail sites that generated revenue) now stands at $40,273, up from $13,260 at the same point in 1997– a dramatic increase. Retail sites are also primary beneficiaries of Web advertising revenue. Advertising flows to sites with many visits, and high-volume retail sites have been quick to recognise the opportunity to build a secondary revenue stream from transient visitors. Advertising for complimentary products allows sites to harvest their primary revenue stream from visitors with a direct interest in the products and services, and to draw the secondary revenue stream from those who may have greater interests elsewhere.[16]

Few companies, however, are yet making profits from their Web-based commercial activities. Pornographic sites and stock traders are supposedly making money, but everything else is making a loss as yet despite high prices for shares in many companies involved in electronic marketing.

## The media oligopoly

The mass media are controlled by a series of oligopolies. As Benjamin Bagdikian points out, "newspapers, magazines, broadcasting systems, books, motion pictures, and most other mass media are rapidly moving in the direction of tight control by a handful of huge multinational corporations. If mergers, acquisitions and takeovers continue at the present rate, one massive firm will be in virtual control of all the major media by the 1990s."[17] The figures he cites are alarming. Despite 25,000 media outlets in the US, twenty-three corporations control most of the output. The number of daily newspapers continues to shrink and there are only three dominant players in the magazine industry. Six corporations control most of the book market, while four lead the motion picture market. In the words of a former US Supreme Court Justice, Louis Brandeis, such dominance with its interconnection to other corporations, is entirely contrary to "a fair field with no favours". It is fair to ask if the Internet will be any different?

## The direction of Internet development

Fifty percent of all traffic on the World Wide Web goes to the top 900 Websites now in service.[18] All of the top ten Internet Service Providers (ISPs) are based in the United States and function as "portals" on "on-ramps" for people accessing the Web. In one sense these portals function as essential gatekeepers for the Web. These top ISPs are listed in Table 2.

Table 2: *The top ten Internet Service Providers (ISPs) (March 1999)*

| Rank | Site | Visitors Per Month |
|---|---|---|
| 1 | yahoo.com | 26,480,000 |
| 2 | aol.com | 23,321,000 |
| 3 | microsoft.com | 20,243,000 |
| 4 | netscape.com | 15,892,000 |
| 5 | geocities.com | 15,238,000 |
| 6 | excite.com | 14,549,000 |
| 7 | lycos.com | 11,831,000 |
| 8 | msn.com | 11,136,000 |
| 9 | infoseek.com | 10,434,000 |
| 10 | altavista.digital.com | 8,956,000 |

The issue of portals has become important because whichever company gains dominance will have a huge "captive" audience for on-screen advertising and various forms of direct and indirect marketing. The portals also make sure that when their users look for particular services (e.g. on-line bookstores), they are first directed to those companies who have paid the portals' owners to promote them. Book purchases are one of the fastest growing dimensions of the Web retail market. Amazon.com, one of the largest book retailers on line, has no retail outlets and sells exclusively via the Internet. It advertises extensively on the Internet, for example, on the frequently used *www.altavista.com* search page. Amazon, in fact, has an advertising banner on the opening or secondary pages of eight of the top ten ISPs, with Barnes & Noble, and Borders having one each of the remainder. This portal connection to advertisers is important because it indicates the power of the Internet to direct users in a specific direction. Amazon exists entirely as an Internet creation and has already been floated on the stock exchange as a result of its unprecedented growth.

Advertising is clearly not limited to books. A large variety of goods are advertised or promoted on the Internet, and if any company can gain a foothold in a particular market, its success will most probably be assured. This only becomes problematic with the issue of cross-ownership, where a given advertiser has dominance in virtue of a vertically integrated market. Such is the case with Microsoft's attempt to create dominance in the Web browser market with the linkage between its operating system, Windows 98, and its associated Internet browser, Internet Explorer. Microsoft is the dominant player in personal computer operating systems, with an estimated 90 percent of the market. Its efforts to build its browser software into its operating system have met with fierce resistance in the US under existing monopoly law. The case is currently before the US courts.

## The promises

Writing in 1992, Howard Rheingold stated that "Today's new communication technologies differ from earlier ones in the greater degree to which, through computer processing power, they span space, time, and pre-existing social arrangements."[19] For many users, one of the most attractive elements of the Internet is its promise to give control of the communications process back to the individual. Users of the Internet, at least in theory, do not even have to identify themselves to their interlocutors. Online anonymity (the ability to adopt a new persona at will and to visit any and all of the Internet's sites) is much appreciated by Net surfers. The vast majority of Internet users do not have video cameras or microphones attached to their computers, so it is almost always impossible to determine the age, gender, race, or physical appearance of other people who are online. Promoters of the Internet see this as an enormous benefit; it removes the taints of racism and other forms of stereotyping and instead promotes the unrestricted exchange of ideas. Because most Internet activity is text-based, there is also a degree of a-corporeality and an ease of a-synchronicity involved with Internet use.

Rheingold, and others of like mind, have promoted the idea that Net surfers could "homestead on the electronic frontier,"[20] establishing "virtual communities" where old rules and old power structures would not apply. Control would pass from the established cultural and social elite to decentralised and radically democratic groups. Internet users are also promised instantaneous access to vast libraries of information with links to causes they are interested in and the ability to search without cost through vast libraries of information.

Other promises of the Internet have included opportunities to avoid business travel through advanced video conferencing; "telecommuting" to work instead of grinding along in traffic jams for hours on end; the possibility of bypassing traditional education through "distance learning"; and obtaining, even in the most remote parts of the world, advanced diagnostic and other medical care through "distance medicine". Businesses, of course, are promised easy access to ever growing millions of literate and prosperous potential customers.

## The reality

It is hardly surprising that the reality of the Internet does not always match the rhetoric of its most ardent promoters. The Internet does still allow the individual a large amount of personal control, but the frontier is getting tamed with considerable speed and fences are going up all over the place. ISPs have installed filters to check for unacceptable language in e-mail messages, they sell demographic and other information about their subscribers, and they have proved ineffective in stopping the delivery of Spam messages (unsolicited bulk e-mail offering goods and services).[21] A recent survey indicated that Spam mail could be hurting British and Irish businesses by as much as $8.2 billion per annum.[22]

The anonymity and personal privacy of online users is constantly under threat. "Cookies", text files which many Web sites place on the hard drives of Net surfers, enable sites to track the usage patterns of those accessing their Web pages. Most users of the Internet are unaware that their Internet surfing is being tracked in this manner; "cookies" are enabled on both the Netscape and Microsoft browsers unless knowledgeable users override them. Moreover, Microsoft prohibits access to some of its pages to users unwilling to enable "cookies." Recently, the Intel Corporation has come under severe criticism over an identifying feature in its new Pentium III chips which would allow

Web sites to monitor Internet usage even if the "cookies" feature was disabled.

There is creditable evidence that some virtual communities are flourishing on the Internet, but that is not where most Net surfers head when they go online. A report by Cyberdialogue, for instance, states that more than two-thirds of active Internet users in the US seek out entertainment content.[23] When movies and the VCR were first introduced one of their most common uses was for the delivery of pornography. The Internet is proving to be another popular source for pornographic materials.[24] Few of these sites allow free and unfettered access; visitors either have to pay to enter the site or else they have to provide personal details which render them liable later on to become recipients of "adult-oriented" advertising and promotions. Children, however, can still easily find their way to sites that present "free samples" or other materials that are unsuitable. They are also vulnerable to approach by individuals who do not have their best interests at heart.[25] There are a number of documented cases where Internet encounters have led to the death of children who were lulled into believing that they were meeting a peer.[26] Other assaults, occurring as a result of Internet encounters, have also been reported.[27]

The Internet does contain vast amounts of useful data and is still an invaluable source for all kinds of research. Search engines (such as Yahoo!) have brought some kind of structure and order to the Internet, but it often remains a frustrating place to do research. More and more, newspapers and other information archives are charging for access[28] and even in free sites it is often difficult to sort out the chaff from the wheat. It is easy to waste hours online looking for information that remains forever elusive. Further, "timed out" messages and other indications of massive Internet congestion are increasingly challenging the promise of instantaneous access. The Internet is in many ways a victim of its own success.

The promises of telecommuting, distance learning and distance medicine remain, for the most part, unfulfilled. Progress continues to be made in all these areas, but there has yet to be any kind of massive switch of resources towards these online activities.

## Specific Internet issues

Access to quality information on the Internet is being threatened by the continued privatisation of Net resources, but the promise of boundless knowledge continues to be promoted as a "bait" to encourage new users to go online. One example of this has been seen recently in Ireland. A new company has been proposed which is based on the premise that knowledge is a tradable substance, and to a certain extent can be commodified or packaged into tradable units or assets, an extension of an idea that began with the telegraph. This company will be encouraging experts in various subjects to form a guild which specialises in that subject. That guild will package knowledge, put it in wrappers which will list the subject matter, the author, the provenance of the knowledge, the currency, and the price to open the wrapper. The guild collection of wrapped packages will be password protected and opening one will cause the buyer's account to be automatically debited. The company will take a slice off the top of the revenue generated. It is envisaged that the Internet will be the medium for delivery of the various packets of information. Such a proposal is clearly a long way from that of a freely accessible library of shared knowledge. The antithesis to this is a project like Project Guttenberg, or the Center for Electronic Texts in the Humanities, which aim to make electronic information available to all.

Anonymity, as already noted, is also under threat but its appeal is still strong to many new users of the technology. Many people buying computers capable of accessing the Internet are parents who are being persuaded that their children are in danger of falling behind at school if they do not have computers to help them with their homework.[29]

There has been a steady increase in the amount of Internet fraud and other crimes. According to the Internet Fraud Watch of the National Consumers League, complaints have increased 600% since 1997,[30] and the FBI reported a 250% increase in cyber crimes over the last two years.[31] The InterGOV International Web site predicts that there will be more than 500 Web crimes reported each day in 1999, although it also notes that less than 10% of Web crimes are ever reported.[32]   It also reports that, according to the accounting firm of Ernst & Young, cyber crimes amount to some $5 billion per year.

Two further issues also arise here. Firstly, the Internet is becoming the sole source of certain information, and its very existence can allow those charged with publication of various materials an easy solution. This is, of course, problematic for those who do not have Internet access and rely on other forms of media for information. Allied to this is a second issue whereby additional costs accrue to non-users of the Internet. One recent example of this is the decision of Delta Airlines to add $2 to the cost of every airline ticket that is not purchased on line.

## The victims

It seems clear from what has been noted above that children are especially at risk when it comes to the Internet. It is true that, in most respects, they are no more at risk in front of the computer screen than they are in front of their televisions or out alone on the streets of any city. Among the threats, besides pornography, that young people can come across on the Internet are ultra-violent computer games, cigarette and alcohol ads specifically targeted at them, pedophiles and others who harass children, racist and other noxious kinds of propaganda, and even instructions for committing suicide. The real issue with regard to children and the Internet is a lack of adequate parental supervision.

The poor in developing countries, and especially those in rural areas, have almost no chance to access the Internet. Indeed, in many parts of the world, the literacy needed for navigating the Internet is far from widespread. The poor are thus at a severe disadvantage in a global economy. Even in the United States, the richest country in the world, a quarter of the nation's children are being raised in poverty and cannot go online with the same ease as those who have direct connections to the World Wide Web from their homes. It is true that some schools and public libraries do provide Internet access, but the number of terminals is usually quite limited and the amount of time people can spend online is sometimes restricted. The development of information "haves" and "have-nots" based upon financial resources continues unabated.

## Ongoing developments

The latest Bill to protect children by requiring age verification for adult sites has been stayed by a federal judge in the US on the grounds that it goes against freedom of speech. Because of the First Amendment to the US constitution, which guarantees freedom of speech, there seems to be little that can be done to regulate content on a worldwide basis, given the dominance of the US in terms of the Internet. The $107 million punitive damages award granted to those who sued the anti-abortion "Nuremberg Project" Web Site because it identified abortion providers and then crossed off their names if they were murdered, is indicative that some elements of speech are not quite as free as others.

## A broader perspective

There are wider concerns relating to Internet development beyond those listed above, which are focused on emerging dimensions of the Internet as it is today. But looking further afield from a different perspective, the Internet appears to be geared specifically at a wealthy western world. The 1995 Panos Media Briefing put it concisely.

The new information age is upon us. Over 40 million people across 168 countries are now wired up to the Internet – a collection of computers around the world linked to cables like ordinary telephone lines allowing the transport of digitised information. Both the speed of that transport – messages can be sent across the world in the time it takes to post an airmail letter – and the fact that information can be sent to one or one thousand people for the same low cost, mean radically new patterns of communication.

And that can empower. Everyone from journalists to indigenous peoples can access a store of information – some reliable, some not so – in a short time. Many Southern based organisations are at the forefront of electronic communications. A publication in Bombay keeps tabs on World Bank funded projects through a worldwide network of contacts. Meanwhile in Zambia, doctors in rural hospitals can seek specialist advice from Lusaka, and the capital's independent newspaper, the *Post*, is available on the Internet.

But costs are a constraint. Individual users need a computer and modem, affordable telephone lines and reliable electricity. On a national level, the need for such a hi-tech infrastructure has seen the rich countries race ahead. More than half the connected computers in the world are in the United States, whereas in Africa less than 10 countries are directly connected to the Internet. In theory the means to handle information are increasingly available and democratic. In practice there is a danger of a new information elitism which further disenfranchises the majority of the world's population. In the short term, the North-South information gap looks set to increase, particularly for Africa.[33]

The Internet is currently geared almost exclusively toward those in the developed world with disposable cash. The concerns indicated in the Panos briefing are not unfounded. Most of the millions of documents on the web are on the 70 percent of US hosts. There are less than 10 African countries on the Internet. Some 80 percent of the world lacks basic telecommunications. And costs in the developing world are both directly and proportionately much higher. A modem in India, for example, costs 4 times what it costs in the US but represents a far greater proportion of a worker's income. Access in Indonesia costs 12 times that in US.

## Africa could use a good net

As the Panos briefing indicates, the problem is especially acute in Africa. About 70 percent of Africa is reached by radio, and 40 percent by television. Less than 0.1 percent of Africa is reached by Internet. And it is in Africa that the developmental need is greatest. Some 87 percent of Swedes own a mobile phone while less than 1 percent of Africans have ever used a phone. Basic telecommunications services hardly exist in many parts of Africa. PC access is an unknown luxury. And so the promise of the Internet as a source of information and as a potential for economic development is almost meaningless. But there is a serious question placed over the notion of Internet development in Africa. As Michael Saradar puts it with the money needed to enter the Internet world, you could feed a family in Bangladesh for a year. The more the Internet develops, the more it will become basically a commercial place. Communities that are rich will become powerful; but the vast majority will be worse marginalised. I think the Internet will be a weapon of economic power and knowledge.[34]

But Hudson points out that the Internet is no longer a luxury:

> Until recently, telecommunications was considered a luxury to be provided only after all the other investments in water, electrification and roads had been made – and after all the demand for telecommunications in the cities had been met. Instead, telecommunications should be considered a vital component in the development process ... in developing regions.[35]

## Development issues

Saradar and Hudson point to a real difficulty in terms of development. On the one hand the Internet, as a fundamental dimension of telecommunications infrastructure, cannot be regarded as a luxury even in developing nations, while on the other every effort must be made to ensure that any such Internet promotion in developing nations must be undertaken as genuinely useful rather than exploitative. The Panos briefing refers to the phenomenon of the rusting tractor:

> The history of development assistance is littered with failed initiatives to transfer technologies to developing countries. Stories abound of huge shipments of tractors – or lorries or turbines or television transmitters – arriving to transform the prospects of developing countries only to end up rusting and useless through want of spare parts or adequate training to operate and repair them. Such failures have almost always derived from a lack of any feelings of ownership or

participation by the groups they have been designed to benefit. If this can happen with a tractor, it can happen with the more delicate and fast-moving technology of the computer. Such concerns are being fuelled by the rapid increase in organisations dedicated to spreading connectivity in developing countries.[36]

The same "rush to wire" is being experienced within education. But what is missing in many cases seems to be any serious analysis of why this is being done. In the educational sphere it is clear that there is a perceived need that every school should be on the Internet. But there is, as yet, little research to validate the idea that children can necessarily learn anything in a superior fashion from the Internet than they can through traditional models. There is certainly a wealth of information now at the fingertips of school children, but it is not necessarily the soundest pedagogical approach to point them in the direction of the Internet as a source of material for projects and other work.

Similarly with developing nations there is a real need to ask what is being done, and why, a modern version of *cui bono*. Reports are already coming back to the west from travelers reaching outposts of civilisation only to find the whole village gathered around a single television set watching "Friends". Is the purpose of Internet development one of resource provision to nations in need or is it more a case of delivering more audience to the advertiser?

The danger to which Saradar, Hudson and others alert us is one of losing sight of other needs in the push for technological development. The real question in this regard is relatively simple: what difference does technology make that cannot be achieved effectively by other means. Perhaps one classic anecdote illustrates this well. It has been reported that during the space race it became quickly apparent that the normal ballpoint pen would not work in space. The American space research team spent enormous sums of money and valuable time on developing a pen that could write effectively in non-gravity situations. The Russians simply decided to use a pencil.

A recent US survey ascertained the importance of the Internet across the US. The first-ever "America Online/Roper Starch Cyberstudy 1998", a sample of 1,001 adult Americans who subscribe to online and Internet services from home, revealed that more than three-quarters believe that being online has made their lives better. According to Bob Pittman of AOL, the Internet has surpassed VCRs, stereos and cable TV as a necessity for those who have access to them:

> Whether it's keeping in touch with friends and family, getting information to make better buying decisions or trading stocks, people are clearly seeing everyday tasks are easier and more convenient when they're done online – and the longer people have been online, the more benefits they notice.[37]

While nobody would want to quibble with the results of such a survey, it does raise questions as to how Internet development will benefit developing nations if its primary life-enhancing benefits in the US are keeping in touch and getting information regarding stock trading.

### What now for the Net?

The development of the Internet provides society with a new powerful technology that is, of itself, amoral. Like any other tool it can be used for weal or woe. This paper has developed the idea that the Internet has great promise but with certain limitations. The fulfillment of its initial promise has, at best, been limited. Of clear concern is the ongoing commercialisation of the Internet and the danger of it becoming an effective oligopoly. Also of concern is the push to promote Internet activity on a global scale, without a clearly defined objective in mind. This runs the risk of allowing the technology to be the driving force without any regard to content or use. Previous experience from other media, most recently television, has clearly indicated the folly of such a move. What is needed is a serious debate about the Internet, its development, practice and ethics, so that all of society is well served by this powerful technology rather than simply the interests of the powerful few. It is the hope of the authors of this paper that such a debate will be seen in the months and years to come, such that the issues are highlighted and debated before they become problematic.

## Notes

1 Breen was conference presenter and is the corresponding author.
2 George Comstock, *Evolution of American Television* (Newbury Park, CA: Sage Publications, 1989).
3 Bruce Sterling, "History of the Internet."
(http://www.dsv.su.se/Internet/documents/Internet-history.html)
4 The authors of this paper, in fact, used the Internet to gather much of the data presented here and through video "Net Meetings" were able to work together in real time both in the drafting and revision of the essay.
5 The Internet, at least in its initial phases, has been an American-led phenomenon. In considering some historical precedents, therefore, emphasis is given to the introduction of communication technologies in the United States.
6 cf. Richard Campbell, *Media & Culture* (New York: St. Martin's Press, 1998) [7]
7 Henry David Thoreau, *Walden* (1854)
ftp://uiarchive.cso.uiuc.edu/pub/etext/gutenberg/etext95/waldn10.txt
8 ibid., [6]
9 Colin Cherry, "The Telephone System: Creator of Mobility and Social Change" in Ithiel de Sola Pool, ed., *The Social Impact of the Telephone* (Cambridge, MA: The M.I.T. Press, 1977) [124-125]
10 Carolyn Marvin, *When Old Technologies Were New* (NY: Oxford University Press, 1988) [107]
11 cf. Howard Rheingold, *The Virtual Community* (Reading, MA: Addison-Wesley, 1993)
12 NUA Internet Surveys: 13ibid.:http://www.nua.ie/surveys/index.cgi?f= VS&art_id=905354630&rel=true
14 ibid.:
15 ibid.: http://www.intelliquest.com/press/release72.asp
16 http:www.activmedia.com/latestnews.html
17 Benjamin Bagdikian, *The Media Monopoly* (Beacon Press, Boston, 1997)
18 InternetWorld Online, 31/8/98
http://www.Internetvalley.com/intvalstat.html
19 Howard Rheingold, "Connections: Book Reviews" in the *Whole Earth Review*, 22/3/92 [77]

20 Subtitle of Rheingold's book. Cf. footnote 10
21 Rich Dean, an "information age specialist" interviewed on National Public Radio's "Weekend Edition" (7/3/99), indicated that his AOL mail account was unusable because of the amount of Spam mail he receives each day. http://www.npr.org/programs/wesun/current.html
22 Benchmark Research survey, cited by NUA. http://www.nua.ie/suveys/index.cgi?f=VS&art_id=893678873&rel=true
23 Cyberdialogue report cited by NUA. http://www.nua.ie/surveys/index.cgi?f=VS&art_id=905354748&rel=true
24 Entering the terms "pornography" and "porno" on a popular Internet search engine [Dogpile.com] in March '99 yielded a combined total of more than 790,000 "hits." Even allowing for some duplication, there can be no doubt that pornographic materials are omnipresent on the Internet.
25 InterGOV International reports that child pornography crimes are the most frequent, covering 35% of all reported incidents. http://www.intergov.org/public_administration/information/latest_web_stats.html
26 The Tulsa World, Oct 28 1998, reported the death of 7-year-old Sherrice Iverson at the hands of Jeremy Strohmeyer in a case fuelled by Internet pornography.
27 http://www.geocities.com/NapaValley/4631/
28 *The New York Times*, for instance, has begun charging for access to portions of its Website.
29 In late 1998, in time for the "holiday season" in the United States, Compaq launched an advertising campaign with a fairly explicit fear appeal to parents; it insinuated that children without Internet access were at a real educational disadvantage.
30 Cf. http://www.fraud.org/news/news.htm
31 cf.http://www.nua.ie/surveys/index.cgi?f=VS&art_id=892650598&rel=tre
32 InterGOV International:http://www.intergov.org/public_administration/information/latest_web_stats.html
33 Panos Briefing No. 28 April 1998, *The Internet and Poverty*.
34 Sardar, Ziauddin and Ravetz, Jerome R., *Cyberfutures: culture and politics on the information superhighway*. London, Pluto Press, 1996.
35 Heather E. Hudson, *Global Connections: International Telecommunications Infrastructure and Policy*, New York : Van Nostrand Reinhold, 1997.
36 Panos Briefing No. 28 April 1998, *The Internet and Poverty*.
37 http://www.roper.inter.net/news/content/news86.htm

## Bibliography

Bagdikian, B., *The Media Monopoly*, Boston, Beacon Press, 1997.
Campbell, R., *Media & Culture*, New York, St. Martin's Press, 1998.

Cherry, C., "The Telephone System: Creator of Mobility and Social Change", in Ithiel de Pool, S., (ed.), *The Social Impact of the Telephone,* Cambridge, MA, The MIT Press, 1977.

Comstock, G., *Evolution of American Television,* Newbury Park, CA, Sage Publications, 1989.

Hudson, H.E., *Global Connections: International Telecommunications Infrastructure and Policy,* New York, Van Nostrand Reinhold, 1997.

Marvin, C., *When Old Technologies Were New,* New York, Oxford University Press, 1988.

Rheingold, H., *The Virtual Community,* Reading, MA, Addison-Wesley, 1993.

Rheingold, H., "Connections: Book Reviews", in the *Whole Earth Review,* 22/3/92.

Ziauddin S., and Ravetz, J.R., *Cyberfutures: culture and politics on the information superhighway,* London, Pluto Press, 1996.